INSIDE THE
CURRENCY MARKET

Since 1996, Bloomberg Press has published books for financial professionals on investing, economics, and policy affecting investors. Titles are written by leading practitioners and authorities, and have been translated into more than 20 languages.

The Bloomberg Financial Series provides both core reference knowledge and actionable information for financial professionals. The books are written by experts familiar with the work flows, challenges, and demands of investment professionals who trade the markets, manage money, and analyze investments in their capacity of growing and protecting wealth, hedging risk, and generating revenue.

For a list of available titles, please visit our web site at www.wiley.com/go/bloombergpress.

INSIDE THE CURRENCY MARKET

Mechanics, Valuation, and Strategies

Brian Twomey

BLOOMBERG PRESS
An Imprint of
WILEY

Library of Congress Cataloging-in-Publication Data:

Twomey, Brian, 1961-
 Inside the currency market: mechanics, valuation and strategies / Brian Twomey.—1
  p. cm.—(Bloomberg financial series)
 Includes bibliographical references and index.
 ISBN 978-0-470-95275-7 (hardback); ISBN 978-1-118-14933-1 (ebk);
 ISBN 978-1-118-14934-8 (ebk); ISBN 978-1-118-14935-5 (ebk)
  1. Foreign exchange market. 2. Interest rates. I. Title.
 HG3851.T88 2011
 332.4'5—dc23

                                                                2011021444

Printed in the United States of America

10 9 8 7 6 5 4 3 2 1

*To the memory of my grandfather,
Richard Francis Schmidt, the greatest stock
trader I've ever known and a man who
taught me not only valuable lessons of life
but foundations of the markets at a young age.*

Contents

CHAPTER 9
  Currency Cycles, Currency Futures,
  Options, and Volatility

CHAPTER 10
  Technical Analysis

Foreword

I met Brian Twomey about five years ago when he came to my office here in North Carolina for a day visit. What immediately struck me about Brian was his "fire-in-the-belly" spirit and go-getter attitude. Brian impressed me with his knowledge of the markets as well as his outstanding analytical prowess. We've kept in touch over the years and I was honored to be contacted by Brian's publisher for the purpose of writing this foreword.

For anybody interested in trading or studying the Forex markets, I would consider this book required reading. I was astounded at the level of detail, especially in terms of the nation-by-nation analyses that is provided. Detailed methodologies, trade strategies, a terrific chapter devoted exclusively to the Libor, and an extensive analysis of currency pairs are also discussed.

At the book's conclusion, Brian explains "My purpose for this book was to address all the various issues involved that comprise a currency pair not only from a strict trading perspective but to bring an understanding from a whole host of perspectives." I believe that Brian has achieved this objective tenfold. I predict that this book will serve as an important reference resource for all those interested in the inner workings of world currencies.

I hope you enjoy this book as much as I did.

JOHN R. HILL
President
Futures Truth Co.

Preface

This book answers the question what are the components, the constituent factors that comprise the second side of a currency-pair equation and how should those factors be considered in terms of a trade strategy. A currency pair comprises two sides, a two-nation perspective. In order to understand a currency-pair combination, both sides of the pair must be considered from the two-nation perspective.

The two-nation perspective was fully outlined in this text with not only the trader in mind but researchers, market professionals, and present and future students of the markets.

The genesis of the book framework was derived from the many biases I saw over the years from the academic journals, trader publications, or years of prior books. Each book, each article, and each journal publication offered a point, an insight that would help the reader further his or her knowledge. But each publication taught a perspective, an insight that would eventually lead to the overall understanding of the two-nation operational framework. Yet years may pass before the full learned concepts could actually become operational in a trade strategy and understanding of the market due to the proper knowledge never advanced in one publication. Publications had biases, toward the U.S. dollar side of the currency-pair equation, with no consideration of the second part of the pair.

Spot-currency prices move in the markets based on factors of interest rates but interest rates between two nations rather than one side of a currency pair. The question must then be asked: How does the second nation calculate and factor interest, and what market instruments are available to track the various rates that trade every day in the markets in order to track a trade throughout the various markets?

To trade Australian dollar/Japanese yen, one must understand Japanese TIBOR and Euroyen rates in terms of bank bills and Overnight Cash Rates in Australia. To trade U.S. dollar/Canadian dollar, one must know the U.S. Fed funds rates in relation to Canada's CORRA and OMMFR interest rates.

How those specific interest rates trade and direction of their movements can have profound effects on currency-pair prices.

This book sets out to outline the two-sided currency-pair trade from a whole host of perspectives as it relates nation to nation. It addresses currency pairs from the eight major nations because that is where the vast majority of trade occurs.

Chapter One is an outline of the Triennial Survey released every three years by the Bank of International Settlements (BIS). While that is not new to any publication, the historical surveys are addressed and analyzed so readers can understand the historical composition of the market in its proper context as well as the rise of many varied currency pairs and financial instruments associated with the historical rise of the markets.

Beside the Triennial surveys, the BIS offers annual and quarterly reviews of the currency markets and each is addressed in terms of the specifics of the markets, types of topics addressed, and factors for consideration to understand and evaluate the market.

Foreign-exchange committees formed in the late 1970s and mimic the work of the BIS. Each nation has an FX Committee, but that committee is specific to the nation of trade. Each nation's FX Committee is fully highlighted.

Chapter Two offers foundation and theories of money and interest. It begins with a historical perspective and answers such questions as supply and demand of money from an operational framework, always highlighted nation by nation. Historically, the demand and supply of money begins with the classical theorist, moves into Keynes, Von Hayek, and Milton Friedman. Theories and perspectives of Purchasing Power Parity are explored in fine detail.

Chapter Three explores trade weight indices from a whole host of perspectives: historical, methodological, index composition, and theories of composition from an economic perspective. Each nation is addressed specifically in terms of formulas, calculations, currency composition, and economic framework, and trade strategies are explained in detail.

Chapter Four begins the open-market valuation and knowledge of interest rates and currency-pair prices from the perspective of repurchase agreements. Each nation is addressed specifically due to the many factors nations consider as they approach their open-market operations. Repo rates establish a floor for interest, yet interest rates rise and fall with markets and economic conditions. Each nation is addressed in all its minute detail to fully understand the operational framework of repurchase-agreement markets.

Chapter Five addresses the most important of open-market interest rates, LIBOR. LIBOR is explained, addressed, and highlighted not only from the well-known British Bankers Association perspective but each nation has its own LIBOR. Each nation's LIBOR is fully explained in terms of factors of interest rates and what moves currency pair prices associated with those LIBOR rates, and historical views are addressed to the best of my ability. Many currency-pair chart examples accompany each nation's LIBOR so readers can fully understand each nation's LIBOR and factors of currency-pair movements and prices.

Chapter Six addresses yield curves first from their historical perspective then each nation's yield curve is explained and calculated with bond examples and historical perspectives offered. The U.S. market is the most important of the four, so currency-pair chart examples accompany yield curve charts. Factors such as how to trade yield curves are also fully highlighted.

Chapter Seven moves further along the interest-rate curve to address swaps in all their various forms from currency swaps, cross-currency basis swaps, and overnight interest-rate swaps. Each nation's swap market is highlighted specifically due to the varied nuances of every market. The chapter then moves into outright forwards and forward points. Formulas and calculated examples are offered. A forward point calculated example includes a yield curve and spot price calculated to a forward point.

Chapter Eight addresses stock markets as they relate to currency prices and the bond/yield interplay. Each nation's stock market is discussed in terms of time of trade, formulas of each nation's stock market, factors for trade consideration, and relationship to bonds and yields in each market.

Chapter Nine addresses currency-pair conversions, volatility and volatility indicators, formulas, and calculated examples as they relate to currency pairs. A full discussion of volatility is offered not only for currency pairs, but currency options are addressed. Futures contracts in terms of standard versus micro contracts are discussed and fully addressed in terms of currency-pair prices and conversions.

Chapter Ten offers technical indicators, ready-made indicators employed to evaluate trade decisions. Simple moving averages, Bollinger Bands, Ichimoku, and pivot points are addressed due to features specific to the markets. Ichimoku is vital to the Japanese and Asian currency markets since it is not only widely employed but its operational framework must be understood in order to trade Asian markets. Bollinger Bands is important to volatility, simple moving averages to means, and pivot points to support and resistance.

Simple moving averages go a step further, as a simple moving average is converted into a volatility indicator. Trend lines are discussed in all their finer details and histories offered. Volume and open interest studies, COT reports, correlations, and the Baltic Exchange is offered due to its importance to the commodity currencies such as Australian dollar, New Zealand dollar, and Canadian dollar.

Acknowledgments

Without the dedicated and efficient help of the Wiley and Bloomberg professionals, this book would not have been possible.

I thank Stephen Isaacs of Bloomberg Press for allowing me an opportunity to write this book. Kevin Commins, Executive Editor of Wiley, assisted in every regard. His decency, dedication, and professionalism is appreciated. Meg Freeborn's dedication to the manuscript deserves my gratitude. A special thank you to Kimberly Bernard who developed the manuscript; she is appreciated more than words would allow. Her efficiency, dedication, expertise, and knowledge in the development process were genius. A thank you to all at Wiley for their work and effort.

I offer my solemn and heartfelt thank yous to many dedicated market professionals who were vitally important in more than one vital detail of this book. My acknowledgments are offered in a nation-by-nation framework.

New Zealand:

Daniel Pringle calculates the NZX indices on a daily basis. His knowledge, his market skills, his access, and attention to my questions were vitally important to bringing the New Zealand information to my text. A sincere thank you is offered as well to others at the NZX. Thank you to the New Zealand Financial Markets Association for help and time.

Switzerland:

Gazmend Maliqi deserves a special gratitude. Gazmend calculates the Swiss SMI, Switzerland's main stock market index. His dedication, his help, and market depth and knowledge is again appreciated.

Canada:

Lois Sperling of Insideinformation.com, a high-quality business-intelligence service in Vancouver, British Columbia, I owe a debt of gratitude. When I was pressed for time in terms of due dates, Lois jumped into action and we literally spent Christmas Eve working on the Bibliography together.

Europe:

Cedric Quemener manages the steering committees at the EURIBOR-European Banking Federation and not only offered his valuable time but shared his market insights, access to research publications, and granted permission for use of the Eurepo, EONIA, EURIBOR, and EONIA Swap Index charts. His dedication, professionalism, and decency are appreciated more than words would allow me to offer here.

Thank you to the dedicated market professionals at the London Wholesale Market Brokers Association in London for access to charts and SONIA and EURONIA information.

Martin Duffell is Head of Dealing at the U.K. Debt Management Office. Martin's time, help, attention, and access to publications to understand gilts in all its finest forms is sincerely appreciated.

Thank you to Euribor-rates.eu for access to charts.

Japan:

Naohiko Baba is one of the most prolific scholar/writers on not only Japan and their markets but his work spans many markets over many years. His work is appreciated.

United States:

A special thank you to Peter Wadkins of Thomson Reuters. Not only is Peter a long-time scholar, trader, and historian of the currency markets but his help over the years with all my questions is sincerely appreciated. Basic questions began more than five years ago and graduated as my own knowledge expanded. Peter's time, effort, and knowledge is most appreciated. I'm not only honored to know Peter but I've looked forward on a daily basis to reading his expert market commentary.

Thank you to Joseph Haubrich at the Cleveland Fed for his years of scholarly work and help to me on my examples.

A special thank you to Jaclyn Sales at FXCM whose dedication is always appreciated.

I'm not only honored to know John Hill, but his dedication as a long time market professional of decency and honesty is widely known throughout the industry of professionals. To John, thank you.

Ron Griess at thechartstore.com I offer my many thank yous.

York County Library:

Special thank you to my friend Troy Beckham, whose computer skills and knowledge helped guide me through well over a year while working on the manuscript. Without Troy's assistance, this book would never have seen the light of day. Kyle Merck as well deserves my gratitude and thank yous for assisting me with my many chart examples. His computer skills are expert and his devotion to my cause gratifying. My friend Page Hendrix, a research librarian, is thanked for her dedication in compiling research for many, many days. Her attention to my research efforts over these many years is appreciated. And thank you to the many dedicated professionals at the library who have a sincere love for books and information.

CHAPTER 1

Foreign Exchange Reports

Foreign exchange (FX) reports are market-intelligence documents that comprise many facets. Bank reports for example address direct and sometimes short-term market variables such as a short- or long-term trade, a possible central bank interest rate change, or economic variable that directly relates to the market.

Institutional reports address bigger-picture issues that comprise market intelligence in terms of overall trading volume, types of instruments traded, and a fundamental or technical aspect that must be addressed in order for the market to function. Yet these reports address overall market fundamentals and functions so traders and market professionals can understand the big picture as it relates to their overall trade plan. Institutional reports are always forward looking and written by market professionals with the ability to understand and analyze big-picture issues. Much information can be derived from professional reports in terms of strategies, risks, and highlighting of possible scenarios with future implications to profit. The key is to understand the various reports and their implications because some reports are nation specific while others address the overall market as it relates from nation to nation.

This section addresses a variety of market-intelligence reports that relate both to a specific nation and overall market picture. This section incorporates not only reports from a market-intelligence perspective but institutional histories, frequencies of reports, and types of information released and addressed.

Bank of International Settlements

Before we discuss the much-publicized implications of the Bank of International Settlements' Triennial Survey and the not-so-publicized quarterly report, here's a quick and basic overview of the role, functions, and historical aspects of the Bank of International Settlements (BIS) due to its profound importance to not only world banking and economic stability, but the markets in particular, both yesterday and today.

Established in 1930 as the world's banker, the BIS today is much more than the facilitator of gold and FX transactions for the 54 central banks that contributed to its 2007 report. It was originally established to repatriate German monies to the Allies after the war at the behest of the Bank of England, which called for its establishment. How to implement further Treaty of Versailles' arrangements between nations after World War I further heightened its need as intermediator to facilitate multilateral payments and currency conversions. Its location in Basel, Switzerland, attests to not only its neutrality but its commitment to carry out its mandate (BIS 2010).

The real existential challenge to the BIS came during the 1930s at the height of the currency wars, when the Bank of England suspended its gold standard in 1931 and the United States did the same in 1933. Gold-backed nations sought stability due to currency price fluctuations by the United States and the United Kingdom as trade imbalances seriously deviated from the norm of gold-backed nations and threatened their economic existence (BIS 2010).

The resolution was the Tripartite Agreement signed by the United States, France, and England in 1936 to ensure price stability and to abstain from competitive economic devaluations of currency prices as long as currency prices didn't destabilize the economic balance of trade. While the world prevented a crisis, the BIS maintained its existence until the bank was rescued by President Truman in 1948 when the United Nations voted for its dissolution in 1944. Ironically, Franklin Roosevelt died shortly after in April 1945, so Truman assumed the presidency and, with the help of the United Kingdom, ensured the bank would remain today as one of the oldest world institutions (BIS 2010).

Moreover, the BIS provides short-term collateral loans to nations through their respective central banks and settles trades every trading day at 5:00 p.m. eastern standard time through its Committee on Payment and Settlements (BIS 2010). Closing spot currency, outright forwards, currency options, and swap prices are established at the 5:00 p.m. settlement to end a full-cycle trading day. Trading institutions must then reflect these changes to all accounts the world over through their respective central banks.

The Committee on Payment and Settlements ensures that world markets not only function properly but further ensures this functionality replicates itself every trading day. Rollover debits and credits are marked to market at the 5:00 p.m. close. Market bid/ask spreads tend to change dramatically at times as traders begin the new trading day during the Asian session. This however depends on the liquidity provided to markets based on trading activity. Robust trading means decreased spreads as liquidity is provided to the markets.

Triennial Survey

Since 1989 and every three years thereafter, the BIS publishes its quite detailed Triennial Survey through its Markets Committee and the Committee on the Global Financial System—established in 1971—that focuses on daily turnover in U.S. dollar amounts and outstanding contracts in FX for the last three years.

Information is reported to the BIS by central banks—54 at the 2007 count up from 52 in 2004, 48 in 2001, 43 in 1998, and 26 in 1995 (BIS 2007 Triennial Survey). Surveys covered data on amounts outstanding of over-the-counter (OTC) FX interest rate, equity and commodity, and credit derivatives. FX, spot, outright forwards, foreign exchange swaps, and currency and interest-rate derivatives are surveyed. Interestingly, the 2007 report included for the first time credit default swaps (CDS).

These surveys feature quite detailed reports that serve as important guides for market professionals and traders because they determine where money flowed to seek its best yield and the types of instruments utilized to facilitate those returns. All have important implications for the spot trade.

Triennial Survey 2007 versus 2004

From the 2007 report provided in Exhibit 1.1, Global Foreign Exchange Market Turnover, we learned that daily turnover of all spot, outright forwards and swap transactions increased to $3.2 trillion, up from $1.9 trillion in 2004, a 69 percent increase. Based on types of instruments from Exhibit 1.1, swaps rose 80 percent in 2007, an increase of 45 percent from 2004. But notice the number of up-to-seven-day swap transactions in Exhibit 1.1 that increased since its full reporting period began in 1995.

From 1995 to 2001, the number of up-to-seven-day swap transactions doubled to the over–seven-day counterpart, while those same transactions doubled from 2004 to 2007 with the number of swap transactions on a continual rise. Why? A swap is primarily an agreement to exchange cash flows. One can look at swaps as a bank simultaneously buying or selling a currency for one maturity and selling or buying the equivalent amount at a later date. They trade

EXHIBIT 1.1   Global Foreign Exchange Market Turnover[1]: Daily Averages in April, in Billions of U.S. dollars

	1992	1995	1998	2001	2004[2]	2007
Spot transactions	394	494	566	387	631	1,005
Outright forwards	58	97	128	131	209	362
—Up to 7 days	—	50	65	51	92	154
—Over 7 days	—	46	62	80	116	208
Foreign exchange swaps	324	546	734	656	954	1,714
—Up to 7 days	—	382	528	451	700	1,329
—Over 7 days	—	162	202	204	252	382
Estimated gaps in reporting	44	53	60	26	106	129
Total traditional turnover	820	1,190	1,490	1,200	1,900	3,210
Memo: Turnover at April 2007 exchange rates[3]	*880*	*1,150*	*1,650*	*1,420*	*1,970*	*3,210*

[1]Adjusted for local and cross-border double-counting. Due to incomplete maturity breakdown, components do not always sum to totals.
[2]Data for 2004 have been revised.
[3]Non-U.S. dollar legs of foreign currency transactions were converted from current U.S. dollar amounts into original currency amounts at average exchange rates for April of each survey year and then reconverted into U.S. dollar amounts at average April 2007 exchange rates.
Source: Bank of International Settlements.

OTC and were once employed primarily when normal markets couldn't offer financing, but their popularity has increased year over year as a regular form of finance. A swap can be an interest rate swap, a commodity swap, an equity swap, or a currency swap.

Yet swaps can be employed as a hedge against an interest rate swap, a currency swap, a commodity swap, or an equity swap. As noted in Exhibit 1.2, a trend developed from 2006 to 2010. As interest rate spreads tightened, implied volatilities decreased and carry to risk rose.

As noted in Exhibit 1.3, clearly the U.S. dollar and other currencies are the most widely traded swaps from 2001 to 2007, followed by the euro, Japanese yen, pound sterling, Swiss franc, Canadian dollar, and Australian dollar.

The number of outright forwards from its up-to-seven-day to its over–seven-day trade has held steady since the full reporting began in 1995. Yet

EXHIBIT 1.2 Interest Rate Spreads, Implied Volatilities, and Carry to Risk

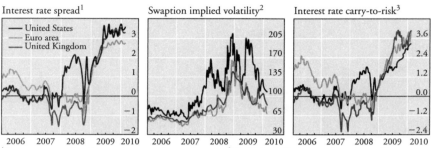

Interest rate spread[1]   Swaption implied volatility[2]   Interest rate carry-to-risk[3]

[1]Ten-year swap rates minus three-month money market rates, in percent. [2]Volatility Implied by three-month swaptions on 10-year swap contracts, in basis points. [3]Defined as the defferential between 10-year swap rates and three-month money market rate divided by the three-month/10-year swaption implied volatility.

Source: Bloomberg, BIS calculations.

swap transactions far outnumber outright forwards by four times in 2007 and five times in 2004. Overall outright forwards increased 73 percent in 2007 from 2004. An outright forward is a transaction where two parties agree to buy or sell a predetermined amount of currency at an agreed rate sometime in the agreed-upon future. Traders trade views based on future exchange rates.

Major world companies doing business across borders trade forwards to take advantage of a particular exchange rate to repatriate money, to lock in rates for future business, to hedge, and speculate.

Spot transactions increased 56 percent in 2007 from 2004, according to latest reports, but this increase was lower than previous years. Yet from 1998 to 2007, spot transactions almost doubled from $568 billion to $1.5 trillion and almost tripled from $394 billion in 1992 to $1.05 trillion in 2007. Notice how swaps slightly outnumber spot transactions from 1995 to 2007. Further notice how swap transactions almost doubled over spot transactions in 2001. Spot traded $387 billion to $656 billion for swaps. Interest rate volatility may be one explanation because interest rate swaps are the most widely traded of all swap instruments. Yet 2001 was the year 9/11 occurred, so much volatility was experienced (Triennial Survey 2004, 2007).

In Exhibit 1.4, the U.S. dollar is by far the most widely traded element of a pair. The number one traded pair is the euro, yen, sterling, Australia, Swiss franc, and Canadian dollar. And all traded against or with the U.S. dollar. An interesting phenomenon is the Hong Kong dollar that traded a daily turnover of $79 billion in 1998 to $175 billion in 2007. The Singapore dollar falls within the same parameters of daily turnover exhibits. Both trade in government controlled trading bands.

EXHIBIT 1.3 Reported Foreign Exchange Turnover in OTC Derivatives Markets by Currency Pair[1]: Daily Averages in April, in Billions of U.S. dollars

| | Total[2] | | | Of Which | | | | | |
| | | | | Options | | | Currency Swaps | | |
	April 2001	April 2004[3]	April 2007	April 2001	April 2004[3]	April 2007	April 2001	April 2004	April 2007
U.S. dollar vs. other currencies	787	1,165	2,055	48	92	158	6	18	27
—Euro	256	345	627	16	31	43	1	7	8
—Japanese yen	169	223	298	17	27	38	2	3	3
—Pound sterling	101	196	282	3	9	19	1	3	4
—Swiss franc	41	60	101	2	3	6	0	1	1
—Canadian dollar	38	55	93	3	6	9	0	0	2
—Australian dollar	38	78	147	3	8	9	0	1	1
—Swedish krona[4]	—	—	51	—	—	0	—	—	1
—Other	143	208	457	3	10	32	1	2	8

Euro vs. other currencies[5]	47	104	185	10	20	37	1	3	3
—Japanese yen	18	38	42	6	10	16	0	0	0
—Pound sterling	14	29	40	2	3	4	0	2	1
—Swiss franc	5	13	29	1	4	8	0	0	0
—Canadian dollar	1	2	5	0	0	0	0	0	0
—Australian dollar	1	3	5	0	1	1	0	0	0
—Swedish krona[4]	—	—	15	—	—	2	—	—	0
—Other	8	20	49	1	3	7	0	—	1
Japanese yen vs. other currencies[6]	3	10	27	0	1	6	0	0	0
Other currency pairs	15	24	53	2	4	10	0	0	1
All currency pairs	853	1,303	2,319	60	117	212	7	21	32

[1]Adjusted for local and cross-border double-counting.
[2]Outright forwards, foreign exchange swaps, currency swaps, options, and other products.
[3]Data for 2004 have been revised.
[4]The currency pairs U.S. dollar/Swedish krona and euro/Swedish krona could not be separately identified before 2007, and are included in "other".
[5]Excluding the U.S. dollar.
[6]Excluding the U.S. dollar and the euro.

Source: Bank of International Settlements.

EXHIBIT 1.4 Reported Foreign Exchange Market Turnover by Currency Pair[1]: Daily Averages in April, in Billions of U.S. dollars and Percent

	2001		2004[2]		2007	
	Amount	Percent share	Amount	Percent share	Amount	Percent share
U.S. dollar/euro	354	30	503	28	840	27
U.S. dollar/yen	231	20	298	17	397	13
U.S. dollar/sterling	125	11	248	14	361	12
U.S. dollar/ Australian dollar	47	4	98	5	175	6
U.S. dollar/ Swiss franc	57	5	78	4	143	5
U.S. dollar/ Canadian dollar	50	4	71	4	115	4
U.S. dollar/ Swedish krona[3]	—	—	—	—	56	2
U.S. dollar/other	195	17	295	16	572	19
Euro/yen	30	3	51	3	70	2
Euro/sterling	24	2	43	2	64	2
Euro/Swiss franc	12	1	26	1	54	2
Euro/other	21	2	39	2	112	4
Other currency pairs	26	2	42	2	122	4
All currency pairs	1,173	100	1,794	100	3,081	100

[1]Adjusted for local and cross-border double-counting.
[2]Data for 2004 have been revised.
[3]The U.S. dollar/Swedish krona pair could not be separately identified before 2007 and is included in "other".

Source: Bank of International Settlements.

The interbank market in 2007 accounted for 43 percent of all foreign exchange transactions, down from 53 percent in 2004. The retail currency broker may be one explanation, as well as the number of swap and forward transactions that occur on the OTC market.

While the Triennial report may have a three-year look-back period, it has profound effects for currency markets. We learned that spot and swap transactions account for the majority of foreign-currency trades around the world, about $2.7 trillion in 2007. The U.S. dollar by far is the most widely traded instrument, followed by the euro, Japanese yen, British pound, Swiss franc, Canadian dollar, and Australian dollar. All other currencies of the world are thinly traded and can't compare to the amounts traded of these major currencies. One reason is the convertibility factor.

Of the vast majority of the world's currencies, 150 of 200 can't be directly converted, so conversion is facilitated through the major currencies because they are more liquid. Another reason is larger economies where trade and investment not only flow freely but gross domestic product (GDP) levels are high. Add a robust economy and stable political system to the equation, and traders have a recipe for success when the focus is trade in these major pairs.

With rising GDP levels in the major economies and an increasing supply of money earned, imagine what the supply of dollars will be in the future and future dollar amounts of trade. Trade the major currencies because currency prices are allowed to free float where the market sets the price.

BIS Annual Report

While the Triennial Survey may have a three-year look-back period, the BIS publishes a very detailed annual report. The 79th annual study was released in March 2009 (BIS Markets Committee 2009). These reports are consequential, an imperative for market professionals because of the detailed orientation with which the BIS approaches topics from a world perspective. Because the prior period focused on implications for world economies, examining markets and banking systems from a global perspective due to the collapse are just a few aspects of the report.

Since the collapse, there are many implications for spillover effects around the world. This was viewed in terms of interest rates and imbalances across the world. Spillover effects can be viewed in terms of contagion. Contagion asks the question, Does a crisis in one nation have ramifications for other neighboring nations, or worse, does a crisis have implications for all world economies? What that meant for investment bankers, banks, and insurance companies is profound in terms of investments, cash flows, and profits and is highlighted extensively in this report.

Such questions had to be answered to align proper funding and ensure profit margins. Questions such as: Where does money flow to seek its yield, and how can investors take advantage of those situations? Bank capital was the greatest question, because as credit spreads widened an increase in the price of capital available to lend became an issue. Where do hedge funds and insurance companies fit into this equation? What are risk opportunities? Where should monies *not* be invested is the question. What about possible policy responses to the collapse? A detrimental policy response can cost a nation and their markets irreparable harm for years. Those decisions must be viewed with a discerning eye.

The annual report is 250 pages, complete with charts, graphs, and many statistical measures that outlined pre crisis to the crisis and beyond. It has a one-year look-back period, but its reports can be profound in terms of exchange rates and spot trades.

BIS Quarterly Review

As noted in Exhibit 1.5, more important on a shorter-term basis is the Quarterly Review published by the BIS, where a glimpse of the last three months of trading activity and highlights can be viewed.

Equity prices recovered, credit spreads fell as the cost of borrowing decreased, and bond prices rose with equity markets. Two major market occurrences materialized during this period that sent the markets reeling: The Lehman Brothers collapse and the announcement of the Volcker Rule in January 2009. The Volcker Rule was the proposal by former Federal Reserve Chairman Paul Volcker and current economic assistant to President Obama,

EXHIBIT 1.5   Major Market Developments

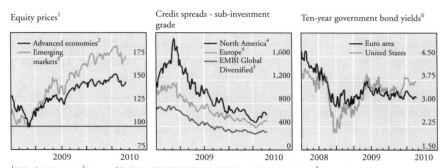

[1] 3 March 2009 = 100. [2] Average of S&P 500, DJ EURO STOXX, TOPIX, and FTSE 100 indices. [3] Average of Asian, European and Latin American emerging market equity indices. [4] Five-year on-the-run credit default swap (CDS) mid-spreads on sub-investment grade (CDX High Yield; ITraxx Crossover) quality, in basis points. [5] Stripped spreads, in basis points. [6] In percent.

Source: Bank of International Settlements Quarterly Review, Jan–Mar 2009.

EXHIBIT 1.6 Equity and Commodity Markets, January to March 2009

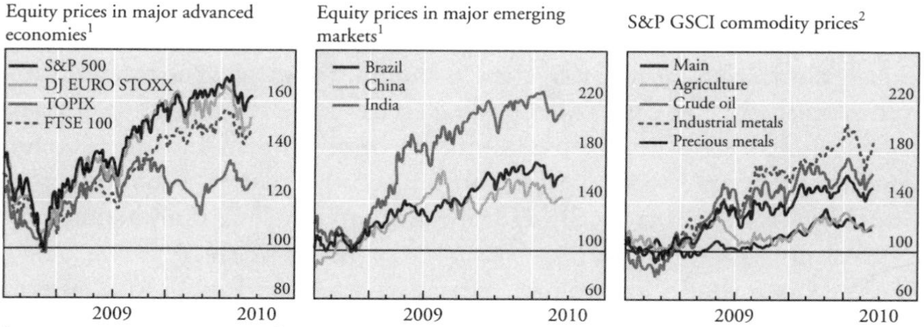

Equity prices in major advanced economies[1]

Equity prices in major emerging markets[1]

S&P GSCI commodity prices[2]

[1]In local currency; 9 March 2009 = 100. [2]Goldman Sachs Commodity Index; 9 March 2009 = 100.

Source: Bank of International Settlements Quarterly Review, January to March 2009.

who proposed that banks limit proprietary and speculative trading if the trade wasn't implemented based on client desires.

As seen in Exhibit 1.6, January 10, 2009, saw equity prices, especially bank stocks, in Europe and in the U.S. dive, credit spreads widen, yields fall, and the safety of government bond prices soar upwards.

Finally, see Exhibit 1.6, and notice as equity prices rose in 2009, agricultural, crude oil, and metals prices fell. This equation is not only a common denominator of market developments since the crisis hit in August 2008, but a common occurrence of historical intermarket movements.

FX Committee in the United States

In addition to the BIS FX reports, each central bank of the major nations has its own FX committee that imitates for the most part the work of the BIS.

For example, the FX Committee was formed in 1978 under the sponsorship of the Federal Reserve. An annual report published every year since 1979 highlights past yearly market activity in foreign exchange. Earlier reports focused on advisory roles of the FX Committee and processes of market activity because free-floating exchange rates recently began, so questions of structure and process had to be defined by both the markets and the committee.

As spot-market structure began and settled into a system, new investment vehicles such as forward interest-rate agreements, interest-rate swaps, and currency options had to be addressed. For example, what happens to an options delta 25 hedge when the market expects volatility? According to the recently introduced 1973 Black-Scholes Model of option pricing, the hedge could be at risk due to market volatility. Delta hedging was addressed in the 1984 annual FX Committee's Report as a study of risk assessment with the recent introduction of currency options.

Legal issues are addressed by the FX Committee such as the recent introduction in the United States, and trading arrangements of, the Chilean peso, the Columbian peso, the Peruvian sol, the Brazilian real, and the Chinese renminbi. Not only spot rates are introduced, but currency options, forwards, swaps, and other legally agreed terms are set. This is all handled by FX committees.

The Committee's first volume survey was published in 1980 as a trial, and was published every three years thereafter until 2005 when the committee proposed a semi-annual survey. The 1982 committee discussed adoption of volume surveys as a regular practice due to the increased volume of the market. For example, the Japanese yen traded $8 billion a month in 1976 and increased to $75 billion a month by 1981. Such issues had to be addressed.

The 1980 survey highlighted a 64 percent market share for spot transactions and 51 percent in 1983. Swaps traded 30 percent of market share in 1980 and 48 percent in 1983. Forwards accounted for 6 percent of market share in 1980 and 0.5 percent in 1983. The low volume in 1983 was caused by a ruling by the Financial Accounting Standards Board (FASB) in Rule 52 that stated forwards should be treated as stockholder equity rather than current earnings (1980 report).

The German mark was the most widely traded currency in 1983 with 32 percent of all spot, forwards, and swap transactions, and 31 percent in 1980. The yen was second in 1983 with a 22 percent market share, up from fourth in 1980 with a 10.2 percent turnover. The pound sterling was second in 1980 with a 22.2 percent share and third in 1983 with a 16.6 percent share. The Swiss franc was fourth in 1983 with a 12.2 percent share and fifth in 1980 with a 10.1 percent market share. The Canadian dollar was fifth in 1983 with a 7.5 percent share, down from third place in 1980 with a 12.3 percent share. Cross currencies accounted for $1.5 billion in April 1983 (FX Committee 1995).

Since 2005, the FX Committee has published its semi-annual volume survey that highlights forwards, swaps, option, and spot transactions. Volume surveys focus on monthly volumes, dollar changes year over year, and volumes by currency pair, by counter-party, and by maturity.

Notice Exhibit 1.7 of the pie chart from the most recent survey. Spot transactions accounted for $388 billion, 57 percent of all FX transactions, while swaps garnered 26 percent of the market with a volume of $176 billion. Forwards accounted for 13 percent of the market with a volume of

EXHIBIT 1.7 FX Committee Pie Chart

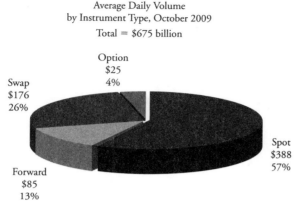

Average Daily Volume
by Instrument Type, October 2009
Total = $675 billion

Option
$25
4%

Swap
$176
26%

Spot
$388
57%

Forward
$85
13%

Source: U.S. FX Committee, 2010.

$85 billion, and OTC options garnered 4 percent of market share with a volume of $25 billion.

Worldwide FX Committees

Major trading nations of the world established their own counterparts to the FX Committee through their respective central banks. The United Kingdom, through the Bank of England, established the U.K. Foreign Exchange Joint Standing Committee, Singapore adopted the Foreign Exchange Market Committee, Canada through the Bank of Canada established the Foreign Exchange Committee, Australia through its Royal Bank of Australia adopted the Foreign Exchange Committee, Europe through the European Central Bank established the Foreign Exchange Contact Group, Japan established its FX Market Committee through the Bank of Japan, Hong Kong established its FX Committee through its Hong Kong Monetary Authority called the Treasury Markets Association, and Switzerland established the Federal Supervisory Markets Committee from the Swiss National Bank.

The purpose of reports such as those issued by the BIS and the various FX committees is not to wholly focus on volume and types of trades, but that in itself is an important function. More important are the types of instruments traded, where money flows to seek yield, who the major players in the world are, and where the economic growth is in terms of a specific nation or region.

The major questions answered by these reports are where should resources be allocated, how should portfolios be adjusted, and what are the risks? Is a certain nation's currency overbought or oversold, is a certain region over-bought or oversold, and will past strategies work in the future? For example, of the seven major widely traded currencies, three are considered commodity currencies, Australia, Canada, and New Zealand. If all three had long runs based on prior reports and their respective natural resources sold well, will those same strategies work in the future?

Conclusion

Traders and market professionals must understand the constant attention paid to overall industry changes in these reports by consummate market professionals who look at forward changes and market developments through reports, statistics, and market studies. Volumes are just one side of the overall equation. Yet we know from past volume histories that the spot transaction is the dominant instrument traded yesterday, and chances are good that spot will dominate foreign currency transactions long into the future.

Professional market reports provide an insight, an intelligence of a market that may undergo changes in design, structure, or some feature that may enhance or limit a market's overall ability. Yet reports can answer questions as to present strategies and possible tactical changes. Reports serve as market guides, a road map that can hint at direction of a currency pair, highlight an overbought region, gain insight into a new trading instrument, and even provide insight into a government position on tax and fiscal policies. Many reports exist nation to nation and all are released at various times throughout any given year. Because of the forward nature of various reports, much can be gained due to the depth and detail professionals devote to every issue.

CHAPTER 2

Currency Trading Beyond the Basics

This chapter will address the many foundations and theories of money and exchange rates as well as the histories behind those theories. The chapter begins with concepts of the currency market, participants, and foundations that comprise currency pairs. The belief is that understanding currency pairs must equate to an understanding of how other nations view their own currencies and how those currencies are traded in their respective markets. Concepts such as margin, rollover interest, and how that interest is debited and credited to accounts is important to denote amounts of revenue that may be earned or lost. All is highlighted from a nation-to-nation perspective. Histories of economic formations are addressed as they relate to an economic structure, and concepts such as interest rates that hold economies together are detailed. Purchasing Power Parity is a turn-of-the-century concept that still has relevance today, so it was addressed in detail. All concepts have relevance to not only understand the currency markets but to understand the markets in relation to gaining profits.

One common theme that should be stated, promoted, and understood throughout this text is that currency trading is about money, the cost of money, the demand and supply of it, and the price in relation to the various currency pairs and assets it mimics. How much does money cost and can demand meet supply or supply meet demand are just a few questions that will be answered. These answers can only be determined in the interbank market through interest rates and financial instruments associated with interest. Interest-rate formulas have as their foundation:

$$\text{Simple Interest} = \text{Principal} \times \text{Rate} \times \text{Time}$$

From nation to nation, central bank to central bank, the answers are different because cost factors and funding needs are distinct. A commodity currency has different cost and funding needs as opposed to a manufacturing currency nation and economic situations allow various pairs to move differently from each other. Larger nations are different than smaller nations. Export nations are distinct from import nations. Cross pairs and U.S. dollar pairs are quite different in movement and cost structure. Each economy varies in size, shape, cost, and finance needs. Yet these factors are aligned as currency pairs. Historic currency pair terminology referred to pairs as commodity/terms and terms/commodity. To bring these factors into balance and understanding, I explore the numerous factors involved to answer these questions, because not all currency pairs are the same. All have a distinctness, a purpose, a reason for existence, and a reason for movement. And many have a market interest in these factors.

Banks, governments, central banks, major companies throughout the world, importers and exporters, traders, speculators, hedge funds, pension funds, cross-currency investors, traders and speculators, carry traders, organizations, and tourists, to name a few, are all involved in this market on a daily basis. A trading indicator won't necessarily help to understand this answer because it looks at these factors in the short term and from the inside out without a look at the whole picture of a nation and its particular pair.

The important answer to understand is what makes a currency turn to strength or a sell and what are factors that force market weakness—a long. A currency price is based on the cost factor, the price of money, and the price that others are willing to buy or sell for in terms of an interest rate. Any market implications that hamper a currency pair's funding or cost structure means that that pair will be sold to reflect the new cost and funding structure. Inversely, a pair will be bought if funding and cost aren't hindered. From a single-nation perspective, internal funding is conducted through sales of bonds, notes, and bills and it connects to external factors of foreign exchange such as Spots, swaps, and forwards. Failure to connect can hamper the overall structure.

For example, a spot trader in Great Britain would want the British pound/U.S. dollar pair to trend toward weakness, to trend upward. This means England's economy must have strong economic output, rising wages, rising consumer prices, rising producer prices, rising exports, and rising interest rates. In this instance, the cost and funding structure is cheap and the Bank of England can easily meet these funding needs while its nation's manufacturers and consumers enjoy good economic times. Any problems along this journey and the British pound/U.S. dollar pair will be sold as the cost of money rises and funding needs can't be met.

Most important is the idea that a currency pair is a two-sided equation that must be understood from a two-nation perspective in terms of price, cost, funding structures, and reasons when, how, and why pairs move. To understand is to profit.

Pips and Lots

Spot-currency trading is conducted through pips. A pip is a percentage interest point. A 100 pip move up or down in any currency pair equates to one penny, a common occurrence on any given trading day. The market term for a 100 pip move is a Big Figure, slang is big fig. Just like a Milliard is equal to one billion units of currency, the market term is Yard to equal a billion units.

The value of a pip depends on the type of lot traded. A standard lot equates to control of 100,000 currencies; it is one one-hundredth of a point, one basis point, or $10 per pip. For most pairs, this is found in the fourth decimal place, second decimal place for the Japanese yen. For example, British pound/U.S. dollar is the British pound sterling versus the United States dollar. So British pound/U.S. dollar is equal to 0.0001 multiplied by 100,000 and equals $10.00. A mini lot is British pound/U.S. dollar is equal to 0.0001 × 10,000 and equals $1.00. A standard lot is $10.00 per pip, two lots are $20.00 per pip, three lots are $30.00 per pip. No dollar limits exist on the amount of lots to buy or sell. A mini lot is 10,000 trades at $1.00 per pip, two lots is $2.00 per pip, three lots is $3.00 per pip. There are no limits to dollar amounts or number of lots to buy or sell. The advantage of a mini lot is that one can buy or sell 15 mini lots or one standard lot and a half. One standard lot is equal to 10 mini lots. It is perfect for a small trader with limited funds.

Micro Lots are equal to 0.10. Each lot trades at 1 cent a pip. Quotes here are in U.S. dollars because the base currency is in U.S. dollars. Suppose we have U.S. dollar/Swiss franc. How much does each pip earn? Divide by the exchange rate. For example, U.S. dollar/Swiss franc exchange rate is 1.0570, equal to $10.00 divided by 1.0570, so it is $9.46 per pip based on one standard lot. How much does a lot cost? The price of a lot is different from market to market and it depends on which market to trade, how much liquidity is available, how much bids and offers cost, and the amount of narrowing or widening of the spreads.

Bid/Ask—The Difference Is in the Spread!

All traders once paid a per-lot price, but recent changes now stipulate traders pay a spread between the bid and ask. Currencies are now quoted in bid/ask thanks to retail brokers that sell currencies back to the interbank market. Bid/ask can also be viewed in the context of bid/offer, buy/sell, borrow/lend, and even deposit/lend where deposit rates create a floor and lend rates create a ceiling. The difference is the spread.

The *bid* appears on the left side of a currency pair and that is the quote to sell while the *ask* is the price to buy and appears on the right. The ask always exceeds the bid. Ask minus bid equals the cost of a trade per one lot. The price of a spread depends on liquidity of the market and the particular currency pair. Fast markets and high volatility will see small spreads generally. Illiquid currency pairs or illiquid markets will see higher spreads.

Some pairs such as the British pound/Japanese yen or U.S. dollar/South African Rand may see higher spreads due to wide-ranging movements. The U.S. dollar/South African Rand can cost as much as 200 to 300 pips for the spread and as little as 70 pips depending on volatility. Trading the majors against the U.S. dollar and even the cross pairs should cost between 2 and 10 pips, as a general range in the United States and Canada, double easily in Switzerland and the vast majority in Europe and Hong Kong. Japanese broker pip spreads are as competitive as the United States.

To determine percentage terms Ask Rate – Bid divided by the Ask rate. Directional determinations of spot prices based on smaller bid/ask spreads are not as easily determined today. With recent changes from a per-lot price to a spread, it is hard to answer because it is not an area of great interest to researchers presently. Recent studies focused on volatility in relation to spreads, so general assumptions can only be rendered presently. One aspect widely employed in the past to determine direction was to calculate bid/ask spreads in terms of arithmetic means, but because the spreads are so minuscule the best answer would be to employ percents. The analytical eye would also determine direction as a bid or ask price would be supported on any price divergences. Sometimes an indicator may hint at direction but the overall market may have other purposes and it shows within the bid/ask spread.

Punishing the United States with Margins

Most margins in the United States allows for a 100 to 1 leverage and a 1 percent margin. One standard lot to control 100,000 currencies requires traders to maintain the 1 percent margin. To fall below will mean a trader must add money to the account or the broker will sell out the position by a margin call and a trader will suffer the loss. A current proposal by the Commodity Futures Trading Commission (CFTC) to limit margins is underway as this is written. And this has happened yet again as the war against currency markets continues. Leverage is now 50:1 with a 2 percent margin, 20:1 leverage with a 5 percent margin for exotic pairs such as U.S. dollar/South African Rand and U.S. dollar/Turkish Lira. Taking this into account, the United States is the most punished nation in the world.

Mrs. Wantanabe and the Margin Japan

About 120 currency brokers exist in Japan, down from 500 in 2005 and all offer leverage that can be as high as 400 to 1. Japanese accounts traded $302.5 billion a day according to the 2007 Triennial Report. The Japanese have a long, long history of active trading and the modern day is no different. Yet the governing arm of the currency markets, the Financial Services Authority in Japan is currently proposing to limit margins to 50 to 1 in 2010 and 25 to 1 in 2011. The Bank of Japan released a report in 2008 and found that one tenth of all spot trades were transacted by margin traders, so the trading public is firmly against these proposals almost by a 70 to 30 margin according to recent polls. The most famous person in Japan is Mrs. Wantanabe, a fictitious person representative of a vast group of everyday traders who comprise a vast majority of the Japanese public. The idea is as Mr. Wantanabe works during the day, Mrs. Wantanabe is helping earn income by trading.

Margin: Europe, Switzerland, England, Australia, Hong Kong, and Canada

Spreads are higher through European brokers compared to the U.S. but leverage is 100 to 1 with a 1 percent margin in some nations. Generally brokers apply automatically a 5 percent margin that can be changed higher at the request of the trader. This equates to a 50-to-1 margin. The British pound/Japanese yen will cost easily a set nine-pip spread and higher throughout any trading day, 70 pips for U.S. dollar/South African Rand.

Switzerland is no different in set spread prices, yet some Swiss brokers also charge a volume commission. Traders pay the least amount of these three categories: volume according to net deposit, volume based on equity, or volume based on traded volume. The price paid is based in U.S. dollars, not Swiss francs. The higher the equity and the more volume of trades, the less a trader pays. Another way to view this is in terms of volume versus price quotes.

If a foreign currency is the quote (bottom) and the local currency is the terms (top), this is called a price quote. The foreign currency is priced in terms of the local currency. If a foreign currency is the terms (bottom) and the local currency is the quote (top), this is called a volume quote. Other firms offer spreads without a commission but the spreads are higher than the United States. The competitiveness may be derived because the Swiss tout their low capital-gain rates.

England is by far the best throughout the world in all categories, including pip spreads, taxes, hedging, rollovers, and margin. London is the home of currency trading and it lives up to its reputation. Australia encourages traders as well and offers a decent system for traders.

Canada offers a 25-to-1 leverage with a 4 percent margin. Pip spreads are slightly higher than the United States, but still competitive.

Hong Kong sets margin at 20 to 1, 5 percent of open positions, 3 percent to maintain, and below 1 percent means the position will be liquidated for a loss. These rules are set by the Securities and Futures Commission. Some nations help and encourage traders and markets, others punish.

Rollovers

In the United States, rollover interest is debited or credited to accounts at 5:00 p.m. eastern time for positions held overnight. This process began in 1994 to settle spot prices so a standard system of exchange rates could be established to settle old contracts and enter into new agreements. The prior time was 4:00 p.m. in conjunction with the New York Stock Exchange close, but changed to 5:00 p.m. in later years.

At 5:01, the opportunity to gain interest is lost until the next trading day at 5:01 p.m. Rollover interest works based on interest rates, short and long term. Suppose a trader is long Australian dollar/U.S. dollar, meaning a trader bought the Australian dollar and sold the U.S. dollar pair. The interest rate in Australia is currently 4.25, and the interest rate is 0.25 in the United States. Based on the formula to calculate interest, a positive account will receive the difference of 4.25 minus 0.25, so 4 percent. Four percent multiplied by 100,000 for one standard lot equals $4,000. $4,000 divided by 365 days is equal to $10.95. This interest amount is credited to the account, per lot, on a daily basis as long as the position remains open.

Suppose a trader sold British pound/Australian dollar. Here a trader sells the Australian dollar and buys the British pound. England's interest rate is 0.50 and Australia's is 4.25. This account will always receive a negative rollover due to negative interest. Monies will be debited daily on a per lot basis.

There is one caveat to this interest-rate trading strategy. During the course of any trading day, short-term interest rates ebb and flow based on market events such as news announcements, volatility, and liquidity. The quoted rollover on the Australian dollar/U.S. dollar position is based on a per-annum basis. It is the benchmark interest rate between two nations and used by many brokers as accepted and legal practice. But rates will ebb and flow throughout the day. If for some market reason U.S. dollar rates traded higher, Australian dollars would receive less interest for the day. It is the factor, how each broker debits and credits rollover.

Rollover Rates and LIBOR

Rates are factored based on the London Interbank Offered Rate (LIBOR), which is released by the British Bankers Association every day at about 11:30 a.m. London time, about 5:00 a.m. eastern time. It is the reference rate for the following currencies: Swiss franc, British pound, U.S. dollar, Canadian dollar, Australian and New Zealand dollars, Japanese yen, euro, Danish krone, and Swedish krona. The majority of the world's trading nations follow these rates, but this is just the start of rates as the New York markets begin. Where these unsecured borrowed LIBOR will go based on the course of any trading day can at times be unpredictable. This is due to the factors of the LIBOR.

LIBOR is the offered rate, a rate at which banks will lend unsecured funds. LIBID is the bid rate, the rate at which banks wish to borrow unsecured funds, and LIMEAN is the average rate of LIBOR and LIBID. What usually transpires is a rate based on an arithmetic mean or a rate agreed, plus or minus the spread. Normally the highest and lowest bids and offers are discarded and the middle rates are averaged to derive the day's LIBOR. The question for rollover and trading purposes is how much does money cost on that day and from nation to nation, because all nations have different cost structures and liquidity needs.

The most notable effect for residents of these nations is LIBOR are connected to residential housing finance, especially in Singapore. With every new day, rates change as finance needs change with a top LIBOR and a lower LIBID rate, a ceiling and floor. See Exhibit 2.1, overnight LIBOR.

The U.S. dollar rates traded higher one day and lower the next. Notice further how Australian dollar rates edged up in the yesterday column

EXHIBIT 2.1   LIBOR Charts

	Current	Yesterday
U.S. dollar	0.250250	0.249000
British pound	0.541250	0.540630
Euro	0.278130	0.278130
Japanese yen	0.117500	0.117500
Swiss franc	0.046670	0.046670
Australian dollar	4.320000	4.332500
Canadian dollar	0.250000	0.250830
New Zealand dollar	2.737500	2.750000

as the U.S. dollar rates traded down. Further notice overnight LIBOR in Exhibit 2.1 and notice how far the U.S. dollar rates dropped against their Australian dollar counterpart.

Australian dollar LIBOR continues to trade at a premium to its benchmark rate and may be a sign of either the market anticipating a further rate hike because borrowing costs are higher or the rate is overbought. Liquidity and funding needs will determine the answer. For rollover purposes, this represents continued positive interest payments. Some brokers, particularly in Europe and Asia, will use swap points instead of the benchmark interest rate between central banks to determine rollover.

Swap Points and Rollover

Swap points, or forward points, are the bid/ask prices of forward contracts traded in the interbank market and must be viewed as an interest rate. But foreign exchange (FX) swaps, particularly interest rate swaps, also incorporate swap points in their terminology and trade in the interbank market. The formal definition of swap points is the difference between interest rates on currencies. All currency pairs have different swap rates due to the differences in interest rates between pairs. Swap points are also termed forward points, FX points, or spot points. Positive forward points are added to the spot rate while negative points are deducted. Forward points equate to basis points by multiplying by 100 or 1000. If a swap point appears as 0.0084 and is positive, basis-point terms are already derived. The multiplication determines how much. The Czechoslovakian central bank factors forward points by dividing forward points by 1000 and adding the result to the spot rate. Future spot prices and future interest is factored based on forward implied rates.

The formula:

$$(1 + r)\#days/12 = [(1 + Spot)month/12] \times [(1 + y)p/12]$$

where

p = number of periods in the implied period.

A last method to look at forward points is by forward margin.

Forward margin is derived from forward rates and expressed as the future value of a currency pair in terms of the terms and quote. Forward margin equals the forward rate minus the spot rate and is expressed as swap or forward points. The reason to employ forward points in rollover accounts is to debit or credit actual market rates rather than benchmark interest rates.

For example, Europe debits and credits rollover accounts based on swap points. Swap points are derived from euro LIBOR, a LIBOR rate released by the British Bankers Association (BBA) at 6:00 a.m. exclusively for the European markets. euro LIBOR is used because it is the basis of swap contracts, the basis of interest rates, and the basis of unsecured borrowing for the trading day in the European interbank market traded in London and overseas. It is the interest rate more closely aligned to the overall market.

Beside euro LIBOR, the British Bankers Association releases LIBOR for 10 different currency markets with 15 various maturities ranging from overnight to one year.

Yet each nation releases its own LIBOR to accommodate interest rates for their own interbank market. For example, Japan releases it's TIBOR at 11:00 a.m. Tokyo time, 11:00 p.m. eastern standard time. This rate is released one hour after the Japanese stock market opens. It is a common convention for nations to release rates just after market openings. So the swap point basis will change from nation to nation due to the rise and fall daily of LIBOR within the various nations. Swap-point basis can be derived directly from bid/ask spreads in the interbank market, LIBOR, or LIBID. What is credited or debited to a rollover account can range from broker to broker around the world. Some brokers list their swap points. Others factor the swap rates and list to view on their trading screens.

Currency Fixing

When LIBOR is released by the BBA and when nations, through their top bankers, release their own rates, this is called fixing. Fixing times occur many times throughout any trading day and represent at times trading opportunities. BBA fixings represent one time and one fix, the external unsecured borrowing rate for a nation's bank doing business in London, while each nation must set its own fix to represent its internal unsecured borrowing rate. All times for the internal fix of nations are different due to the various time frames in which nations trade. Because these rates are the shortest and most sensitive of all interest rates, trading opportunities may occur based on new bids and offers.

For example, the fact that Tokyo releases its fixing rates one hour after the Japanese stock market opens is constructive for short-term gains. Markets will reflect LIBOR immediately. Central banks that experience an interest-rate change are another trading opportunity, because all interest rates short and long must be reflected in the market through financial instruments because the cost to borrow, lend and liquidity needs changed. What is important is that LIBOR must be priced to the currency. See Exhibit 2.2.

BBA LIBOR and internal nations' LIBORs must be viewed as an offshore and onshore interest rate. The offshore rate allows business and trading to be conducted overseas in a nation's currency at a particular BBA rate while the onshore rate is the rate priced to the currency in the home market. To factor an interest rate for the home market, take BBA LIBOR and divide it by the internal rate to obtain an effective interest rate. That rate will be the basis to trade a currency pair in the home market while the market is open. If a nation has two internal interest rates, as is the scenario among the major pairs, divide the two internal rates to obtain an effective rate.

Factor Swap Points

In our Australian dollar/U.S. dollar example, factor closing price by the difference of interest between pairs divided by 360 multiplied by the number of lots.

$$1.9336 \times 0.04/360 \text{ days} \times 100,000 = \$2.1484$$

Brokers may charge a fee, 10 percent for some, to handle this and any rollover transaction. Why? Because brokers must employ a Tom/Next trade. Tom/Next is the short-term terminology to mean Tomorrow Next. Tom/Next rates are found in the interbank market and don't widely vary from day to day. Spot/next or spot/starts are further terms. In order for the account to be debited or credited, the trade must be closed then reopened for the

EXHIBIT 2. 2 Internal LIBOR Currency Fixing Times by Nation

Country	Opening Fix	Closing Time	Rate Term	Market that Releases Information	Number of Banks Involved in the Process
Australia	10:00 a.m. Sydney time/ 8:00 p.m. EDT	4:45 p.m. Sydney time, 6:45 a.m. EDT	Bank Bill Reference Rate	Australia Financial Markets Association	8
Japan	11:00 a.m. Tokyo/ 9:00 p.m. EDT	6:00 p.m. Tokyo/ 6:00 a.m. EDT	TIBOR	Japanese Bankers Association	16
New Zealand	2:00 p.m. Wellington/ 10:00 p.m. EDT	4:00 p.m. Wellington/ 10:00 p.m. EDT EDT	Bank Bill Reference Rate	New Zealand Financial Markets Association	8
Canada	10:00 a.m. Toronto/ 10:00 a.m. EDT	4:00 p.m. EDT	Overnight Money Market Financing Rate also referred as CDOR, Canadian Dealers Overnight Rate	Bank of Canada never releases survey	Never released by the BOC
Hong Kong	11:00 a.m./ 11:00 p.m. EDT	5:00 p.m. Hong Kong, 5:00 a.m. EDT	Hang Seng Interbank Offered Rate	Hong Kong Association of Banks	20 Banks (close estimate)
Singapore	11:00 a.m./ 11:00 p.m. EDT	5:00 p.m./ 5:00 a.m. EDT	Singapore Interbank Offered Rate/Swap Offer Rate	Association of Banks in Singapore	17 (close estimate)
Europe	11:00 a.m. Frankfurt/ 5:00 a.m. EDT	6:00 p.m. Frankfurt/ 11:00 a.m. EDT	Euro Interbank Offered Rate, called EURIBOR. Euro Overnight Index Average	European Banking Federation	42
Switzerland	8:30 a.m. Zurich/ 1:30 a.m. EDT Noon Zurich/ 5:00 a.m. EDT	6:00 p.m. Zurich/ 11:00 a.m. EDT	Swiss Average overnight Rate	SIX Swiss Exchange	Unknown
Great Britain	11:00 a.m. London/ 5:00 a.m. EDT	6:00 p.m. London, 11:00 a.m. EDT	BBA LIBOR	BBA LIBOR	16
United States	11:00 a.m. London/ 5:00 a.m. New York	4:00 p.m.	BBA LIBOR	BBA LIBOR	16

next day's trade. If Tom/Next is not employed, a trader would have to take delivery of the currencies in the account.

Day-Count Convention

The original example factored interest payments based on 365 days a year. After the BBA administers LIBOR, the International Swap and Derivatives Association (ISDA) sets the benchmark—since 1998—for fixed rates on interest-rate swaps and other instruments through its ISDAFIX. They set rates for the euro, Hong Kong dollar, Japanese yen, Swiss franc, British pound, and the U.S. dollar. For the U.S. dollar, they also provide swap spreads. Day-count convention asks how to factor accrued interest for traded instruments. The United States, Switzerland, and the euro zone administer an actual/360 basis, Great Britain and commonwealth nations administer an actual/365 basis. To factor leap years, actual/actual is used. Other instruments such as bonds are factored on a 30/360 basis. The formula is BBA LIBOR is equal to Interest equal to the principal sum multiplied by the BBA LIBOR divided by 100 multiplied by the number of days in the interest period divided by 360.

Accrued interest asks the question how are bond coupons factored? Japan, Great Britain, Australia, New Zealand, and Canada factor coupon payments based on 365 days while the United States, Switzerland, and Europe employ 360 days. Financial instruments may trade based on different day-count conventions.

For example, Japan factors TIBOR based on 365 days while Euroyen factors based on 360 days. It is the difference between an offshore and onshore rate. Eurodollars trade based on a 360-day convention. Effective interest must be factored.

Financial instruments quoted 360 converts to effective interest by 360 divided by 365 and 365 converts by multiplying 360 by 365.

Triple Rollover

Wednesdays are triple rollover days when accounts are debited or credited with triple interest to account for the weekend and holidays. Rates are published on any trading station as they are released and when closing prices are issued for the trading day so any trader can determine early and exactly how much rollover rates pay for the day. Our rollover strategy is called the carry trade and is popular to earn rollover on a daily or longer-term basis. Yet this is only one aspect to the carry trade that will be addressed in later chapters.

Trade Strategy

Fix flows are released by banks and research companies so market professionals can gauge direction of interest rates. View the three-month LIBOR. Look for crosses to determine where one nation's rates trade above or below another. For example, suppose U.S. dollar LIBOR traded above Japanese yen. This is a sell U.S. dollar/Japanese yen trend trade because U.S. dollar rates are not only higher, but they may be higher for purposes of expectations of future higher benchmark interest rates or an economic boom to follow. Suppose three-month U.S. dollar rates crossed above British pound rates. Buy British pound/U.S. dollar. If U.S. dollar rates crossed below British pound, sell British pound/ U.S. dollar. View correlations from overnight rates to three month and determine trends to find good rollover rates plus capital appreciation. If rates held steady for both overnight and three-month LIBOR for a particular pair, chances are good that the trade is a range trade. So sell the range tops and buy the range bottoms and always allow LIBOR to be the overall guide.

Swap Points versus Rollovers for World Wide Traders

Not all nations employ LIBOR or benchmark interest to credit rollover accounts. It is important to understand how brokers factor rollover, what instruments are employed, and how much is debited or credited.

Market Orders

Market orders are defined as an entry order, an exit order, a limit order, an order to hedge a trade, and a stop order to exit a position at a predetermined time. All historic market orders were changed by the National Futures Association in 2009 due to Rule 2-43. Markets orders to enter and exit a position were changed as well as rules to manage lot and lot rotation. Lot rotation is managed by a system of first in, first out, which says that if 10 lots were bought to go long the British pound/U.S. dollar, the first lot must be addressed before the second lot, then third lot, up to the tenth lot. If a profit is earned on the tenth lot, a trader must rotate through the prior nine lots before the tenth lot's profit is allowed to be taken from the market. Rules to exit a position are done by a one-cancels-the-other order (OCO). This means an order above or below the market must be entered in order to exit a position. All rules apply to only U.S. traders in their own market. What was once a standard and easily applied system to trade has now radically changed. This convoluted system applies only to U.S. residents in U.S. markets. All nations highlighted in this text are not subject to such convoluted rules in their own nations of trade. The main polemic is that markets may run fast at times, so profits may be realized for fleeting instances. This system can slow down profits in fast markets. Examples of each type of order are provided.

United States

- National Futures Association (NFA)—Regulates currency and other markets in the United States in conjunction with the Commodity Futures Trading Commission. In April 2009 with issuance of Rule 2-43, order rules were changed, hedging rules were changed, and rules were changed for lot rotation.
- One cancels the other—Once a lot is bought or sold for any pair, an OCO order must be entered to exit the trade. If the Australian dollar/U.S. dollar was bought at 1.9336 and exited at 1.9376, a limit order must be placed above the market at, say, 1.9386. If a short was entered at 1.9376 and exited at 1.9336, a stop loss order must be entered at, say, 1.9326 to formally exit the trade.
- First in, first out (FIFO)—If a trader bought 10 lots of any currency pair, the first lot must be addressed and settled before the second, then third, and onward.
- Hedging—Traders can't enter a buy or sell at the same time in the same pair in the same account. To hedge, traders can hedge with two separate accounts or hedge in another market. For example, the euro/U.S. dollar can be hedged in the oil market, the currency option market, or the gold market to name just a few examples.

National Futures Association and Currencies

The adverse decisions to traders and currency markets in particular may be based on a number of factors. The NFA, as a regulator, has pondered the question of what is a currency without asking what are currency pairs. Can one currency be classified as a security or as a derivative, and how should it be treated in relation to other traded instruments?

NFA regulators haven't objectively answered these questions, so they treat a currency as a security—a stock—and place limits on its trading ability just as a stock would trade. To treat one currency as a derivative is just not objectionable either, due to the lack of an underlying instrument, so that concept doesn't exist unless the decisions were rendered based solely on the views of the U.S. dollar Index, the only single-currency index.

A currency pair's value is based on the corresponding pair it aligns to in relation to the nation that it trades. Only the economic situation of a nation can determine that value through the free markets. In economic terms, this is called international parity conditions where interest rates, prices, and exchange rates are linked to form the market-price model. Therefore, a currency cannot be viewed as a single entity in isolation because it detracts from the concept of currency pairs as trading vehicles, funding mechanisms, and a measured value of a nation's economic conditions and worth. Further, a currency pair is a money-market instrument and priced against other instruments in the money market. To hinder a currency-pair trade ability can only hinder other priced instruments in the same money market.

Orders: Europe, Australia, New Zealand, Hong Kong, Japan, Switzerland, Canada, and England

Several nations are governed by their own NFA that sets policies and regulations according to the nation's desires.

Japan has the Financial Services Authority; the United Kingdom has the Financial Services Authority; Hong Kong has the Securities and Futures Commission; New Zealand has the Securities Commission of New Zealand; Switzerland is home to the Swiss Financial Markets Supervisory Authority; and Canada has the Investment Industry Regulatory Organization of Canada.

The United States is the only nation that placed restrictions on currency trading. In other nations, hedging is allowed, straight limit orders are allowed, stop orders are allowed, trailing stops are allowed, and there are no restrictions to lot rotations and FIFO.

The recently passed 2010 Dodd-Frank Wall Street Reform and Consumer Protection Act section 743 and 744 prevents account openings in the countries listed previously for U.S. citizens. Any accounts held in these locations at the time of passage were closed and funds repatriated. This says that traders anywhere in the world can trade U.S. markets as they desire but U.S. traders can't trade their own markets as they desire due to adverse restrictions.

Brokers: Yesterday and Today

Since 1998, the Securities and Exchange Commission (SEC) has allowed the implementation of Electronic Communication Networks under Rule 600 b 23 of Regulation NMS and found in the Securities and Exchange Act of 1934, 11A (SEC 2010).

The National Market System (NMS) was formed to promote fair-market competition and efficient markets and is regulated by Congress and enforced by the CFTC. The focus of NMS in its infancy addressed trade of stocks when, for example, the 1975 rules facilitated linkages of systems that traded stocks. All U.S. stock markets connected to one system. Time passed and NMS was again the focus to ensure fair market access, order protection, inter-market price competition, fair price protection, and access rules, as was the case with the 2005 updates (SEC 2006).

As new financial instruments developed, retail brokers, traders, and hedge funds developed with fast computers. NMS was again the subject of debate and hearings in Congress. Congress, the SEC, and CFTC are currently addressing the May 6, 2010 Flash Crash when Greece announced horrendous economic news and the New York Stock Exchange dropped 1000 points on the day. What will occur to further enhance efficient markets or slow the speed through the NMS system is a guess at this stage. The questions are speed of computers and fair access.

Originally, networks facilitated trade through a network of buy and sell orders routed through NASDAQ. All electronic communication networks (ECNs) had to register with the SEC as a broker dealer and became subject to regulation as an Alternative Trading System. Early debates included questions of access to the network and whether fees should be charged for access. Questions of trading commissions came next, as well as fees for dormant accounts.

As time progressed and old issues settled, the personal computer and increased access to the networks allowed retail and professional traders access to the markets. Today retail traders can trade many types of financial instruments from futures to options to currencies to stocks on any exchange around the world and even at the same time.

Currency brokers found their purpose as middlemen to support the trade of currencies from retail traders to the interbank network. In the beginning, they charged a fixed price on a per-lot basis. With better and faster computers, the fixed-lot price was reduced to a spread price as trading outside the interbank market exploded.

Today the majority of currency brokers earn their revenue from the spread. Traders must be aware of brokers that make markets in certain currencies. Their role changed from facilitator to dealer. Unsuspecting retail traders in these instances trade against their own broker. As retail traders buy and sell lots from these brokers, dealers facilitate separate trades for profit in the interbank market and may earn the same revenue twice.

Exchange Rates: The Impact of Keynes and Mundell-Fleming

When one ponders the question of what is or what should be the price of one currency in relation to another, the modern day and accepted answer is the nominal or real exchange rate, the purchasing power parity, or balance of payment models. How these models were derived should be the question, as well as their validity. A brief walk through history will help to explain.

Classical theorists focused their attention on monetary policy as it relates to the level of prices in an economy in terms of the money supply. They believed that as the money supply increased, price levels would increase along with the exchange rate without any dramatic effects to an economy in terms of growth and output. If growth in the money supply increases inflation, interest rates and the currency price would reflect these economic variables but still not affect an economy's growth rates. Then John Maynard Keynes turned this theory upside down.

No discussion of macroeconomics can neglect John Maynard Keynes. Keynes believed that economies always move toward equilibrium. How equilibrium finds its place in an economy was the source of contested debate for classical economists and Keynesians in the 1930s. This debate is continuous; it is argued today on a higher order.

Building on this premise, 1972 Economic Nobel Laureate John Hicks in 1937 introduced the Investment Savings and Liquidity Preference for Money Supply (IS/LM) Model. It is actually two equilibrium models linked together, income to interest rates and expenditures to income. Equilibrium is the intersection of nominal interest rates to gross domestic product (GDP) or income. The measure is not only economic equilibrium and interest rates, but the proper output of goods and services. Aligned properly, one can determine how an economy fully functions to its perfect capacity.

The IS curve measures interest rates on the vertical axis and income on the horizontal axis. Income in 1937 was a measure of GDP, beyond 1937 it measured, for example, exports, savings, and government spending. The IS curve is a quantity of equilibrium as it relates to total spending to total output. It is measured by the equation:

$$Y = C + I$$

The premise is that interest rates ebb and flow with investment along the curve. Higher interest rates equate to a higher return on investments. But if investment in terms of profitability is uncertain due to high interest rates, the investment is scrapped. For these reasons, the IS curve is downward sloping.

The Liquidity Preference and Money Supply (LM) curve measures demand for money on the vertical axis and the supply of money held by banks on the horizontal axis. The measure is the demand for money and investment. Equilibrium occurs when demand equals the supply on the money markets. The positive is if money demand is uncertain, consumers will be cautious. If money is cheap in terms of a low interest rate, consumers will buy assets. With high interest rates, they will sell assets. Two types of money were identified by Keynes—speculative and uncertain.

Uncertain money is used for basic living, and speculative money is used for investment. This equation is represented by M/P where M = the money supply and P = the fixed price level or interest rate. So

$$M/P = L(Y) + L2\,(I)$$
$$L2\,(I) = M/P - L1\,(Y)$$

This curve points upwards.

Equilibrium occurs when IS is equal to LM and answers the question where does supply equal demand in terms of money and interest rates? The method of determination is to plot points to further specify the balance of monetary policy. To accommodate for fiscal policy, Income is equal to consumer spending (Income minus Taxes) plus Investment multiplied by the interest rate as a function of real interest rates plus government spending.

While this equilibrium model was presented in its basic form, inputs can be mixed and matched, as the case has been since 1937, to determine equilibrium of an economy. The glue that held this model together and the method employed to fully understand an amply functional economy is interest rates.

If this economy would have been fully functional today, a nation's economy would have been reflected in its currency price since interest rates, above all, are what drive spot prices. Although this model and the classical model may have an inward bias that determines a look at an economy at one moment in time, it led to the understanding of the level of bond prices, asset prices, and construction of yield curves. It was the beginning of understanding exchange rates but it wasn't enough since only one side of a currency pair was understood.

Robert Mundell and Marcus Fleming revolutionized the IS/LM Model in 1962 with an introduction of a balance of payments component that would change not only the GDP income element of the model, but the money supply, domestic versus global interest rate, government expenditures, and exchange rates would all become important factors to determine an economy in equilibrium. It completely altered what was understood for 25 years as an economy in equilibrium and shifted the IS and LM curves exponentially to form a new model.

The balance of payments net-export function would change the curves due to the purchase and sale of foreign securities to complete transactions. Income would change due to the factors of net exports and the cost of transactions in terms of interest-rate differentials. Both would affect the domestic and global interest rate and all would affect government expenditures. For the first time in history, exchange rates and the proper balance of rates were tied to a macroeconomic view of the world due to capital flows across borders. No longer would economies be viewed from an inward perspective without the consideration of Mundell-Fleming. Robert Mundell would receive the Nobel Prize in Economics in 1999 for this model, and would later become instrumental in the development of the forward market.

While these models were presented in their basic form to understand the historical aspects of the development of exchange rates and all have their critics because the gold standard was still in effect in 1962, Mundell-Fleming set the world on a new course of study for governments, researchers, traders, professionals, and academics to understand exchange rates in terms of the balance-of-payment model. Nearly 50 years after this valuation model was introduced, world governments and international organizations adopted a reasonably uniform standard of a balance-of-payment model employed not only to determine trade but to gauge the proper balance of exchange rates. The effects of Mundell-Fleming are still a crucial element of the international system today.

U.S. Current and Capital Account

For the United States, the two most important components of the balance of payment are the Current and Capital Accounts. The Current Account measures trade in goods and services based on inflows and outflows, a standard measure that traces back to the classical model. It is a measure of the value of imports to exports. The term *merchandise trade* is used by the popular media to characterize these numbers.

Next, the Capital Account measures the total outflow of net capital account payments. Income Accounts measure receipts and payments of foreign-owned assets in the United States and U.S.-owned foreign assets. The last category is the unilateral account that includes transfer payments to foreigners, such as grants. Together, a trade deficit or surplus is derived and released by the Bureau of Economic Analysis every three months and an exchange rate is determined by the markets based on the released figure.

A deficit or surplus will see a revaluation among spot currency pairs to reflect the increase or decrease in prices among nations. A surplus will see a devaluation of the U.S. dollar while a deficit will see appreciation to reflect the various degrees of price. The U.S. dollar has an inverse relationship to its economic releases.

With price variables, the theory is that eventually equilibrium in the trade balance will reach parity as prices adjust to the reported deficit or surplus within nations. Due to the many variables in the above models such as GDP, prices, income, and interest rates, many models to gauge spot prices developed over the years to streamline the various factors.

The long-run model and one popularized by Keynes is the monetary approach with a focus on elasticities highlighted by demand. This approach is generated by government money and investments that create societal demand. Critics would argue that it eliminates the focus on capital flows, so many would rule out the possibility to find equilibrium within the above variables and a proper exchange rate.

The Austrian School of Economics popularized by Von Mises and more recently Von Hayek in the 1940s would argue cash balances, income, and prices rather than GDP, money supply, or price levels is the equilibrium determination.

Milton Friedman and the early Monetarists School of Economics believed monies should target the money supply on a weekly basis in rising and falling economies to find equilibrium. While these arguments may appear outdated, the Monetarists actually won the argument by adoption when Ronald Reagan became president in 1980. Von Hayek, Keynes, and Friedman still live within today's economic studies because their research forms the foundation of today's worldwide economic system.

Von Hayek and Ludwig Von Mises are descendents of the Austrian School of Economics, an offspring that dates its history to Thomas Aquinas in the fifteenth century. The last argument not considered until now are nations such as Canada and the United States that traditionally ran deficits knowingly and willingly.

The argument suggests that foreigners would finance deficits by the purchase of government bonds. The Japanese traditionally ran trade surpluses with the United States as far back as World War II, while the Europeans and Great Britain ran surpluses sporadically as deficits and surpluses waxed and waned with spot prices. Equilibrium or exchange rates were never factors to consider in this model.

GDP models to determine equilibrium and exchange rates operate on the assumption that if surpluses are reported, GDP is greater than consumption, investment and government expenditures, and total income exceeds investments. A deficit in the current account means GDP is less than consumption, investment, and government expenditures, and income is then less than expenditures. All are basic models that nations adopted in a uniform manner today.

A widely popular model is the Taylor Rule where $i = r^* + pi + 0.5 (pi - pi^*) + 0.5 (y$ minus $y^*)$ where $p^* =$ target inflation, $i =$ nominal fed funds rate, $pi =$ rate of inflation, $y =$ logarithm of real output and $y^* =$ log potential output. No coherent equation can be derived without Gustav Cassel, considered the founder of purchasing power parity (PPP), also termed the Law of One Price.

Purchasing Power Parity

Swedish Economist Gustav Cassel set out in the early 1920s to determine a true exchange rate between nations at various price levels when the gold standard broke down at the outbreak of World War I. Exchange rates were allowed to free float, causing an anomaly never understood—inflation. The Law of One Price asks the question how much does a tradeable good in nation A cost in relation to nation B? The Law of One Price says goods expressed in one price in one market should sell for the same price in another market or an arbitrage would exist to equalize prices.

Suppose a bushel of wheat costs $15 in the United States and $30 in Japan. The spot price of wheat in United States divided by the price of wheat in Japan is equal to $15 U.S. dollars divided by $30 Japan is equal to a 0.50 exchange rate. This is termed absolute purchasing power parity. It is a measure of price levels. The formula:

$$\text{Spot Rate} = \text{Price in nation A/Price in nation B}$$

is an implied rate that will determine if one side of a spot pair will appreciate or depreciate based on the price of goods and the Law of One Price. It is a measure to determine and possibly encounter misalignments and equilibrium from the previous examples. Cassel believed that either the exchange rate or purchasing power would adjust until parity existed.

Relative purchasing power parity measures the real effective exchange rate (REER) measured by inflation between two nations. Suppose inflation in Nation A was 8 percent and 2 percent in Nation B. REER is supposed to reflect the difference and the market will equalize the rates. The formula is:

$$\text{Real Effective Exchange Rate} = (\text{Actual Exchange rate P foreign price})/ \text{P domestic price}$$

Cassel believed the higher prices in one nation, the lower the purchasing power. His absolute PPP example is a measure of price levels, while the relative PPP compares price changes. The relative PPP is employed today by central bankers because it reflects market conditions and spot rates more quickly than the absolute method, especially if the correct price index is used as the gauge.

OECD-Eurostat PPP Program

Since the 1960s, the Organization of Economic Cooperation and Development (OECD) in conjunction with Eurostat established the PPP Program to determine exchange rates for euro zone- and OECD-member nations. 2008 marks the ninth round of the PPP (OECD 2010).

The program gauges exchange rates among nations by a comparison of prices paid for products and services between nations' GDPs. By a comparison of prices paid within the basket of goods measured for GDP, the PPP Program can determine an approximation of the health of an economy in terms of future GDP levels and exchange rates.

With floating exchange rates, a whole new body of knowledge has developed over the years to explore the validity of Cassel's PPP, only to determine that prices may equalize in terms of exchange rates but would take a few years to do so and that would depend on the spot pair. Some pairs can find imbalances for many years. Another factor is the measure of prices employed.

Suppose relative PPP through the REER was employed against the Consumer Price Index (CPI) that measures inflation. The International Monetary Fund (IMF), central banks, and other world organizations use the REER approach against a basket of trade weights. The weightings could be a number of factors that incorporate REER such as the GDP deflator, producer prices, wholesale prices, or manufacturing output because of its focus on inflation. The OECD reports that every 10 percent fall in the euro trade weighted exchange rate lifts nominal output 1.8 percent. Real effective exchange rates are usually factored as:

$$Q_t = S_t\text{-}P_{1,t} + P_{1,t} \text{ to represent a spot rate in}$$
$$\text{logs in relation to quantity to price}$$

The monetarists approach represented by Von Hayek to exchange rates and equilibrium can be defined by the equation

$$\text{Spot rate} = V \times Y \times MS$$

where
$$V = \text{Velocity of money, domestic} \times \text{foreign,}$$
$$Y = \text{Real Output, and}$$
$$MS = \text{Money supply.}$$

$$\text{Spot} = (Vd/Vf) \times (Yf/Yd) \times (MSd/MSf)$$

Von Hayek believed this formula would maintain a stable price, provided that the speed of velocity of money was orderly without the production of inflation.

Irving Fisher introduced the Fisher Effect and the International Fisher Effect in the 1930s to further gauge the correct spot-currency price based on inflation. Inflation is a measure of the general price level. High inflation erodes the purchasing power of money by its ability to purchase fewer goods and services. This can only be measured by interest rates.

The Fisher Effect says the nominal interest rate is equal to the real rate plus the expected rate. Suppose the interest rate in Nation A was 8 percent and Nation B was 5 percent and the expected rate was 2 percent. The real rate would be 1 percent. The International Fisher Effect then compares spot rates based on inflation. The formula is:

$$E_1 - E_2/E_2 \times 100 = 1\$ - 1 \text{ yen}$$

Where E is the exchange rate, and I$ and 1Y are national interest rates.

$$E_1 - E_2/E_2 = 1\$ - 1Y/1 + 1Y$$
$$1\$ - 1Y = \text{Spot rate}$$

Conclusion

This chapter addressed quite detailed concepts in terms of currency pairs, margin, rollover, brokers, and histories as they relate to exchange rates and PPP. It is the basic chapter to understand how exchange rates factor within the larger concept of today's currency market. More important is the concept of how a currency and how currency pairs are viewed in the context of each nation that it trades. This chapter was the foundation as currency pairs will begin the process to be priced in the traded markets. Now that an exchange rate is understood, the next chapter will address theories and foundation of effective exchange rates.

CHAPTER 3

Exchange Rates and Trade Weight Indices

This chapter will address all the necessary conditions and formulas to understand a true exchange rate and factor that true rate in terms of a basket of currencies in an index based on weights in the index according to each nation's currency and weight. These are known as trade weight indices (TWIs). To factor another nations's currency in a TWI sometimes holds the key to gauging the proper levels of exchange rates between nations. Many formulas and index-construction methodologies are provided for each nation to allow a true picture of an exchange rate but enough information is provided to allow anyone to form their own desired index.

The last factor of exchange-rate determination is to survey real-world examples of individual nations and ascertain how they factor real effective Exchange Rates (REER) in relation to their TWI, also known as an effective exchange rate index.

Effective exchange rates are employed so one nation can measure trade against a basket of weights assigned to another nation's currency in the index. This process can be managed on a daily basis much more easily than managing the volatility of spot rates. To manage spot rates means the market must be monitored on a constant basis around the clock so entries and exits can be obtained in relation to a preferred spot price in order to lock in a rate to export a good. Days may pass before a market price can be obtained.

The REER formula in its basic yet effective form is employed and factored as a basic purchasing power parity (PPP) model by

$$Q^t = Spot^t - p^t + p^t \times p^t$$

because it is the preferred method for central bankers and world organizations due to its focus on inflation and as a more rapid measure of changes to prices within nations. The measure is a spot price in logs in relation to quantity and price within a nation. The formula can be rewritten as

$$Q_t = Spot_t - p_t + p_t \times p_t$$

Log spot prices or exchange rates always allow a truer picture of a price rather than for example a correlation formula that measures exchange rates in relation to quantity and price.

TWIs are relatively new and became a function of floating exchange rates the world has experienced since the breakdown of the Louvre Accords in the early 1980s. It was the path to determine exact dollar terms of merchandise trade, identify trade partners, and effects on spot prices. The first constructed indices for some nations were fairly primitive, but today the importance and value of a nation's spot price and the importance of TWIs are a vital function of a central bank and the nation it serves. It gauges an overall economic picture of a nation even when that picture is not so clear.

For example, too high a spot price may mean a nation may gain in their exports but gain nothing in their imports. What if the spot price of the U.S. dollar/Japanese yen was 125 yen to dollars? Japanese vehicles sold in the United States would sell at a high value. That's great for the Japanese because they earn revenue. Now the Japanese repatriate their monies home and they find an overabundance in the supply of yen. This overabundance of yen leads to an erosion of prices in Japan and deflation takes over. The true purchasing power of the yen in Japan erodes as new money loses its value to old money. Credit then paid in new money deteriorates against the old money. So the Japanese lower their prime interest rate to accommodate consumers. But the Japanese continue to export and earn even more revenue. The downward spiral continues; as interest rates drop so does the value of the yen.

In a different example, deflationary yen is exported while inflationary yen is repatriated home instead of the reverse scenario. In this instance, a balance must be found, an equilibrium of spot rates that is conducive to both export revenue and consumer health. This is one reason why PPP failed as a model under floating exchange rates because every nation has economic factors that may not match against another nation's economy.

Japan is dependent on trade but it must import the resources for its manufacturers in order to export those goods, so it may never experience parity against the United States nor any nation under their normal trade circumstances. To deflect this conundrum, Japanese companies established satellites in all the major export nations of Japan to alleviate a deflationary environment at home. Japan in 2007 began to then view their currency as fair effective exchange rate (FEER) rather than REER. FEER allows a target range that is set by the markets due to world interest rates among the major nations at their historically low levels and monetary policy contained within those levels. The answer to this conundrum for nations was TWIs.

TWIs forced nations to view their economies from an import and export perspective of competitiveness. From an export perspective, nations determined their strengths, resources, major companies, cost of production, export goods and services, trading partners, and revenues earned from exports. Imports determined necessary resources for the health of the economy and the general population.

Many nations rely on export revenue to fund their domestic needs. Central banks of each nation were tasked with construction of a proper index, the correct measures employed to ensure a timely monetary policy that would balance inflation against change in prices and imports to exports based on exchange rates. Due to the uniqueness of various economies, TWIs vary in size, scope, and measures.

When indices were first constructed in the 1970s, factors such as fixed and floating exchange rates and taxes and tariffs had to be considered. Major trading nations today are quite different from those considered in the early 1970s. China is one nation that factors into this equation, but a whole host of emerging-market nations now exist as trading partners that weren't considered in the 1970s.

With the introduction of the euro in 1997, all nations overhauled their indices to reflect new trading arrangements. The standard indexes constructed then remain the common practice today, with an annual review by all central banks.

One difference is the overhaul of indices around 2005 by nations to reflect a growing need to include services in trade calculations. An advanced trader could possibly factor a balance-of-payment determination and profit as the TWI is factored on a daily basis and released at the same time every day. The release is a factor of the price of the respective nations' exchange rate against the U.S. dollar for the most part. Yet cross rates play an equally important role.

Think of these indices as a measure of one currency against a basket of other currencies. It is an external measure of prices as the Consumer Price Index (CPI) is an internal measure of prices. Think about the spot yen or euro that may trend upward against the U.S. dollar but trend down against another currency. The implication for overall direction of the trend of exchange rates against a basket of currencies says much in regard to overall direction of the yen or euro and may bring into question or reinforce the intensity of that trend.

What influences any TWI is spot and other market rates. Yet what influences spot is any TWI and other market rates such as short-term interest rates. This is why market rates are monitored constantly by central bankers—their economies depend on healthy rates.

The TWI fluctuates on a daily basis and on occasion it trends because it is a measure of a nation's internal cost and external price competitiveness. That trend is real because it is gauged against a basket of currencies. A high index number says cost measures may be too high for the health of an economy. In other instances, a high index number may be appropriate. Fixing times occur daily at a predetermined time.

For example, New Zealand fixes its TWI at 11:10 a.m. Wellington time. This means the daily funding for contracts is paid at 11:10 a.m. New Zealand time, 7:10 p.m. eastern daylight time. Great Britain publishes its rates on its Exchange Rate Index (ERI) every two hours London time with a close at 4:00 p.m. London time, 10:00 a.m. New York time. Trade weight numbers reported throughout any trading day are called indicative rates and will be covered in the next sequence. The euro zone is one circumstance where the reported trade numbers are reported as a reference rate, also covered in the next section.

Trade-Weight Methodology

The first question for any nation is how should an index be constructed to reflect imports and exports with trading partners and who should be included? Also, how should competitiveness of nations and prices be reflected? Should a nation target inflation, prices, exchange rates, reserves, interest rates, or none of the above? Central banks first constructed nation weights that included trading partners.

Each nation receives a share of its value to trade within the index. Some nations use trade shares, others utilize a percentage. Some nations fix their weights; others use a chained-link index. Some nations report an official index and quantify that index against a broader list of cross rates within the official index so that a market event doesn't capsize the index and the official reported figure is correct.

Broader indices are backdated and tested against the U.S. dollar and against other price measures to ensure integrity of the official reported number. Cross rates are always tested by home nation/trade partner.

The derivation of cross pairs occurred in the 1990s as new nations became members of import and export markets and the U.S. dollar wasn't a factor in those exchanges. Think about the Japanese that export to the euro zone. The euro/Japanese yen is more of a factor in the transaction than the U.S. dollar. Prior to cross pairs, only U.S. dollar pairs existed, so money was repatriated through a triangulation of euro/U.S. dollar to Japanese yen/ U.S. dollar. Cross pairs eliminated the U.S. dollar and streamlined imports, exports, and repatriations. An extraordinary amount of money depends on the accuracy of index numbers.

Some indices measure strictly bilateral trade, others incorporate a variable to capture a competitor's competition by a chain link. This is the International Monetary Fund (IMF) approach, and it first incorporated this model when it became a formal organization at the signing of Bretton Woods in 1944. The IMF monitors world trade by its own trade weight index. All IMF members are listed in the index and held together by a chain link.

Some nations fix their indices once daily, others fix throughout the day at regular market intervals. All report daily index prices on their central bank sites. All report historical prices. An index is used because spot prices are too volatile for true evaluation of trade, price, and exchange-rate measures.

What is incorporated is a price index that measures the rate of change of prices over time based on a base period. Proper measurement incorporates number theory as not only a measure of prices as quantified, but a scale factor must be incorporated. Which index to employ as a true measure depends on the quantification of the index and the scale factor. Some indices are fixed, some are chain weighted. Research suggests chain-weighted indices work best because of their gauge against another economic index, but as periods move further out from their base years, problems may develop in their accuracy. So they must be adjusted every few years. An example of CPI as a scale factor works like this following formula.

$$V = \sum_{i=1}^{n} = P^i Q^i$$

where

$p^i =$ ith item in national currency units,
$q^i =$ corresponding quantity in the time period, and
$i =$ ith item in the group of n that comprise the aggregate v.

The question is the base period.
In 1871, Ernst Louis Etienne Laspeyres invented this practical formula:

$$\frac{\sum_i \dfrac{P_i^{i,t}}{P^{i,o} W^{i,o}}}{\sum_i W^{i,o}}, \quad W^{i,o} = p^{i,o} q^{i,o}$$

This is a weighted average of price ratios of each item weighted by expenditures at the base period. Quantities are fixed at the base period.

Along came Hermann Paasche in 1874 and identified this formula:

$$\sum_i \frac{P_{i,t} q_{i,t}}{P_{i,0} q_{i,t}}$$

For individual item i, price at the base period to be pi/o, at observation period to be pi/t and quantity at the base period to be qi/t.

The denominator and numerator are total expenditures for all items at the base and observation period. Quantities are fixed at the observation period. Earlier fixed-weight formulas were identified in 1823 by Joseph Lowe, considered the father of the CPI Index.

The formula is:

$$Pl_o(P_o, P_t, Q_b)$$

This formula compares prices in a base month O, P_o, with those in month t, P_t using a quantity vector O, Q_o as weights.

IMF Price Indexes and History

Others came along in the 1920s such as Irving Fisher and Correa Moylan Walsh to further build on Lowe, Laspeyres, Paasche, and others to form more advanced models. The difference between older and newer indices is the older indexes fix weight using an arithmetic mean while the newer indices use a chain link or fix weight with a geometric mean.

The Hermann Paasche Index in a longer form:

$$Pp(P_o, P_1, Q_o, Q_1) = \frac{\sum_{i=1}^{n} P_{1,i} Q_{1,i}}{\sum_{n} P_{o,i} Q_{1,i}}$$

Irving Fisher Ideal-Pf $(P_o, P_1, Q_o, Q_1) = (PL(P_o, P_1, Q_o, Q_1)$
$Pp\ (P_o, P_1, Q_o, Q_1))^{1/2}$

The Fisher Quantity Index is a chain link of the Fisher Ideal index and identified by this formula:

$$F_{q,t} = (L_{q,t})^{1/2} \times (P_{q,t})^{1/2}$$

This formula is employed by governments to factor gross domestic product (GDP). Many employ the Fisher Ideal and quantify it with the Fisher Quantity Index.

Nominal effective exchange rates are then utilized and factored against each nation's currency. Think of this as Cassel's Absolute PPP. Why nominal effective exchange rates? So the index isn't jolted by one nation that may have, for example, a high inflation rate against other index members' currency or a one-nation calamity won't shake the index price. Further, the nominal rate is used because whatever scale is utilized to measure the index against other nominal exchange rates can be deflated. Nations have various scale factors.

New Zealand scales its index based on the nation's GDP, while some nations scale their index based on the CPI to measure prices and inflation at the same time. Some use producer prices. Australia utilizes a price deflater. The reason for deflating the scale against nominal exchange rates is to capture the REER accurately. And this is our intention, to capture the true rate to understand further the spot rate.

REERs can only be factored on a monthly basis as nations release their economic reports. Economic reports are then scaled against the respective index to form a REER. In many instances, this occurs at month end and a time to really watch exchange rates as refunding and refactoring efforts occur. Central banks must replenish their supply of foreign and domestic currencies in the spot market, termed reserve diversification. Month end is important in the spot market because it may experience volatility due to rebalancing. All nations have various methods and reasons for managing their economies, and that reason is measured within their index.

Following is a list of the major trading nations and their index construction and formulas. One will notice that variations exist from central bank to central bank. The determination is to consider a REER based on the given data methodology in order to profit. It also helps to know that all central banks report their TWI factored numbers directly on their web site every day while some emerging market nations, if they have a TWI, do not.

While all nations report single-index numbers, it is important that each individual nation within the index is also reported along with their historic rates. This is not only where a trend can be found, but in which pair, what direction, and how far can also be determined. Following is a list of each major nation, major trading partners, percentages for each partner within the index, trade strategies, and major exports. This is all the necessary information to evaluate a spot-trade decision.

Further, the indices listed are the foundation for all modern-day indices in terms of factoring consumer price indices for many nations: Paasche in particular is employed by Japan and New Zealand, for example. The United States employs a Laspeyres Index with a geometric mean to factor the 8,018 CPI items in their index.

Some nations factor stock market indices based on Laspeyres while others factor balance of payments using one of the previously discussed indexes. Slight variations may exist from nation to nation, but the basic formulas haven't changed since inception. The measure for all indices is the relationship between quantity and price and the means to handle an exorbitant amount of items. No limits exist with the proper index.

Finally, a spot trade against a TWI must always be factored as home currency/foreign currency. Both can be confirmed as foreign currency/home currency. As one pair bottoms, the other tops.

Australia

Australia adopted a free-float currency in December 1983. The Australian dollar was pegged against the British pound from 1971 to 1974, then against the U.S. dollar for many years. At one point, the Australian dollar was employed as a crawling peg to their TWI. A peg to the United Kingdom meant that Australia's dollar would almost mimic the moves of the British pound while a crawling peg meant that any exchange-rate movement in the Australian dollar would be adjusted with their TWI due to the fixed nature of that index. This however caused volatility swings so Australia adopted their trade weight index in 1974 and revised it in 1988 to reflect their free-float status.

Based on 2008 and 2009 trade weight data, Australia's TWI was comprised of 22 currencies that reflected 93.2 percent of imports and exports with 22 nations.

Country (Currency)	Initial Trade Weight	Updated Trade Weight
China (renminbi)	18.5	22.5371
Japan (yen)	17.1	14.9356
Euro zone (euro)	10.4	9.9174
United States (dollar)	8.9	8.5423
South Korea (won)	6.2	6.4074
Singapore (dollar)	4.6	4.3425
Great Britain (pound)	4.99	3.5337
New Zealand (dollar)	4.7	4.0894
India (rupee)	4.2	4.9052
Thailand (baht)	3.8	4.6668
Malaysia (ringgit)	2.9284	3.1598

Taiwan (dollar)	2.9	2.7943
Indonesia (rupiah)	2.2	2.4527
Vietnam (dong)	1.3	1.2292
United Arab Emirates (dirham)	1.3	1.1617
Papua New Guinea (kina)	1.1	1.3340
Hong Kong (dollar)	1.1	1.0461
Canada (dollar)	0.9	0.8213
South Africa (rand)	0.8	0.7530
Saudi Arabia (riyal)	0.7743	Not enough trade flow for consideration
Switzerland (franc)	0.7	0.6820
Sweden (krona)	0.7	0.6885

Notice the 4 percent increase in the Chinese weight, the Japanese decrease of 2 percent, and the U.S. dollar and euro each decreased by one half of a percent.

Exports include coal, iron ore, crude, aluminum, copper, zinc, gold, nickel, wheat, sugar, wool, beef, and milk powder to name the vast majority of commodities listed in Australia's Index of Commodity Prices. Crude accounts for 5 percent of total export commodity receipts. This constitutes Australia in the category of a commodity currency based on IMF standards of 50 percent exports of commodities.

From 1970 to 1988, Australia calculated its index based on an arithmetic mean. Since 1988, a geometric mean has been used. Australia's TWI is based on trade shares of the 22 nations with which it trades. If Australia conducts 20 percent of its trade with the United States, the United States would receive a factor that represents 20 percent trade in its TWI. Each trading partner receives a percentage of trade shares to eventually normalize the index to equal 100 although that may not always occur because of an occasional import or export from a nation outside the index. The goal is to reach proximity to 100.

Formulas are calculated using REER based on a ratio of the implicit price deflator for exports and imports of goods and services. Australia factors price deflators two different ways to ensure integrity of the final index number.

For the first method, divide current price estimates by constant price estimates for imports and exports. The base period is 1989 to 1990 and is equal to 100. For the second method, divide imports by exports. Finally, Australia calculates consumer prices, unit labor costs, and the GDP deflator as a ratio of Australia's "cost measure against the weighted geometric average of the exchange rate adjusted cost measures". The base period is 1989 to 1990 and is equal to 100. An increase in the index says cost measures are too high and must be adjusted. What is most important in Australia's calculation is the factor of exchange rates.

Please note the following formula:

$$
\begin{aligned}
TWI_t &= (A\$_t/A\$_o)^{a1} \times (E^2_t/E^2_o \times A\$_t/A\$_o)^{a2} \times \ldots \times \\
&\quad (E^{23}_t/E^{23}_o \times A\$_t/A\$_o)^{a23} \times TWI_o \\
&= (E^2_t/E^2_o)^{a2} \times \ldots \times \\
&\quad (E^{23}_t/E^{23}_o)^{a23} \times A\$_t/A\$_o \times TWI_o
\end{aligned}
$$

A\$ = Units of U.S. dollars per Australian dollar
Ei = Units of foreign currency i per U.S. dollar. (i = 2, ... , 23)
a1 = Weight of U.S. dollar
Ai = Weight of foreign currency i (i = 2, ... , 23)
o = Base period 1970 = 100
t = current period

Another view works like this. The index is a ratio of the Australian cost or price weighted to the geometric average of the exchange-rate adjusted price or cost measure of Australia's trade partners with an Index equal to 100. An easier way to look at the above equation may be:

$$
TWI_t = 100 \times TT\,(E_{j,t}/E_{j,o})^{w,j}_{j-1}
$$

where

    TT = Product operator,
    $E_{j,t}$ = Number of Australian dollars per unit of foreign currency at time t,
    $E_{j,o}$ = Number of Australian dollars per unit of foreign currency for nation j in the base period, and
    w,j = Weight of nation j.

It should be noted the prevailing market rates will be factored and released 10:00 a.m. Australia time, 7:00 p.m. New York time.

In 2010, Australia introduced another trade weight index termed ATWI that incorporates sub weights and includes services, commodities, and manufacturing. The trade partner weights are:

Country (Currency)	Weight
Japan (yen)	11.56
Euro zone (euro)	17.41
China (renminbi)	10.26
United States (dollar)	16.48
Korea (won)	3.87
New Zealand (dollar)	4.10
United Kingdom (pound)	7.27
Singapore (dollar)	4.28
Malaysia (ringgit)	2.49
Taiwan (dollar)	2.11
Thailand (baht)	2.35
India (rupee)	1.99
Hong Kong (dollar)	2.31
Indonesia (rupiah)	1.95
Canada (dollar)	2.63
South Africa (rand)	1.23
Sweden (krona)	1.21
Switzerland (franc)	1.42
Denmark (krone)	1.00
Brazil (real)	1.00
Mexico (peso)	0.94
Russia (ruble)	1.25

What was found is divergence of Australian dollar/U.S. dollar in the index will see cross-rate divergence.

The most important currency pairs to Australian trade are Australian dollar/U.S. dollar, Australian dollar/New Zealand dollar, Australian dollar/Japanese yen and Australian dollar/euro, Australian dollar/British pound, Australian dollar /South Korean won, and Australian dollar/Singapore dollar. Most would note that the euro/Australian dollar is a widely traded pair with most brokers, especially in the United States. Australia would like to see that pair move down as Australian dollar/euro rises to reflect profits in exports through favorable exchange rates. When Australian dollar/U.S. dollar spot traded at .9100 on May 5, 2010, Australia's TWI was 71. 5. When Australian dollar/U.S. dollar traded at 8524 on May 28, 2010, the TWI was fixed at 67.8. Does a correlation exist? Absolutely. The TWI fix occurs at 10:00 a.m. and 4:00 p.m. Australia time, 7:00 p.m. EDT and 1:00 a.m. EDT.

New Zealand

One of the most advanced central bankers among the family of nations is by far New Zealand. With passage of the Reserve Bank of New Zealand Act in 1989 and the Markets Act in 1988, New Zealand was one of the first nations to target inflation within a range, leading other nations to follow suit. New Zealand is also known for its high quality and always-reliable cutting-edge research.

New Zealand's dollar, called the Kiwi, free floated in March 1985. Yet New Zealand first introduced its five-nation TWI in 1979. That TWI accounted for its five major trading partners, the United States, Great Britain, Japan, Germany, and Australia. With the introduction of the euro, the deutsche mark was replaced to hold the index at five nations.

With increased import and export trade from a whole host of nations and the introduction of cross pairs, New Zealand expanded the size of its TWI in 1997 to cover 14 nations' currency cross rates. But this index remains separate from the original and official five-nation index. This method allows New Zealand to capture market highs and lows more accurately and ensure integrity of the official reported figure (Kite 2004).

Before 1997, New Zealand targeted inflation as a measure of its exchange rate, but the weight of the TWI was based strictly on trade shares, the same method Australia currently employs. When TWI prediction errors occurred by an under- or overforecast of exchange rates, New Zealand changed the index-construction methodology (Kite 2004).

New Zealand now employs a 50-50 methodology: 50 percent of the index comprises trade shares based on a nation's share of imports and exports with New Zealand, while the other 50 percent is based on each currency area's share of the combined nominal GDP of the five-currency area. New Zealand uses this methodology because of a belief that trade shares alone didn't capture inflation in New Zealand and in the larger economies of their trade partners (Kite 2004). GDP allows New Zealand to measure prices and inflation, especially inflation in the medium term, a direct and indirect effect on exchange rates. Further, GDP methodology allows New Zealand to capture third-nation competition by a chain link. This method was derived from the IMF's methodology. GDP shares are calculated using GDP in the local currency then converted into U.S. dollars.

New Zealand employs export weights based on GDP volumes and converts to index form with a base period set to 1995 Q1 to equal 100. Export weights are expressed as a portion of the partners in the index. A Fisher Ideal Index is then employed because it captures the geometric mean of Laspeyres and Paasche. The formula is:

$$Q_f = (Q_l \times Q_p)^{\frac{1}{2}}$$

the geometric mean.

Laspeyres export shares of the base period: $Q_l = Q_1 W_o / Q_o W_o$

Paasche: $Q_1 W_1 / Q_o W_1$ = export shares of the current period

Q = GDP index at time t = 0 and 1. W = export weight in time t = 0 and 1.

The formula $TWI_{y,t} = \prod I (E_{i,t} / E_{i,o})^{wy} \times TWI_y$

$E_{i,t}$ = Bilateral exchange rate with region I on date t, suppose weights wiy are used in year y.

Australia accounts for 21 percent of trade with New Zealand and is the largest trade partner followed by euro zone 15 percent, U.S. 14 percent, Japan 10.5 percent, and China 5 percent. 71 percent of New Zealand's exports are shipped to APEC nations such as Australia, Brunei Darussalam, Canada, Chile, China, Hong Kong, Indonesia, Japan, Korea, Malaysia, Mexico, Papua New Guinea, Peru, Philippines, Russia, Singapore, Taipei, Thailand, the United States, and Vietnam. New Zealand's major exports include milk powder, salted butter, cheese, logs, wood, and crude.

The most important pairs to New Zealand are New Zealand dollar/U.S. dollar, New Zealand dollar/euro, New Zealand dollar/Japanese yen, New Zealand dollar/British pound and New Zealand dollar/Australian dollar. Notice the relationship with New Zealand dollar/Australian dollar for New Zealand and Australian dollar/New Zealand dollar for Australia. Both are major trade partners to each other and both want to reap the benefits of their respective trade. Australian dollar/New Zealand dollar is the normal pair offered by brokers in the United States. Either way these pairs are offered, always expect volatility. Australian dollar/New Zealand dollar is an especially volatile pair due to push and pulls by each nation who vie for a certain price. New Zealand's TWI is reported as an indicative rate at 11:10 a.m. New Zealand time, 7:00 p.m. New York time.

TWI weights: U.S. dollar 0.3023, euro 0.2797, yen 0.1425, AUD 0.2126 and GBP 0.0629.

Notice the wide differentiation of time and the disconnection to the American markets. To connect to American markets and especially money markets, New Zealand introduced its BKBM 14:00 fix on July 1, 2008. The BKBM is New Zealand's Bank Bill and represents the shortest interest rate in New Zealand that encompasses Certificates of Deposit and Bills of Exchange.

The BKBM rate is connected to the New Zealand dollar/ U.S. dollar and the various rates between the two nations. The formal name is the World Markets Company WM/Reuters New Zealand Fix and reported as B1 rates on the New Zealand Central Bank site, one of the easiest and most user-friendly central bank sites. The 14:00 fix refers to 2:00 a.m. New Zealand time, 10:00 a.m. New York time to reflect a 16-hour difference in time. The purpose of the new fix was to secure a benchmark rate for currencies used in contracts and to connect with the forward market in other time zones.

Nine currencies are factored as mid rates, U.S. dollar, British pound, Hong Kong dollar, Singapore dollar, Australian dollar, Swiss franc, Canadian dollar, euro, and Japanese yen. Approved banks offer buy and sell rates on one- to six-month maturities that are representative rates for New Zealand's Prime Bank Bill, the top interest rate.

A January 2010 development is the fix during New Zealand market-trading hours for the following currency pairs: New Zealand dollar/Australian dollar, New Zealand dollar/Canadian dollar, New Zealand dollar/Swiss franc, New Zealand dollar/euro, New Zealand dollar/British pound, New Zealand dollar/Hong Kong dollar, New Zealand dollar/Japanese yen and New Zealand dollar/Singapore dollar. The purpose of the fix is to set a price for contracts settled between New Zealand and the respective nations. It allows for the TWI to be more accurate. See Exhibit 3.1 for an historic view of New Zealand's TWI as it tracks New Zealand dollar/U.S. dollar.

Japan

Japan is a nation that must rely on its exports because it lacks natural resources. Commodities such as oil are crucial elements that must be imported to fuel the machinery of Japan's productive processes.

EXHIBIT 3.1   Historic Chart of NZ TWI and New Zealand Dollar/U.S. Dollar

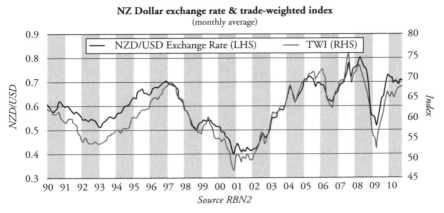

Source: New Zealand Central Bank.

What held Japan together as a nation through the centuries was its focus on education, which became a boon for their manufacturers. Because exports are so vital to the Japanese economy, the records and statistics to evaluate their exports and ensure a proper level of exchange rates are phenomenally detailed.

Today, Japan's largest export trading partner is China followed by the United States. The Japanese yen began a free float in 1973 under the Nixon administration that forced currencies off the gold standard. In order to earn a place on Japan's TWI list, at least 1 percent of Japan's exports must go to that particular nation. Currently, 15 nations are on the list that covers 87.3 percent of Japan's exports: the United States, China, euro zone, Korea, Taiwan, Hong Kong, Thailand, Singapore, Great Britain, Malaysia, Australia, Indonesia, Philippines, Canada, and Mexico. Each nation earns a percentage share of the TWI based on the average export share of each trading partner. This calculation is factored against Japan's Domestic Corporate Goods Price Index (DCGPI).

The DCGPI is an index comprised of many indices such as the Import Price Index, Export Price Index, Commodity Index, and Index by Stage of Demand and Use. The purpose of this index is to determine supply and demand in the production process within Japan. The index as a whole is a determination of domestic produced goods. The DCGPI is calculated based on a chain weight so it is a continuous calculation. Further, it is calculated minus Japan's consumption tax. The DCGPI is a regular economic release at the end of every month.

To calculate exchange rates, Japan first calculates a nominal effective exchange rate. The weighted average calculated as a geometric mean of the yen's exchange rate against other nations currencies are calculated using the annual value of Japan's trade with other nation's as weights, then converted into an index. The base period index has equaled 100 since 2005, as this index is updated every five years.

A real effective exchange rate is then calculated by deflating the nominal exchange rate by the DCGPI and the correspondent nation's indices. For the United States and most trading partners, producer prices are utilized. China is factored by the Price Index of Industrial Products with an estimated year-over-year change. For Australia, manufacturing output is used. The weighted average is then factored as a geometric mean and calculated using annual values of Japan's trade with respective nations as weights, then converted into an index with a base period 100 since 1973.

Nominal effective exchange rates in month m of year t (Cit_m) =, year = I $1973/1974_1$, × I $1974/1975_1$, × 1975/1976, 1, × ..., × I $_{t-1}$ t, i × I − t − 1. T1 = Change rate of the effective exchange rate from January year t − 1 to January Year t calculated with the year t − 1's weighted value of trade and Itt, m is the change rate from January year t to month m of year t with year t's weighted value of trade. The formula for Itt, m follows using a geometric mean.

$I_{t,t}$, m = Cartesian j $(e_{j,t}, m/e_{j,t}, 1)$ $w_{j,t}$. $E_{j,t}$ m = Nominal exchange rate of the yen in relation to foreign currency j at time t month m of year t and $w_{j,t}$ is the weight of exports to nation j in year t. The base period is March 1973.

Most significant currency pairs to Japan are Japanese yen/U.S. dollar, Japanese yen/euro, Japanese yen/British pound, Japanese yen/Australian dollar, Japanese yen/Canadian dollar, Japanese yen/Hong Kong dollar and Japanese yen/Singapore dollar. Normally pairs are classified for trade and positive exchange-rate purposes as Japanese yen/Trading Partner to reap the benefits of trade and exchange rates. But this is the Japanese, who not only must export but they must reap the benefits of those exports to ensure a healthy economy. So it is important to watch the Japanese because they calculate to the nth degree all factors of calculations.

Secondly, the Japanese are probably the world's best and smartest traders. For these reasons, the key pairs for any trader to watch are the U.S. dollar/ Japanese yen, euro/Japanese yen, Australian dollar/Japanese yen, Canadian dollar/Japanese yen, Hong Kong dollar/Japanese yen and Singapore dollar/ Japanese yen. Evaluation of the reverse pairs should always be the first essential element in any trade evaluation.

Great Britain

Great Britain, like other nations, revamped their ERI trade weight index in 2004 and implemented it in 2005 to reflect trade in services. Originally, its index was based on a fixed weight but has been revised to incorporate a chain-linked index, which means that new nation weights had to be recalculated. This also meant a formal review of trading partners.

Any nation with a 1 percent trade over a three-year period with the United Kingdom earned rights on the narrow ERI, the Effective Exchange Rate Index. Others fell into the 0. 5 category and were listed on the broader index. For example, the 2004 review revealed that Poland and Russia met the new criteria and South Korea did not. Russia has since lost but then regained its right to be listed in the narrow index (Lynch and Whitaker 2004).

The Bank of England (BOE) updates the ERI annually while the Office of National Statistics calculates Exchange Rates. London is truly the home of currency trading, so the British pound sterling needs no introduction.

Despite 22 nation's currencies listed in the ERI, the vast majority of the index—about 50 percent—comprises trade with the euro zone and 16 percent with the United States. So the two most important currencies are the British pound/U.S. dollar and the British pound/euro.

Index weights are published five times daily by the Bank of England in two hour intervals from 8:00 a.m. to 4:00 p.m. London time. The nations' currencies and trade weights factored in the ERI narrow index according to 2009 updates are:

Country	Weight
Australia	1.4%
Belgium/Luxembourg	5.3%
Canada	1.5%
China	6.4%
Denmark	1.2%
Germany	12.9%
France	7.9%
Hong Kong	1.1%
Japan	4.1%
India	1.8%
Ireland	5.6%
Italy	4.8%
Netherlands	6.2%
Norway	1.1%

(Continued)

Poland	1.5%
Russia	1.3%
South Africa	1.1%
Sweden	2.0%
Singapore	1.7%
Switzerland	3.0%
Turkey	1.5%
Spain	5.2%
United States	16.7%

Nations' currencies on the Broad Index are:

Country	Weight
Austria	0.8%
Cypress	0.3%
Slovenia	0.2%
Greece	0.8%
Saudi Arabia	0.9%
Portugal	0.8%
Malta	0.1%
Finland	0.9%

Despite the revamp of the ERI, imports and exports in the United Kingdom had an abysmal record from 2000 to 2009. The United Kingdom had more imports than exports of oil from 2005 to 2009 while overall imports exceeded exports from 2000 to 2009. The top export markets, in order, for 2009 were the United States, Germany, Netherlands, France, Ireland, Belgium, Spain, Italy, China, and Sweden. The peak importers for 2009 include Germany, the United States, China, Netherlands, France, Norway, Belgium, Ireland, Italy, and Spain.

The major commodity exported and imported is oil. Exports include oil, pharmaceuticals, road vehicles, power equipment, and chemicals. Imports include oil, road vehicles, office machines, telecommunications equipment, office machines, clothing, and electrical machinery.

Not only was a chain linked index included in the new ERI but a whole new methodology was incorporated. The new index now represents third nation competition just as the model of the IMF. Third nation competition models capture competition of UK from imports, factors UK exports and competition in export markets and catches competition between the UK and competitors from third markets. It is the direct and indirect approach to trade.

From Whitaker and Lynch 2004, the formula with new weights has three locations for ERI weights that represent three locations. The formula is:

$$Wit = \lambda m, t\, MW\, it + \lambda BX, t\, Yi\, BXW\, ti + \lambda TX, t\, TXW\, ti$$

where
MW = UK Imports,
BXW = Bilateral export competition,
TXW = Third market competition,
λm = import competition,
λBX = Openness of trading partners, and
λTX = UK home markets supplied by third markets.

Wit = total competitiveness weight of trade partner, MW = competition in the UK market from imports, BXW = bilateral export market competition weight, TXW = 3rd market competition weight, λ weights = λm import competition, proportion of UK total contact with trade partners in home market, λBX = trade partners supply competitor home market, λTX = home market supplied by third nation competitor.

Weights are assigned trade shares based on trade flows. λ and y are fixed elements so exchange rates and trade flows are accurately reported.

The new base-year period is 100 from 2005.

An earlier chain-link model by Armington in 1969 looked at the above formula as:

$$WJ = (\text{Imports of I/Imports and exports of I}) \times (\text{Share of I imports from j})$$
$$+ (\text{Exports of i/Imports and exports of i}) \times \text{Overall export weight}$$

A number of components exist to figure exchange rates based on this model.

The Bank of England releases every month and reports on their web site a table of effective interest rates thanks to the Bank of England Act of 2001.

It is calculated as a function of average loan/deposit balances and interest payable/receivables on those balances. The formula is:

$$\frac{\text{Interest Flows}}{\text{Average daily balance}} \times \frac{\text{Number of days in a year}}{\text{Number of days in a month}} \times 100$$

An effective interest rate is a weighted average of all interest rates across all the deposit accounts. Viewed another way, this helps to understand England's M4 growth rates. Growth rates are equal to the rates of increase or decrease in a series from one period to the next. For a one-month period,

$$Y = (\text{Flow period}_t/\text{Level period}_{t-1}) \times 100$$

The Monetary Conditions Index (MCI) is a weighted average of changes in an interest rate and exchange rate relative to their values in a base period. The MCI is employed as a target by central banks or an actual versus a desired result. It is an indicator and used many ways. For example, the Bank of England factors LIBOR to the 10-year gilt effective exchange rate or a three-month Treasury Bill to an effective exchange rate.

The formula is

$$MCI_t = A_r(R_t - R_b) + A_s(Q_t - Q_b)$$

where

R_t = the short-term real interest rate,
Q_t = the log of the real exchange rate – the rise = appreciation,
R_b and Q_b = the level of interest rate and exchange rate in a base period, and
A_r and A_s = MCI's weights with the ratio A_r/A_s reflecting the impact of interest and exchange rates.

A_r percent point rise in Rf has the same impact on the goal A_s percent real appreciation of the domestic currency. A ratio of 3 to 1 (A_r = 3, A_s = 1) says a 1 percent point change in the short-term real interest rate has the same effect on the policy goal as a 3 percent change in the real exchange rate.

The ERI is factored in terms of GDP growth, CPI to measure inflation, rates of change, and interest rates. ERI growth rates are then projected three years into the future. The Bank of England anticipated an 83.2 ERI in 2010, 85.3 in 2011, and 85.3 in 2012.

Trade Strategy

The most crucial pairs to England are the British pound/U.S. dollar and British pound/euro due to their abundance of trade.

A fall in the ERI Index is a fall in spot prices while a rise in the ERI is a rise in spot prices. For example, when the housing crisis hit in August 2008, British pound/U.S. dollar spot was trading at 2.0500 while the ERI began the month at 93. By the end of August, spot fell to 1.4536 and the ERI was at 88.58 by the end of August. Spot fell 1.4 percent while the ERI fell 1.04 percent, an enormous correlation. When the Greek crisis hit, British pound/U.S. dollar spot traded at 1.5150 on May 4, 2010, and ended 1.4536 with a touch at 4500 on May 14, 2010, while the ERI began at 79.5064 on May 4, 2010, and ended at 78.8207 on May 13, 2010. May 14 was a Friday and ERI was not yet reported.

What are the consequences to the ERI and spot prices at these levels? Notice the correlation in the first example. What occurs with prices paid by British consumers, what occurs with the cost structure to the British government, what occurs with their finance cost, what occurs with trade figures, and how is the money supply affected are all determinants of the ERI. The overall question is where does supply equal demand or demand equal supply?

Matthew Hurd, Mark Salmon, and Christopher Schleicher published a 2005 paper in the Center for Economic Policy Research entitled "Using Copulas to Construct Bivariate Foreign Exchange Distributions with Application to ERI" in which they determine ERI exchange rates based on option risk reversals by factoring Bernstein Copulas. This methodology has since been adopted and regularly reported in the *Quarterly Bulletin* every quarter since 2005.

Sweden

The Danish krona free floated in November 1992 as they unpegged against the ECU. Currently, 21 nations are incorporated in their Trade Competitive Weight Index (TCW). But the Swedish Central Bank, Risbank, factors rates for 50 nations as well as cross rates. Cross rates are factored for and against the Swedish krona. Their TCW is factored the same as Great Britain and the IMF where exports, imports, and third-market competition is included. They factor their exchange rates as Buy plus Sell divided by two. Exchange rates are reported at 9:30 a.m. Stockholm time and reported at 10:00 a.m. as mid rates Stockholm time, 4:00 a.m. New York time.

Canada

Canada revised their old C-6 and G-10 Index in 2006 to reflect the change in trade conditions that reflected trade in services as well as new trading partners. Today that index is called Canada Effective Exchange Rate Index (CERI) and reflects six nations' currencies based on 2 percent trade or higher with Canada: U.S. dollar, euro, British pound, Japanese yen, Chinese renminbi, and the Mexican peso. The weights in the index work like this: U.S. dollar 0.7618, euro 0.0931, yen 0.0527, renminbi 0.0329, peso 0.0324, and British pound 0.0271. The United States by far holds the largest position in the index due to the enormous import and export business between the two nations.

The United States accounts for 0.7618 of the index so the Canadian dollar/U.S. dollar and the spot U.S. dollar/Canadian dollar are by far the most important pairs for Canada as the Canadian dollar moves almost in lock step with the U.S. dollar. Because Canada is ranked as the world's seventh-largest oil exporter, Canadian dollar/Japanese yen is a great oil trade because this pair tracks so well with the price of oil. Approximately $100 billion in Canadian dollars are traded on any given trading day.

Canada's major exports are wheat, petroleum, natural gas, lumber, metals, chemicals, plastics, fertilizers, agricultural machinery, and automotive products. The effective rates fixing time is between 12:15 and 12:30 eastern time or New York time. The index is factored against each nation's CPI except China, which always receives an approximation. The index formula is the exact same as England, the IMF, and Sweden as all account for third-market competition, as can be seen in Exhibit 3.2, a 2007 to 2010 chart of CERI against Canadian dollar/U.S. dollar.

Switzerland

A minor polemic exists in Switzerland because of their limited translation of official documents and research publications to English. Most are published in French and German, reflecting historic ties to both nations that date to the Middle Ages. Most important government documents are published in German, representing the capital in Zurich in southern Switzerland, while North Switzerland represents French areas such as Geneva.

Four currencies represent prime economic value for Switzerland because these currencies comprise the majority of trade with Switzerland. In order of importance, Swiss franc/euro, Swiss franc/U.S. dollar, Swiss franc/Japanese yen, and Swiss franc/British pound. Switzerland's index is titled the TWI.

The fixing time for these currencies is 11:00 a.m. Zurich, 5:00 a.m. New York. The following effective rates are reported in order of importance: Swiss

EXHIBIT 3.2   2007 to 2010 chart of CERI against Canadian Dollar/U.S. Dollar

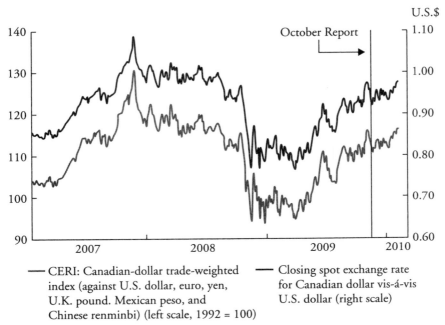

— CERI: Canadian-dollar trade-weighted
index (against U.S. dollar, euro, yen,
U.K. pound. Mexican peso, and
Chinese renminbi) (left scale, 1992 = 100)

— Closing spot exchange rate
for Canadian dollar vis-á-vis
U.S. dollar (right scale)

Note: A rise in the index indicates an appreciation of the Canadian dollar.
Source: Bank of Canada

franc/euro, Swiss franc/U.S. dollar, Swiss franc/Japanese yen, and Swiss franc/
British pound.

Notice the relationship Swiss franc/U.S. dollar. This order is by far more
important to the health of Switzerland's trade with the United States than
the U.S. dollar/Swiss franc pair offered by most brokers. Switzerland would
much prefer to see a rise in Swiss franc/U.S. dollar rather than a rise in U.S.
dollar/Swiss franc, especially during times of market and economic stress.
francs are earned by Swiss franc/U.S. dollar.

When U.S. dollar/Swiss franc rises to levels not acceptable to the Swiss
Central Bank, they will intervene and drive those prices down so any U.S.
dollar/Swiss franc longs should always be treated with caution. Consequently,
Swiss franc/euro for Switzerland is their most important pair due to the over-
whelming trade they conduct with the euro zone. Most brokers offer euro/
Swiss franc. Both central banks play a push and pull tug-of-war game as they
vie for the correct pricing mechanism within this pair.

Exports to the euro zone comprise by far a vast majority of trade for
Switzerland. Following is a list of top import and exports nations in 2009
for Switzerland.

Country	Imports	Exports
Germany	65.8	42.5
Italy	21.7	18.8
France	18.6	18.5
United States	11.4	20.7
England	7.2	11.1
Netherlands	9.0	6.3
Austria	7.9	6.0
Spain	3.9	7.4
Japan	4.2	7.1
Belgium	6.6	4.5

Trade Strategy

For all of 2009, the Swiss exported more to the United States than it imported. On January 1, 2009, the effective rate for the Swiss franc against the U.S. dollar was 1.0852 and ended December 2009 at 1.0283. Spot U.S. dollar/Swiss franc began trade January 1, 2009, at 1.2271 and ended the year at 0.9852. Where the Swiss profited was Swiss franc/U.S. dollar since effective rates are quoted for the TWI in this manner. Where a spot trader profits goes either way. The same scenario occurs with the Japanese yen.

On January 1, 2009, the effective rate began the year at 1.1610 and ended the year at 1.1463. The Swiss franc/Japanese yen began trade January 1, 2009 at 87.144 and ended the year at 90.725. The sell yen and buy Swiss franc was a profitable strategy throughout 2009. One caveat is that this pair was never known for its big movements. Another significant pair is euro/Swiss franc or aptly quoted by the Swiss as Swiss franc/euro.

Intervention

An important caveat to consider in any trade strategy is that all central banks value, and heavily monitor daily, the price of their currencies of interest against their TWIs to ensure profitable trade flows to earn foreign reserves for the government and to ensure profits for each nation's export companies. When a currency pair reaches critical levels unsatisfactory to a central bank's trade flows, spot-market intervention is always a possibility to bring prices back to profitable levels.

Central banks intervene in the markets all the time, ready to spend the necessary amounts, so risk always exists for a bet against the direction of a currency pair in which a central bank has an interest. Many can't compete with the amount of money central banks are willing to spend to intervene.

Central banks such as New Zealand and Australia usually utter a verbal warning in some form before intervention with hope that the market will adhere to the warning so that intervention won't be necessary. In this instance, the market corrects itself and in the interim, an easy and profitable trade may exist. Others such as the Swiss and the Japanese have been known to intervene without warning. Yet the Japanese have not intervened significantly in recent years due to rearrangement of offshore tactics such as the establishment of Japanese companies in other nations, purchase of commodities in other nations' markets, and a new repatriation system that allows companies to now become profitable so foreign-exchange risk to the yen is reduced.

The Swiss however have intervened many times with significant amounts of money to gear their currencies of interest in their desired direction. Recent interventions occurred in early morning New York trading before the stock market opened. Yet they have been known to intervene to adjust euro/Swiss franc to better reflect Swiss franc/euro prices during European trade. The question for traders must be where is the imbalance in a currency price and in what market would it be cost effective for central bank intervention? In this instance, the Swiss will buy francs and sell euros.

Central banks find comfort within certain ranges for their pairs of interest so a ranging market is acceptable. When pairs trend in an unacceptable direction for a central bank, caution is advised. Smaller nations are more prone toward intervention because the sale of their exported goods is paramount to the health of their economies, especially Australia and New Zealand who export commodities and Japan who exports manufactured goods. U.S. dollar/Swiss franc, Australian dollar/U.S. dollar, New Zealand dollar/U.S. dollar, and U.S. dollar/Japanese yen are the premier pairs to monitor because the United States is the largest destination for exported goods of these nations.

Canada is the questionable nation because as a commodity nation and dependent on exports to the United States, they are not prone toward intervention because they rely primarily on oil exports and their present supply will last for a considerable time in the future. Yet due to its close relationship with U.S. banks, U.S. markets, and sales to U.S. manufacturers, Canada can weather any economic storm.

Euro

The European Central Bank (ECB) revamped its TWI in 2004 to reflect trade in services, identify new trading partners, and indicate a clearer picture of manufacturing. Their index is chain linked to indicate imports, exports,

and competitor nations. They readjust their index every three years so the
new chain link from 2004 is properly reflected. The new link occurred in
2010 with completed 2009 trade data.

Due to the size and complexity of euro zone nations, the ECB formulated and categorized many indices in order of importance to euro zone trade.
The standard 12-nation currency index incorporates major trading partners
of the euro zone. The list and their weights are:

Country	Weight
Australia	1.0
United States	19.6
United Kingdom	17.8
Switzerland	6.4
Sweden	4.8
Canada	1.7
Denmark	2.7
Hong Kong	2.0
Japan	8.3
Singapore	1.8
Norway	1.3
South Korea	3.9

The next index, the EER 12, incorporates the 16 nations of the euro zone
against the 12 nations above. Next is the EER 22 (Slovakia drops from 23rd)
that factors the 16 European nations against 22 more trading nations. The
nations of the euro zone do not hold a position in the index since they are
represented by the euro.

This last set of nations includes China with a trade weight of 13.6, Poland
4.8, Hungary 3.1 and the Czech Republic 4.1, Bulgaria, Hungary, Estonia,
Latvia, Lithuania, Romania, Croatia, Russia, Turkey, Brazil, Indonesia, India,
Philippines, Mexico, Malaysia, New Zealand, Thailand, South Africa and
Iceland. All nominal indices are calculated against CPI, PPI, and the GDP
deflater to form real effective exchange rates. Rates are published as reference
rates at 2:15 a.m. Frankfurt time, 8:00 a.m. New York time.

Most representative currencies for the euro is euro/Canadian dollar, euro/
South Korean won, euro/U.S. dollar, euro/British pound, euro/Japanese yen,
euro/Swiss franc, euro/Swedish krona.

United States

The United States holds a unique position in the world due to not only enormous trade with its trading partners, but the dollar is the foundation for all world transactions in commodities and other trade. It is the premier economic barometer so many nations depend on the economic health of the United States for their own economic welfare.

USDX

As a measure to the world, the United States created a unique situation for its dollar index. It allowed the dollar index to trade almost as if it were a single free-floated currency. But it is actually a compendium of currencies.

The dollar index trades on the New York Board of Trade, now called the Intercontinental Exchange (ICE), as DXY. It trades for 22 hours as a futures and option contract on the Intercontinental Exchange and is quoted as DX. It also trades on the Chicago Mercantile Exchange (CME). The polemic with this scenario is this particular dollar is not today's official trade-weight dollar index. The DXY index originated in 1973 and formed along with all other nations' TWI as currencies began a free float. This dollar index is what is officially recognized by the world as the price of the dollar in the markets, the measure against all other currency prices. A need existed then to keep some semblance of balance for the dollar due to its paramount importance as the foundation of exchange throughout the world, as all other traded products on any exchange are quoted in dollars, such as commodities.

The DXY dollar index incorporates six nations' currencies. Following is a list of the six nations' currencies and their weights: euro 57.6, yen 13.6, British pound 11.9, Canadian dollar 9.1, Swedish krona 4.2, and Swiss franc 3.6. The euro, yen, British pound, and Canadian dollar comprise about 92 percent of the index. The six currencies are calculated as a geometric average. Note the following formula:

$$50.14348112 \times \text{euro/U.S. dollar} - 0.576 \times \text{U.S. dollar/Japanese yen}$$
$$0.136 \times \text{British pound/U.S. dollar} - 0.119 \times \text{U.S. dollar/Canadian dollar}$$
$$0.091 \times \text{U.S. dollar/SEK} \; 0.042 \times \text{U.S. dollar/Swiss franc} \; 0.036$$

The base period is equal to 100 from 1973. If the dollar is used as the base, the value is positive. If the dollar is used as the quote, the value is negative. What is missing from the USDX as opposed to the official U.S.

government dollar index is the Australian dollar. For this reason, the USDX and the official Major Index have similarities. On a correlation basis against the U.S. dollar, the euro, British pound, and Australian dollar correlate together in movements but against the dollar in market movements while the Canadian dollar, Japanese yen, Swiss franc, and Swedish krona all move together with the U.S. dollar. The difference between the two indices is that the official Major Index numbers released today represent one week prior's results. So information collected today and factored are not released until one week later. For this reason, any trade strategy should involve contemplation between both indices.

U.S. Major and Broad Index

This dollar index is called the Major Index and consists of seven currencies: the euro, Canadian dollar, Swiss franc, British pound, Australia dollar, Japanese yen, and Swedish krona. The value of the Major dollar Index is derived by its value of trade weights in the Broader dollar Index that consists of 26 nations that includes the seven currencies in the Major Index. For the Major dollar Index, weights are distributed as follows:

Country (Currency)	Weight
Euro zone (euro)	17.792
Canada (dollar)	14.701
Japan (yen)	8.265
United Kingdom (pound)	4.133
Switzerland (franc)	1.535
Australia (dollar)	1.280
Sweden (krona)	0.961

Rates are released as mid rates. For the Broader Index, weights are issued not to include the original seven:

Country	Weight
Mexico	9.621
China	17.934
Taiwan	2.459

South Korea	3.503
Singapore	1.910
Hong Kong	1.283
Malaysia	1.796
Brazil	2.096
Thailand	1.383
Philippines	0.559
Indonesia	0.988
India	1.579
Israel	1.170
Saudi Arabia	0.988
Russia	1.457
Argentina	0.565
Venezuela	0.551
Chile	0.849
Columbia	0.591

The Major and Broad Index is factored so it accounts for third-market competition. So its exports, imports, and a third weight are factored to capture third-market competition. The Federal Reserve publishes not only the overall trade weights but import, export, and third weights for each currency.

- Import weights for the Major Index are as follows: Euro = 16.719, Canada = 16.784, Japan = 9.046, United Kingdom = 3.266, Swiss = 1.175, Australia = 0.615, and Sweden = 0.761.
- Export weights: Euro = 17.993, Canada = 23.606, Japan = 5.862, United Kingdom = 4.328, and Sweden = 0.761.
- Third Market competition weights: Euro = 19.736, Canada = 1.629, Japan = 9.106, United Kingdom = 5.671, Swiss = 2.562, Australia = 1.955, and Sweden = 1.875.
- Real exchange rates are factored by the United States using Consumer Price Indices by use of this formula:

$$E_{j,t} \times P_t/P_{j,t}$$

where P_t and $P_{j,t}$ are CPI for the U.S. and economy j. The Major Index has a base period from 2003 equal to 100.

CME Dollar

The Chicago Mercantile Exchange began trade of a new dollar index. The index is based on a simple average. The weights are as follows: Euro 45.2840, yen 22.1649, British pound 14.5479, Swiss franc 5.9359, Australian dollar 4.1163, Canadian dollar 3.6097, and Swedish krona 4.3414. The 2009 to 2010 multiplier was 34.9870792920 (CME Rulebook 2010).

International Monetary Fund: Role and Function in Trade

The IMF was born at the United Nations Monetary and Financial Conference at the Washington Hotel in Bretton Woods, New Hampshire, in 1944. The IMF was charged with stabilizing exchange rates, securing financial stability, facilitating international trade, and fostering economic growth. Today, the IMF claims 186 members, up from 45 in 1944.

After 66 years of existence and many years of growth, the IMF today fulfills the role as the foundation of the world economy due to its many years as monitor, mentor, and facilitator. This role was accomplished due to the multitudes of studies the IMF performed over its many years. Its country studies are by far the most detailed in all aspects of any nation. The research it performs and the quality of the research that is published periodically is without question extraordinarily valuable. Yet it is the world role it facilitates that is most important.

When nations revamped their TWIs, the IMF provided the model and research. When nations report their TWI numbers every day, trade is monitored and reported to various nations by the IMF through invoices of imports and exports that cross borders TWIs can be factored. All is accomplished electronically. When currencies went from a gold fixed dollar to a free float, the IMF was instrumental in assisting nations through the transitional periods. This role comes at a price to nations as they must pay dues, yet without the IMF the world would be a very different place in its external and systemic functions and operations because the IMF bails out nations whose finances fall below international standards.

Imagine what the world would be like without the IMF. Thomas Hobbs' Leviathan would be rectified and life would be nasty, short, and brutish.

The IMF's TWI is the model for the world because it captures third-market competition. It can monitor effectively the whole world's trade by the use of various weights assigned to each nation. What was learned from this early formed model in the IMF's history is a concept called exchange rate pass through.

Exchange Rate Pass Through and the U.S. Dollar

Exchange rate pass through says a change in the value of a nation's currency induces a change in the price of a nation's imports and exports, a proven methodology due to extensive records maintained by the IMF and thanks to Linda Goldberg whose 2008 paper, "Vehicle Currency Use in International Trade" I quote and summarize: "Every time a good or service crosses a nation's border, customs records the type of product, its value, and the currency used to import or export. This invoiced information is transmitted to the IMF who further transmits it to each nation so each nation can factor their TWI. Currently, the U.S. dollar dominates the choice of currency in trade through-out South America, Asia, Australia, and Eastern Europe. The euro dominates the remainder of the world." For this and other reasons, the U.S. dollar and euro are two of the most widely traded currencies in the spot market. The choice of currency to be used in trade however is a matter of a clear and broad choice. Nations aren't locked into a particular currency. "They choose the currency that favors their own exchange rate, one that will enhance their profits. This is why U.S. dollar indices factored today are held for release one week later. The information is too sensitive for immediate release and can skew markets.

Indicative versus Reference Rates

When a nation releases its trade weight effective exchange rate every day, this is called by most of the world an indicative rate. The ECB refers to its trade weight effective exchange rate as a reference rate. Both are slight semantical references. What is important is that the major nations factor their TWI based on a set formula with set weights and a set fixing time daily and released at the same time as mid rates. For emerging-market nations such as Brazil, the story is quite different because emerging-market nations lack a TWI. Instead, they negotiate currencies based on currency spot auctions. The currency is negotiated rather than an index price. The best example is found at the Bank of Mauritius (intnet.mu). Indicative rates, as they are termed, work as follows.

Indicative rates for most of the world's nations are negotiated through bankers. An exact time is set every day that opens bid and ask prices for currencies. This process, called Indicative Rate Surveys, lasts about 20 minutes depending on the nation but this time is strictly enforced by those that administer this service. Normally an FX Committee or a particular nation's market committee administers this function. Once the exact time to close bid and ask occurs, highest and lowest bids are thrown out and the remaining bids are averaged to derive an indicative rate. This is the rate released at the fixing time every day so banks and markets must rebalance their structures in order to meet these new funding and cost needs based on the negotiated currency price.

This fixing-time rate is also called mid rates because fixing times generally occur just after market openings in the respective nations. Mid rates refer to middle rates between wholesale buy and sell quotes.

Banks that bid on currencies have various reasons for their bids and various means based on a bid or ask price. A bank may bid due to a trade-finance transaction that awaits, dollar transactions may await, bids may be based on spot prices or a spot price implied in an offshore nondeliverable forward foreign-exchange market. Rates are then dealt in the interbank market. If a spot auction fails in its first attempt, another auction is held until a spot price is established.

Major companies may use these rates for payments to another nation, some transfer money, some buy travelers checks, some trade one currency for another, others denominate bank accounts in various currencies, and others adjust spot prices. Still others may plan future developments by locking in a price in a financial instrument. All markets adjust to the fix. An indicative rate can be released as an exchange rate or spot price.

Factor Exchange Rates

The formula is base – term or variable/fixed. For New Zealand dollar/U.S. dollar spot price, it costs 6830 at this time to buy one U.S. dollar. The reverse asks how many dollars does it take to buy one New Zealand dollar. The formula is one U.S. dollar divided by 6830 New Zealand dollars for an exchange rate of 0.000146.

The euro/U.S. dollar spot price traded at 2384 so 1 euro divided by 2384 is equal to 0.00419. It costs .00419 to buy one euro. Euro/New Zealand dollar trades at 1.7667 so New Zealand dollar to euro is equal to 0.56602 New Zealand dollars to equal one euro. Are exchange rates overvalued or undervalued? That would depend on prices of products, the cost of business at these rates, and how one viewed this question. Europeans may see 2384 euro to one dollar as expensive while an American may view this rate as cheap. Bloomberg factors PPP over a yearly period to gauge prices between nations.

Trade Weight Indices and Spot Trades

The foremost reason central banks switched from an arithmetic to a geometric calculation of TWIs is because they can track percent changes in the TWI to percent changes in spot-currency pairs without affecting the base period. Both coincide perfectly. This allows many possibilities to trade spot against trade weight indices.

In the United States, the St. Louis Federal Reserve, through its Federal Reserve Economic Data System called FRED, tracks the U.S. Broad Index based on change, percent changes, and compounded rates of change. FRED can be factored for any TWI against any currency pair using the same methodology. Charts can be constructed based on TWI to the most interested pairs to a particular central bank. TWI prices would be listed on the left side and currency prices across the bottom. Then draw a trend line to monitor prices. Look at the most interesting pairs in this manner.

The Swiss want U.S. dollar/Swiss franc not to rise and not to turn weak in price; they want Swiss franc/U.S. dollar to rise. Why? Businesses that earn profits in the United States can more easily repatriate their monies and earn foreign reserves. Earnings in U.S. dollars means that the Swiss will earn more in Swiss francs when the funds are transferred and this is an economic good for Switzerland.

U.S. dollar pairs can be charted against any TWI based on percent changes. The Bank of England charts its ERI among other methods based on a probability scale of implied volatilities. British Bankers Association (BBA) LIBOR and specific nation LIBOR can be tracked against any TWI.

Any policy rates can be tracked against any TWI. TWIs can be tracked against each other and correlated. A TWI is an index and indices can be tracked against any other index.

View correlation within one nation's TWI as a one-point move up or down in the TWI represents an *X* move in exchange rates. New Zealand once factored its TWI against 90-day bank bills and the Monetary Conditions Index. They found an *X* point move represented a *Y* move in the TWI. This indicator is not published anymore.

TWIs ebb and flow over the years. Current policy rates and TWIs are currently low, so the abundance of liquidity that sits idle will eventually be absorbed with higher rates that will send TWIs back up and in turn send currency pairs back to trend. Think about the BOE's ERI and the two most interested pairs, British pound/U.S. dollar and euro/British pound.

A rising ERI can only send the British pound/U.S. dollar long and euro/British pound short. Yet British pound/euro will go long along with British pound/U.S. dollar. A rising CERI in Canada will send the Canadian dollar/U.S. dollar long and U.S. dollar/Canadian dollar short. A rising TWI in New Zealand sends New Zealand dollar/U.S. dollar and New Zealand dollar/Japanese yen long. Notice the positive correlation of base pairs. Yet New Zealand dollar/euro doesn't correlate with the base pairs, nor does it properly correlate to a rising New Zealand TWI, so expect much volatility as this pair settles into acceptable central bank and market ranges. Yet can New Zealand sacrifice New Zealand dollar/euro in exchange for the profits of New Zealand dollar/U.S. dollar and New Zealand dollar/Japanese yen? The same question applies to Australia. A rising TWI in Australia will send Australian dollar/U.S. dollar and Australian dollar/Japanese yen long, but what about Australian dollar/euro and Australian dollar/British pound—that doesn't correlate to a rising TWI nor to the two base pairs of Australian dollar/U.S. dollar and Australian dollar/Japanese yen.

If TWIs are at high levels and economic times turn down, then the reverse scenarios will hold. Previous longs become shorts. This is just a small portion of the many possibilities that exist to profitably trade currency pairs against any TWI.

Conclusion

Effective exchange-rate indices and effective exchange rates are just another means to trade spot currencies. The only difference is the index, but a currency price factored within an index may prove to be a more powerful indicator as to direction of a particular pair because it is gauged against other currencies in the index. Each nation has various factors to achieve its desired trade and currency price goals due to the uniqueness of each nation. Indices are constructed to reflect the economic parameters of each nation's trade circumstances.

CHAPTER 4

Short-Term Interest Rates and Money Market Instruments

The purpose of this chapter is not necessarily to know how to trade repurchase agreements although a full outline is presented. Instead, repurchase agreements represent the shortest-term interest rate within a nation, the prime mover of a spot price. These shortest-term interest rates can connect to a currency price through factors of interest. Factors of interest for repurchase agreements represent the shortest-term deposit rates and deposit rates represent the bid side of a currency pair. It determines the cost of money. A bid side rate represents the floor for rates, so it is imperative to understand this market.

Repurchase Agreements

Repurchase agreements comprise two forms, a repo rate and a reverse-repo rate. The reverse-repo rate can, depending on market conditions, represent an ask side of a currency, a ceiling. But that is one currency. Each nation must be understood due to the various factors to achieve its repo rate and the day-count factors of interest.

Crisis economic conditions forced not only the normally reported and understood general collateral (GC) rate, but a government rate was established as borrowers were forced to borrow from central bank facilities. This chapter outlines all the various aspects of the repurchase agreement market from nation to nation. What was once a rate hidden from the market has, in the last 10 years or so, become a regularly reported rate with updated rates published periodically throughout any trading day.

What were once popularly known as *repos* since the inception of central banks before World War I have now become known as repurchase agreements and reverse-repurchase agreements that serve a vital function of the daily operation of banking systems throughout the world.

Traditionally, repos were employed as a monetary tool by central banks to add or subtract liquidity from the banking system as needed to manage the supply of money that flowed through banks. This was conducted through sales or purchases of respective nations' treasury bonds, notes, and bills. When central banks bought repos or bonds, they added liquidity, and they drained liquidity when they reversed the transaction. This occurred traditionally when rates were misaligned such as a misaligned Fed funds rate to other short-term interest rates or, as in days past, when the discount rate was misaligned with the prime rate to offer a U.S. example. The system was a simple process.

Central banks opened a bidding process to their primary bank dealers registered with the central bank, currently 19 in the United States, a rate was agreed upon, and the market acted upon this rate by a sale or purchase.

Repo and reverse-repo rates were reported daily in the financial press. Typically, both rates were reported along with the spread so any trader could determine a direction to these shortest of short rates. A repo rate is always higher than a reverse-repo rate.

Repo markets determine not only the direction of interest rates, but the yield curve in fixed-interest markets is also ascertained to serve as a guide to longer term interest-rate instruments. Repo rates determine prices for swaps, forwards, and fixed-income products such as government bonds.

As time progressed and the popularity of repos increased to finance operations, mortgaged-backed securities, stocks, commercial paper, corporate and municipal bonds, and government securities of all maturities were offered as collateral in exchange for cash to finance an institution's cash needs on a daily basis.

Eventually clearing and settlement companies formed due to the automation of U.S. Treasury Market Auctions in 1993 and automation of Treasury Open Market Operations in 1994 and increased in size due to the increased number of transactions handled on a daily basis (New York Federal Reserve 2010). Australia switched to automation with passage of the 1998 Payment Systems and Settlement Act (RBA 2010). This changed the repo market from a bilateral transactional system to a match book or tri-party repo system where orders were matched with secured computer connections by size of transaction, bid/ask, available participants, and rates. These were blind transactions as neither party was familiar with their match.

The identification of the transaction for a bond in the United States is done by a CUSIP (Committee on Uniform Identification Procedure) number that is the nine-digit character identification number on every bond that is registered with the Committee on Uniform Identification Procedure as part of the CUSIP Service Bureau, which is also involved in clearing and settling trades in the repo market. Other nations adopted similar identification conventions. Those conventions are called ISIN numbers, termed the international securities identification number.

The Bank of International Settlements (BIS) reports in the December 2008 *Quarterly Review* by Peter Hordahl and Michael King that $10 trillion in repos were transacted by the United States and euro zone in 2007 and $1 trillion in the United Kingdom. The New Zealand Central Bank reports 7,000 daily transactions totaling about $40 billion daily. Yet this figure is the total for swaps, fixed interest, equities, and repo transactions. The Federal Reserve's 19 primary bank dealers reported $570 billion in daily average trading volume in 2007. Repos became the newest and easiest source of finance for all nations around the world in the last 12 years or so because of the range of rates various banks and dealers charged based on the particular transaction and because the market was safe due to the collateralization of the market.

Prior to the explosion of this market, central banks transacted repos based on British Bankers Association (BBA) LIBOR. That was only one rate, today many rates exist that form a viable market for dealers, banks, and broker dealers. Money was earned by dealers based on the *haircut*, the fee charged to handle transactions. Haircuts depended on market risk and length of time in the transaction. Down economic times saw shorter-dated repurchase agreements with volatile repo rates, a boon for dealers. Crisis economic times saw a higher demand for liquidity but lenders were skeptical, so haircuts and rates rose.

It is imperative for the currency spot trader to check longer-dated repurchase deals and turnover to gauge activity and determine where this market may be headed. Shorter-dated deals and higher repo rates are a sign of economic downturns. Another method is check the spreads between the repurchase and the reverse repurchase, as wider spreads are an indicator of down economic times as the cost to borrow increases. The unforeseen polemic to this market materialized when economic calamity gripped the world in 2008, interest rates dropped to near zero for many nations, and stimulus funding was the order of the day to prop up failing economies and institutions. This led to failed repo transactions when the price of loaned instruments lost their value. In repo-market parlance this is called the *fail*, and fails occur all the time but more so during crisis situations.

Dealers and banks then turned to lending only the safest and most liquid securities. The golden system of finance for so many banks, central bankers, and major companies froze and was limited to only the most credit-worthy customers with only the most liquid of government securities. The cost to lend with uncertain economic conditions and uncertain interest rates became too great a risk.

Questions of default became a huge concern for lenders. Central banks then established special lending facilities to accommodate the shortage of liquidity. Central banks swapped less-liquid securities for government securities for a fee that was marked to market daily. Assets that fell below the threshold loan value were charged a margin fee to bring the asset price back to market value or the position was sold. The United States established the Term Securities Lending Facility (TSLF) with 28-day terms to lend. Under the Federal Reserve Act section 13 (3) the Fed can become the lending authority under emergency conditions. This allowed the Fed to further establish the temporary Primary Dealer Credit Facility so broker dealers could obtain loans from the Fed. Other nations followed.

The Bank of England (BOE) established the Special Liquidity Scheme, the Swiss established the Liquidity Shortage Financing Facility, New Zealand established the Overnight Reserve Repo Facility, the European Central Bank (ECB) established the Marginal Lending Facility, and the Japanese established the Complement Deposit Facility. All facilities brought the repo and lending system back to life, however the majority of transactions were conducted for much shorter terms than what was once the norm. What was once a highly liquid market to fund credit and risk positions with stable repo rates disintegrated and liquidity dried up, so without central bank intervention, the banking system around the world was under severe threat.

Many smaller and medium-sized banks failed under this scenario because either the larger banks refused to lend or smaller and medium-sized banks didn't have the necessary collateral and could not meet liquidity needs. The Federal Deposit Insurance Corporation (FDIC) reports approximately 314 banks failed in the United States alone during this period from 2008 to 2010.

Questions of confidence had to be restored to this market with the proposition that default was not an option, a position only central banks could perform. Since the crisis originated in the United States, the contagion spread to other nations' funding operations since the majority of the world relies on U.S. dollar funding and direction to meet its own bank liquidity needs.

Insurmountable problems arose when requests for funding through central bank facilities had an effect of almost draining the reserves of each central bank. Central banks then offered special financing instruments with various maturities to account for reserves. The Bank of England offered Bank of England Bills with maturities of one to seven days, the ECB offered Debt Certificates for 12 months or less, the Bank of Japan (BOJ) offered Financing

Bills with six month or less maturities, and the Swiss offered Swiss National Bank Bills with seven-, 14- and 28-day maturities.

This section will highlight the repurchase agreement and the reverse repurchase agreement due to its valuable importance to the spot trade and interest rates, the prime mover of spot prices. This discussion can't be limited to the GC market for repos even though the GC rate is the market in which central banks, dealers, and broker dealers transact their business and because it is the rate most scrutinized by the trading public because it represents the private market. The public market through central bank facilities must also be highlighted.

Instead, the many types of repos will be highlighted due to their value and implications for other various transactions such as the prediction of future interest rates. Repo rates vary from nation to nation due to varying interest rates in each nation and because each nation performs transactions for the most part in its own currency. The main reason why various repo rates are different in each nation is different day-count conventions; the United States uses 360 days, Australia and New Zealand use 365, and Great Britain uses 365 days as well.

To fund positions, many banks conducted repo operations in other nations' markets, while some central banks transacted deals in only U.S. Government securities. Of the 19 primary bank dealers registered with the Federal Reserve, HSBC from England, Nomura Securities and Mizuho from Japan, UBS from Switzerland, and RBS from Scotland conduct repo operations in the United States. Yet JP Morgan, Nomura Securities, Goldman Sachs, and Citi Bank are registered to conduct repo operations in Europe, while Citi Bank also conducts repo operations in New Zealand.

Primary dealers in the United States must comply with Tier-1 and Tier-2 capital requirements outlined by the Basel Capital Accords that seek to standardize banking across borders. Currently $100 million is required as Tier-1 capital for banks and $50 million for broker dealers. All report weekly trading activities, cash on hand, futures, and Treasury positions, as well as participation in Treasury Auctions, a requirement for dealers to maintain their primary status (U.S. Treasury 2010).

U.S. Treasury Auctions are conducted through the Treasury's Bureau of Public Debt and report on dealer participation. The current proposal by the Fed is to increase the number of primary dealers. The main problem with repo rates is the reportability of rates and number of transactions.

From the United States' and most nations' central banks and settlement companies, we find one flat U.S. rate reported in the *Wall Street Journal* minus the number of transactions, minus dollar amounts, and minus types of repo transactions and terms of agreement. One must now search each nation's financial press or search each nation's central bank to determine an individual nation's repo rate.

For the United States, a change will occur as the Depository Trust and Clearing Corporation (DTCC), the major clearer and settlement company in the United States, will begin to report a GC rate during the day's trading as well as an end-of-day rate as part of the increased transparency of this market recommended by the United States and adopted as policy by other central banks around the world. The DTCC constructed the DTCC GCF Repo Index Trade Mark™, to report repo rates. The index is a weighted average of interest rates paid each day on GCF repurchase agreements based on U.S. government, federal agency, and mortgaged backed securities. A repo rate is reported as an end of day rate through the index. Since December 2010, anyone can view a chart on the DTCC site. The index coincides with the Repurchase Overnight Index Average Index introduced by the London Wholesale Market Brokers Association April 2010 to gauge overnight secured funding in sterling.

RONIA is a weighted average rate to four decimal places of all secured sterling overnight cash transactions transacted between 12:00 midnight and 4:15 a.m. EST, 7:00 a.m., 10:00 a.m. London.

Due to the unforeseen dilemma of frozen markets, many central banks are currently studying issues of past repo-market failures in order to offer more transparency so future markets won't suffer past effects. The European Repo Council in Europe is one of the most forthright in their openness of rates and terms of lending. This is because Europe is home to the International Capital Markets Association (ICMA), which publishes official European repo information through the European Repo Council such as number and types of transactions, maturities, dollar amounts, and each nation's currency settled in all transactions. The European Repo Council was established by ICMA when the euro was introduced, and extensive repo market information has been published in their biannual report every six months since 2001. Currently the 19th report is slated for publication.

This report is the only true and reliable source to understand the repo market. The problem is that the reports cover only the European markets. To understand the direction of this market overall, however, is to determine what currency repo transactions are settled. More U.S. dollar settlements may hint to increased down economic times ahead as confidence wanes in the home nation's currency. For other nations, one must consult each nation's central bank web site, Thomson Reuters, and Bloomberg market information. For Great Britain, the Wholesale Markets Brokers Association is the expert in all sterling markets.

Repo-Market Definition

The repo market involves a trade between a purchaser of a security and a seller of a security. The buyer offers cash to the seller and the seller offers securities as collateral. The two parties then agree to reverse the trade at an agreed-upon day at an agreed-upon rate. This is a contract trade. This transaction involves a spot sale for the security and forward contract on the repurchase date to lock in the agreed rate. Rates depend on the type of repo market, type of repo transaction, length of time for the trade, and whether the trade involved a third-party clearing agent or a bilateral deal. Tri-party repos are handled by a settlement company that manages trades for a fee.

The various legs of repo trades offer dealers a chance to profit on each leg of the transaction by charging a fee, a haircut, to perform the deal. Ownership transfers to the buyer in case of a default. Many utilize this market because loan rates or repo rates are always lower than unsecured borrowed Fed funds or LIBOR and the transactions are more secure due to collateralization.

The real purpose to borrow and lend in the repo market is to borrow at sub LIBOR rather than the high cost of the Fed funds market when we consider the U.S. example. Yet this example holds for all other nations. Repo rates however tend to track Fed funds and LIBOR in the United States. This example as well holds for other major trading nations including Call rates and TIBOR in Japan. All factor into a viable trading environment for the spot currency trade most importantly because it establishes a floor for rates.

In the United States, a high LIBOR, high Fed funds rate, and high repo rate will drive the dollar down because funding costs are elevated. Conversely, the euro/U.S. dollar, British pound/U.S. dollar, Australian dollar/U.S. dollar, and New Zealand dollar/U.S. dollar will rise and head toward weakness, while the U.S. dollar/Canadian dollar, U.S. dollar/Swiss franc, and U.S. dollar/Japanese yen heads down toward strength.

Repo Rates and Repo Interest

A repo rate is an annualized rate based on a 360-day year in the United States. This convention is common in European repo markets. To factor, a U.S. repo rate is equal to dollar interest divided by the Principal × 360 divided by the repo term in days. Repo rates are calculated and reported throughout the day in a few nations.

The Swiss report their repo rate every three minutes. Interest is factored as the difference between the sale and purchase price or the difference between

the forward and the spot price. The settlement date of the forward equals the
maturity date of the loan. To factor interest is equal to the repo rate multiplied by the price on purchase date multiplied by the days divided by 360
[(Purchase date divided by the sale date) divided by 360]. Accrued interest
began in the 1980s as the number of debt issues increased. Cash loaned and
value of collateral is equal to the haircut or margin.

Types of Repo Transactions and Spot-Currency Trades

Many types of repo transactions exist around the world that all have huge
implications for the spot-currency trade. For example, Europe and Great
Britain traditionally traded a floating-rate repo where the repo rate and maturity of the repo were left open. A rise in these transactions usually signals an
interest-rate change, usually an anticipation of a rate hike. This was an easy
trade for spot-currency traders as a rise in floating-rate repos was the first sign
that central-bank borrowing costs were too low and a rate hike was imminent. Once the hike was announced, traders settled their repo and currency
transactions with a profit. Currency traders could act accordingly based on
floating-rate repurchase agreements, but these transactions are phasing out in
nations.

Currently, Great Britain just announced a 6-to-12 month phase-out of
the floating-rate repo in their U.S. dollar repo market. It is being replaced
with an unlimited fixed-rate term.

Europe has adopted the same policy, but Europe's repo rate will be
indexed to their euro Overnight Index Average (EONIA). It is the overnight
rate for the euro and a weighted average of all overnight unsecured lending
in the interbank market. This ties repo rates to inside nation LIBOR. This
is interesting because the popularity of early repo lending was based on sub
LIBOR rates.

The United States terms floating rate repos Open Purchases where the
repurchase rate and maturity is left open. Once this trade is settled, it must
be re-rated and factored to its maturity date. It is questionable how long this
type of transaction will continue to exist.

Japan employs a Spot/Next, Tom/Next, then an overnight repo. The
vast majority of repo transactions are fixed term, 88.9 percent according to
the December 2009 European Repo Council Report, but predominately the
same in major nations' markets.

Forward-start repos reflect interest-rate positioning and are employed in
Europe. Suppose an interest-rate announcement is imminent, forward-start

repos position the announcement to a higher priced repo rate and represent a profit. A higher prime rate rebalances shorter-term rates higher.

Buy/sell-back repos in Europe are a spot purchase and a forward sell that is not tied to the deal based on the repo rate. The commonalities of repo markets vary slightly from central bank to central bank. All employ the GC market, all report the rate in the GC market, and all prefer to deploy government securities strictly in down economies. As lending increases, dealers accept other types of collateral.

U.S. Repo Market

The U.S. repo market began in 1918 when the central bank sold Bankers Acceptance Certificates to the private market only to buy them back at a later date (Treasury 2010). Bankers Acceptances are timed drafts sold at a discount in the money market and represent one of the oldest money market instruments. The Federal Reserve conducts Open Market operations through the New York Fed by its System Open Market Operations but reports through the SOMA account, termed the System Open Market Account. The Fed uses this account to manage currency in circulation, manage reserves, and provide liquidity in emergency situations. This is conducted through trade of the Fed Funds Rate.

The Monetary Control Act of 1980 allowed the Fed to exchange maturities in open-market operations as needed. As of July 7, 2010, the SOMA account measured in thousands, held T-Bills 18, 422, 636.7, Treasury Notes and Bonds 712, 023, 185.2, Treasury Inflation Protected Securities 41,125, 445.7, Fed Agency securities 164,762, 000.0 and settled mortgaged backed securities 1,118, 290, 404.9. The account holds a total of 2,054, 623, 672.5 with a weekly change of 163, 506.3. The Federal Reserve Bank of New York reports weekly changes to the SOMA account on its web site, newyorkfed.org. The second SOMA account is used for foreign currency investments denominated in euros and yen. The account is measured at par value daily.

The most important repo market in the United States is the General Collateral market that begins at about 7:30 a.m. New York time and ends at 3:30 p.m. with the close of Fedwire Securities Service. 7:30 is the start because that time occurs after the BBA releases their LIBOR for the United States and U.S. banks end their auction rate of U.S. LIBOR, a perfect methodology to determine the day's repo rate because repo rates will always be below LIBOR. This allows dealers who are among the 19 big banks that are registered by master agreements with the Federal Reserve to begin the 15-minute auction process that includes bids and offers for money to inter-dealer brokers.

Master agreements in the United States are called BMA agreements and began in the late 1980s for ability to trade in government securities. After the bidding process ends with the New York Federal Reserve Bank who manages the Fed's Open Market Operations, highest and lowest rates are discarded and remaining bids are averaged to form the day's traded repo rate.

The GC market expanded with the rise of clearing and settlement companies and the sophistication of computers that allow bids and offers to be viewed by registered banks and broker dealers, termed a Tri-party repo due to the third leg of the transaction. Today, it is the largest market because transaction costs were reduced and liquidity enhanced by netting both legs of the settlement process. Thanks to passage of HR5585, the Financial Netting Improvement Act in 2006, the GC market was renamed the General Collateral Finance (GCF) market and expanded beyond comprehension.

The law allowed banks to reduce their systemic risks by netting, a net valuation versus a gross valuation so markets won't be disrupted. This law applied to repos as well as swap transactions. The Fixed Income Clearing Corporation, an arm of the Depository Trust and Clearing Corporation, nets all lended and borrowed transactions at 3:45 p.m. daily.

Dealers trade these markets all day through the Fixed Income Clearing Corporation based on principal amount of trade, term, rate, and class of acceptable securities. These dealers many times make markets in securities. This is why many trades are negotiated in the GCF market because lending terms and haircuts apply differently to each trade. Haircuts apply on a trea-sury bond at one rate while a mortgage-backed security may be negotiated at another rate. A cash borrower can only seek the best price on borrowed funds.

Trades are settled based on a delivery-versus-payment basis or a Tri-party net. Typically established accounts are credited and settled by a book entry. Banks that clear trades include JP Morgan and Bank of New York Mellon. Before getting into the details and comments of the white paper released by the New York Federal Reserve Bank May 17, 2010, that addresses proposed changes and past problems to the repo market, I borrow two examples from the report of a repo trade, a Bilateral and Tri-party trade. These trades are per-formed in simple dollar terms for example purposes yet imagine these trades performed on $20 million, $30 million, or $100 million, a common daily occurrence in the repo market.

Bilateral Repo Trade

$100 Repo at 1 Percent Repo Rate and 2 Percent Haircut for 30 Days

The borrower sells $102 of securities to the cash lender and receives $100 in cash.

After 30 days, the borrower pays $100 plus 0.083 in interest to the cash lender to repurchase securities. This deal is arranged through a clearer. Step one is negotiation while step two informs the clearer of the trade so accounts can be credited and debited and transfers of cash and securities can occur. To factor,

$$\$100 + (100 \times 1 \text{ percent} \times (30/360))$$

this accounts for the Tri-party aspect.

At 8:30 the next morning, repo trades are unwound by the clearer bank to provide intraday credit to the borrower. The lender's account has $100 cash, the cash borrower has $102 in securities, no cash, and 3 percent clearing bank margin. So allowable intraday credit is equal to the cash borrower total collateral plus cash borrower total cash balance less the clearing margin.

$$\$102 + 0 - (\$102 \times 3 \text{ percent}) = \$98.94$$

End of day repos are again rewound and both accounts are locked based on cash and securities of this trade.

When the term of this trade is complete, the clearer bank returns cash plus interest to the cash lender and securities to the borrower. To calculate:

$$\$100 + \text{Repo rate (1 percent for 30 days)}$$
$$\$100 + (100 \times 1 \text{ percent} \times (30/360)) = \$100.83$$

Tri-Party Repo Infrastructure Reform and White Paper by New York Federal Reserve Bank

Released May 17, 2010, this report derived from a culmination of meetings with repo-market practitioners, regulators, academics, banks, broker dealers, money market participants, mutual funds, borrowers, and lenders. The purpose was to address the deterioration of the repo market during the crisis to assess problems and recommend changes.

This report is historic because the public is given an extraordinary and insightful view of a repo market that has been essentially closed to public viewing due to its closed nature and because it is a market not well understood operationally by the public due to its many nuances. The number of academic articles and books on the topic is not overly abundant due to lack of understanding and the many details needed to understand this market's framework. Michael Fleming and Kenneth Garbade, two economists of the Federal Reserve Bank of New York, gave a solid devotion to the U.S. repo market in their many articles, but few others have followed. This report will open the door to further research. I quote directly and summarize from this report point by point.

The first issue is the conundrum of intraday credit that is explained in step 3 of my example. This credit is made available to cash borrowers by clearing banks that provide the necessary operational infrastructure to this market. "Clearing banks clear and settle trades, so the unwinding of trades leaves a clearing bank exposed to default as lines of credit must be extended, an unlikely scenario yet an exposure nonetheless." The purpose of the unwind is to give collateral to dealers for daily settlement. "The elimination of unwinding of trades would reduce intraday credit by clearing banks 10 percent, $2.5 trillion less risk at the May 2008 peak of this market when $2.8 trillion of securities were financed." Credit and liquidity risk would shift to cash investors.

Instead of intraday credit, it is recommended to allow automatic substitutions by automation of collateralized securities that support the Tri-party repo while the transaction remains in place. This was proposed for February 2011 if computer operations can support this function and occurred as a standardized system. Collateral substitution has always been a factor of this market that was previously left to the market to decide. As long as a substitution met the acceptable securities list, a substitution was acceptable practice.

The second issue addresses risk-management practices of cash lenders and clearing banks that are subject to procyclical pressures. The term *procyclical pressure* derives from a 2009 BIS paper titled "The Role of Valuation and Leverage in Procyclicality" published by the Committee on the Global Financial System, a 31-member committee traditionally chaired by the Chairman of the Federal Reserve. Procyclical pressures can be defined as market practices such as collateral and margin subject to the credit cycle. Further, it is a measure of leverage and risk. For example, when long-term assets are funded by short-term liabilities, a maturity mismatch known as basis risk on dealer's banks can occur or when exposure to risky assets exceeds equity capital. The report outlines leverage in terms of mismatches, degrees of leverage, and the durability of secured financing.

Cash lenders are money market mutual funds among others that make investments while cash borrowers are fixed-income-securities broker dealers who use the repo market for short-term funding because they don't have access to the Fed discount window (frbdiscountwindow.org). They must rely on clearing banks to fund short positions, finance customer orders, and cover hedge exposures such as derivative hedges.

"In the first quarter of 2010, securities financed in the repo market totaled $1.7 trillion, down from the peak of $2.8 trillion in May 2008". Yet this peak saw a majority of overnight deals completed rather than longer-dated term deals, a prediction of a market turn?" From 2004 to 2007, repo markets doubled but term repos fell while 2006 to 2007 saw growth come from overnight deals. In May 2002, $750 billion was financed and a straight trend line existed to the May peak. Since then, the market trended down and appears to be presently stabilized. "The top-10 cash borrowers account for 85 percent of market value of Tri-party repo securities financed. The top 10 cash investors provide 65 percent of funds invested. The largest borrowers finance more than $100 billion in securities, the peak saw $400 billion. Cash investors provide $100 billion in finance daily."

"In the first quarter of 2010, 77 percent of Tri-party deals were financed by Treasury securities that included 27 percent treasuries, 37 percent agency mortgage-backed securities, and 13 percent fixed-income securities." Agency securities are defined as Fannie Mae, Federal Home Loan Mortgage Corporation, and Ginnie Mae. "This quarter saw corporate and municipal securities slowly return." The repo market deteriorated because these securities" values were uncertain.

What really forced a deterioration of this market was the collapse of Countrywide, Bear Stearns, and most prominently Lehman Brothers. Lehman Brothers had $50 million of U.S. debt in repurchase agreements. Through Repo 105 accounting standards, Lehman Brothers treated these transactions as sales rather than finance loans that masked their leverage ratios. This caused a change to their balance sheets. Lehman collapsed, the market deteriorated, and a review of Repo 105 transactions was under way, first by the Securities and Exchange Commission (SEC) and U.S. central bank, and then by all central banks to ensure perpetuity of the repo market.

No anticipation of higher margins was expected. Margins are defined as cash loaned, and value of collateral is equal to the margin or haircut. Stated differently, a haircut occurs when the cash is lower than the collateral value of securities. Yet it was recommended that stress tests be performed on collateral price movements to understand margin capacity and market risks. Any margin increases should be based on asset classes to add market stability. "The question remains how should collateral valuations be valued, based on yesterday's closing prices, today's closing prices, trading ranges of prices, or volatility?" Margin payouts were $1,710.5 billion as of April 9, 2010.

Questions of margin as risk based have not been addressed in prior papers until another BIS paper titled "Role of Margin Requirements and Haircuts in

Procyclicality" was released in March 2010 by the Committee on the Global Financial System. This paper reports that erosion of margin with increased trading activity contributed to the growth in leverage possibility due to competition for business. Further, "high credit ratings, ample liquidity, and low volatility increased borrowers' comfort level." This led to more margin calls as the market began its deterioration due to uncertain value of assets. This polemic was worldwide rather than a specific U.S. example.

Currently, the Basel 2 Accords world framework for haircuts says haircuts are established for each transaction secured by collateral. The Japanese employ this model in their repo market by a list of margins based on classes of accepted collateral. The Basel 2 model employed is the Value-at-Risk (VAR) versus Historic-Volatility framework; "framework periods depend on assets and length of time in the transaction. VAR haircuts estimate risk at a 95 to 99 percent confidence level over a 10-day liquidation period. A trade is factored by the holding period with a 10-day haircut multiplied by the square root of 0.5." To borrow an example, a haircut for a five-day holding period will employ the 10-day liquidation rate multiplied by the square root of 0.5, a ratio of 5 divided by 10. The U.S. Federal Reserve employs this model for borrowers at their discount window but progresses a step further by classifying loans as minimal-risk versus normal-risk loans. Minimal-risk loans are classified as similar to investment-grade bonds, while normal risk is classified as below-investment-grade bonds. The purpose is to further evaluate loans for margins with faster process times. For this purpose, the DTCC is scheduled to expand its cutoff times later than its present 3:00 p.m. close to facilitate transactions, which is scheduled for late 2010 or early 2011. The current proposal is still being addressed. Currently, haircuts are under further review by the Basel Committee on Banking Supervision to determine the acceptable level of margin. Margin changes in the future are an obvious possibility. Any increase in margin requirements or the elimination of a class of security can potentially hamper this market and restrict access to credit that means huge implications for the spot trade. A restriction of credit can only be U.S. dollar, U.S. dollar/Japanese yen, or U.S. dollar/Swiss franc negative and euro/U.S. dollar, British pound/U.S. dollar, Australian dollar/U.S. dollar, or New Zealand dollar/U.S. dollar positive. The Federal Reserve is currently floating proposals to increase the number of primary dealers.

Liquidation. Recommendations included a collateral-liquidation service. Before the market collapsed, prior recommendations included the formation of a bank to handle liquidations and fire sales in case of defaults. This recommendation lends more credence in this report and may soon become a reality.

For mature repo trades, a standard time settlement system was recommended to be implemented in late 2010 and point-of-trade confirmations that would legally bind the parties were also recommended. These proposals are currently operational.

Transparency. A recommendation was issued to publish key market information by clearing banks. Information includes market size, depth and volume, dealer concentration, asset categories, and margin and haircut levels. This point is profoundly important as well as historic because it will inform other markets, particularly the currency markets. No mention of rates. Yet the DTCC proposes to publish a GC rate in September 2010 which has been completed by their index.

These remaining proposals await to be addressed and formally adopted by the DTCC. What this market will look like in the future is undetermined, yet its implications are huge so market professionals may want to monitor this situation for further developments.

Treasury Market Practices Group and U.S. Fails Charges

In a further effort to review the problems of the repo market and ensure market efficiency, a group of market professionals that comprise the Treasury Market Practices Group (TMPG) recommended in 2008 a voluntary fails charge for buyers and sellers that fail to deliver securities based on the contract date, better known as Delivery versus Payment. Since May 2009, thanks to submittal of Rule 2009-03 by the FICC, clearer and governed by the 1934 Securities and Exchange Act, and approval by the SEC, this rule has been formalized as a standard market practice in the repo, options, and forwards markets. The question of fails has been considerable. Consider par value of fails reached its highest levels in December 2009 with $676 million in fails and $624 million in January 2010. August 2009 saw $572 million, September 2009 $312 million, and October 2009 $260 million. July 2010 saw $468 million and May 2010 $280 million. A fails charge also allows a reasonable interest charge subject to agreement by contracting parties.

To calculate a fails charge,

$$\text{Amount} = 1/360 \times 0.01 \times \text{Max}(3\text{-R,O}) \times P$$

R = each day based on the previous day's 5:00 p.m. reference rate in percent per annum.

The reference rate is the most recent Fed Funds target rate.

The amount of funds from non-failing party on a delivery versus payment basis or market value on the date the failure began.

Japanese Repo Market

Traditional Japanese repo markets were quite different from their Western counterparts because the Japanese viewed their repo markets more as a lending market rather than a buy-and-sell arrangement. The Japanese borrow and lend but not through an outright purchase and sale. The modern-day repo began with the General Repo and Special Collateral market. The General repo market was a source for banks to raise funds and served as the link to the money and interbank markets (Baba, Inamura, 2002).

The Special Collateral market was the link for dealers, called Tanshi companies, to the securities markets such as the all-important Japanese Government Bond (JGB). Traders and banks lend cash and bonds and then cash in at the repo rate. The Japanese term this the gensaki market to reflect a special financing method that employs securities and funds exchanged for a fixed period. The market exploded from $18 trillion yen in 1996 to $42 trillion by 2001 (Baba, Inamura). The polemic arose due to contract settlement after the contract date and repo rates hovered above Japanese Call and EUROYEN rates so the modern-day GC market was born in 2002 to reflect a better-managed risk system.

Today's Tokyo repo rate is a reflection of Japan's GC market, a market rate based on a mid rate of bids and offers from an average of 20 banks. Currently 15 to 20 active banks in the market with good credit standing bid at least the mandated $10 billion yen transaction, a standard for any maturities. If half the institutions fail to bid, no rate is issued. The Bank of Japan conducts and manages the bidding process for each maturity promptly at 11:00 a.m. Tokyo time and ends at 11:45 a.m. Quick Corp then calculates the rate by eliminating the highest and lowest 15 percent and averages the remaining bids to three decimal places. The BOJ then promptly reports the Tokyo Repo Rate at 12:30 p.m. on their web site and the bidding institutions report the repo rate on their own web sites shortly thereafter (Japanese Bankers Association 2010).

Bidders termed counter parties bid on yields to purchase or sell the majority and most important asset of Japan and the repo market, the JGB. A purchase or sale price is calculated by dividing the market price by the margin ratios. A resell is calculated by the amount obtained by multiplying the purchase price by purchasing yields to purchase price. A repurchase is factored by amount obtained by multiplying the selling price by selling yields to sell price. Rates are on a 365-day basis.

Overnight rates are settled based on a $T+0$ and $T+1$, spot/next known as day-after-tomorrow trades and settled $T+2$, and one week or longer trades are settled on a $T+3$ basis (Tokyo Stock Exchange). Current 2010 BOJ policy is to settle repo transactions on a T + 1 basis to eliminate fails. Many changes occurred in the last three years in Japan's repo market that required revisions to the Japan Banking Act (BOJ 2010).

At the October 2008 Bank of Japan policy meeting, the bank introduced a Floating Rate JGB, an inflation-indexed bond, broadened the range of acceptable asset-backed commercial paper, and issued a 30-year JGB. All are subject to margin ratios set by the BOJ annually (BOJ Official Reports 2009).

Current 2010/2011 margin ratios for Japan's repo market to sell are as follows: up to 1 year maturities—0.998, more than 1 year and up to 5 years—0.998, more than 5 years, up to 10 years—0.998, more than 10 years and up to 20 years—0.998, 20 to 30 years—0.998. For Floating Rate Bonds up to 1 year—0.992, one to five years—0.998, 5 to 10 years—0.981, and 10 to 20 years—0.981. For Inflation Indexed Bonds, up to 1 year—0.964, one to five years—0.998, 5 to 10 years—0.981, and 10 to 20 years—0.981. For Inflation Indexed Bonds up to 1 year—0.964, one to five years—0.960, 5 to 10 years—0.981, and 10 to 20 years—0.981,. For Inflation Indexed Bonds up to 1 year—0.964, one to five years—0.960, 5 to 10 years—0.954, 10 to 20 years—0.948, 20 to 30 years—0.940 and more than 30 years—0.940. (BOJ web site)

Following is a list of rates for 2010/2011 securities purchased by the BOJ: For JGB's with a residual maturity of up to 1 year maturity—1.003, one to five years—1.007, 5 to 10 years—1.007, 10 to 20 years—1.007, 20 to 30 years—1.007, and more than 30 years—1.029.

Floating Rate Bonds with maturity up to 1 year 1.009, 1 to 5 years 1.013, 5 to 10 years 1.020, 10 to 20 years 1.020. Inflation Indexed Bonds up to 1 year 1.039, 1 to 5 years 1.043, 10 to 20 1.058, 20–30 years 1.068 and more than 30 years 1.068.

Inflation Indexed Bonds up to 1 year maturity 1.039, 1–5 years 1.043, 5–10 1.051, 10–20 1.058, 20–30 1.068 and 30+ 1.068.

Daily volume in the repo market is $53 trillion yen, $39.9 trillion in the Call market, $42.3 trillion in JGB's settled as delivery versus payment, and $11.9 in yen foreign-exchange transactions. Intraday overdrafts are measured every 10 minutes and account for $38.6 trillion.

While trades in the U.S. closely track U.S. LIBOR, Japanese repo rates closely track Yields on U.S. Treasury Bills. The formula to trade Japanese yen/U.S. dollar is found within this framework. For all of 2010 margin ratios, Japanese repo rates stabilized between 0.10 and 0.15, yet the top policy Call rate for Japan is 0.10. Ultimately, the price to borrow must always be below the top rates.

Consistent with the U.S. TMPG, the Japanese Securities Dealers Association formed the Working Group concerning the "Review of Fails Practice for Bond Trading." This ongoing discussion involves the question whether fails charges should be a penalty charge or a simple rate charge. The release of this report is scheduled for late 2010. Current 2010 fails in the Japanese repo market includes 89 fails in April 2010 with a yen face value of 100 million yen that totaled 3406, May 2010 saw 69 fails totaling 1,673, and June 2010 saw 53 fails totaling 694 (BOJ Official Reports 2010). The Japanese decided to apply fails as a market practice rather than a rule equaled to about three percent of the transaction.

Japanese banks are subject to higher margin rates in March 2011 based on a recently released report by the Basel Committee.

Spot Currency and Japanese Repo Rates

Japan's futures market, the Tokyo Futures Exchange, trades a Spot/Next repo rate future whose index is quoted as 100 minus the average GC spot/next repo rate, or better stated as 100 minus the rate of interest. This contract is cash settled. Many employ these contracts to hedge spot against futures or futures against cash markets while others speculate on interest-rate changes by the BOJ (Tokyo Stock Exchange 2010).

No better method exists in Japan to determine interest-rate direction than this financial instrument due to its short-term nature. A rise in rates usually signals a BOJ policy rate increase while a lower rate signals a fall in policy rates. The perfect time to monitor this rate is before a BOJ meeting.

A rate increase or decrease will send the U.S. dollar/Japanese yen skyrocketing up or down in a matter of minutes and represents significant profits for traders. The implication for this trade is to factor an implied repo trade. An implied repo trade is to short one market and go long in another so one position is hedged.

In this instance, suppose one is long the futures contract and short the cash repo market or vice versa. Profits from the long will cover the short with a profit, provided that the security can be delivered for a profit on settlement date. The instrument with the highest implied repo rate would be the cheapest to deliver upon settlement. A formula must account for the price paid/purchase price of bond or whatever instrument × Day count convention, 365 for Japan/days to delivery (Tokyo Stock Exchange 2010).

New Zealand

New Zealand's central bank targets inflation and prices as their market methodology. The only method to manage an inflation target is through the Consumer Price Index to ensure prices are aligned with inflation. Bank reserves must then be further managed so targets are properly aligned and this is done through repo markets.

The Official Cash Rate (OCR) is the top benchmark interest rate in New Zealand. New Zealand's repo market began in 1994. Since 1990, market trades had cleared through Austraclear but the June 2010 introduction of NZ Clear means that New Zealand now conducts repo operations. NZ Clear serves as a real-time settlement system while New Zealand's central bank, the Royal Bank of New Zealand (RBNZ) owns and manages the New Zealand Central Securities Depository Limited who becomes the legal owner of securities during transactions.

NZ Clear settles trades on a delivery-versus-payment basis and trades in certificates of deposit, New Zealand Bank Bills, Bonds, notes, and equities, and are irrevocable once reported on the system. Austraclear once reported approximately 800 to 1200 daily trades totaling about NZ $6 billion, but New Zealand's repo markets in all of 2010 saw about an average of $3 billion daily volume with a vast majority fixed-interest trades (New Zealand Financial Markets Association). Reason for this is the RBNZ conducted more FX swaps for funding, but as that market became illiquid during the crisis, repo transactions became the dominant funding mechanism. So funding occurred between the two markets as funding in markets permitted.

During the financial crisis, the RBNZ offered an Overnight Term Reverse Repo Facility to conduct repo operations for overnight and one-week trades only. The cost is New Zealand's OCR plus 50 basis points, but ironically this facility has not been used often.

The RBNZ also offers a Bond Lending Facility where government securities are lent at OCR minus 150 basis points and repurchased at the OCR rate. Bids begin with $1 million, and maturities and terms last from overnight to one week. Bids must state yields factored two decimal places. RBNZ Open Market Operations begin at 9:30 a.m. New Zealand time.

European Repo Council

Richard Comotto, a noted repo author, scholar, and repo expert has written the International Capital Markets Association-sponsored biannual European Repo Market Survey since its 2001 inception. The 40-year goal of ICMA as a self-regulatory body is to bring efficiency to the capital markets and the European Repo Market Survey is just one of those goals.

A few noted points from the survey to gauge conditions for future economic activity to highlight future spot trades will be addressed. Fifty-eight offices from 53 financial groups reported for the March 2010 survey. This is an imperative as an indicator because it represents 14 European nations, Japanese, and North American banks that conduct repo market business in Europe.

The value of outstanding contracts as of the December 2009 cutoff of the survey was valued at euro 5,582 billion, down from the 6,775 peak in 2007, but still above the December 2008 euro 4,633 billion and euro 4,868 in June 2009. Forward-start repos reflect interest-rate positioning and aren't widely traded. Yet forward-start repos increased from 6.1 percent to 11.2 percent to reflect future interest-rate activity, a prediction of a future downturn. British pound sterling repos fell from 15.3 percent to 12.3 percent as well as use of U.K. collateral, 16.1 percent to 12.4 percent, another future prediction of a downturn. More dramatic is currency composition of repo deals.

The British pound in December 2008 saw a 13.0 composition, 15.3 in June 2009, and 12.3 in December 2009, a clear indication of either a highly oversold British pound or an economy falling into an abyss as credit disintegrated. Yet the most widely traded euro currency composition fell from 70.6 in December 2008 to 64.2 in June 2009, and recovered to 65.6 in December 2009. The safe-haven status of the U.S. dollar covered the gaps as 9.6 percent of U.S. dollar-comprised repo deals in December 2008, 14.2 percent in June 2009, and 15.9 percent in December 2009.

Implications of Survey and Spot Currency

The European Repo Market Survey is a true picture of economic activity because it relates to private banks and markets and because repo rates and lending activity, due to the safety of this market, are a clear sign to determine future economic activity. Higher repo rates and reduced lending activity can only lead to a decrease in the amount of government bonds brought to market by central banks, which restricts their own ability to finance their own operations. It is a downward spiral that leads to periods of deflation where piles of cash stand idle, markets turn down, shorter term finance rates such as LIBOR and Eurodollars in Europe rise, and the value of currencies fall.

Switzerland

Monetary policy conducted by the central bank of Switzerland termed the Swiss National Bank (SNB) is based on a target to ensure prices align with inflation. The target for the Swiss is the three-month Swiss franc

LIBOR called SARON, the Swiss Average Overnight Rate. The current rate is 0.12 and the target range is 0.00 to 0.75. SARON is fixed daily at 12:00 noon and calculated by SIX Swiss Exchange, Switzerland's stock market (SIX Swiss Exchange 2010).

To manage the inflation target in the repo market, the Swiss employ the Swiss Average Rate, the Swiss Current Rate, and the Swiss Average Index. The Swiss Average Rate is volume weighted and calculated and reported every 10 minutes by SIX Swiss Exchange (SIX Swiss Exchange 2010). Fixing times occur at noon, 4:00 p.m., and 6:00 p.m. Swiss time.

The Swiss Current Rate is calculated and reported every three minutes and is based on quotes that appear on the Eurex repo platform and further reported on Eurex Zurich. This is the most important rate due to its market sensitivity and because it creates a floor of rates for Swiss franc/U.S. dollar.

The Swiss Average Index Overnight is based on daily yields of SARON. Repo trades are generated through the Eurex Repo platform for the Swiss General Collateral and Special Repo market, payments and confirmations reported and handled by SIX SIS, properly termed SegaInterSettle, and settled through SIX Interbank Clearing (Eurex Repo 2010).

Both the SNB and Swiss banks perform repos and interbank lending through this system. The SNB conducts daily one-week repo auctions as a function of its open market operations that begin at 9:00 a.m. Zurich time daily with a prior 10-minute bidding process. Through Eurex Repo, the SNB also conducts GC repos with collateral denominated in U.S. dollars, euros, British pounds, Danish Kroner, and Norweigan Kroner. The majority of these transactions are Swiss franc, euro, British pound, and U.S. dollar (Eurex Repo 2010). Kraennzlin and Schlegel report in a 2009 paper titled "Bidding Behavior in the SNB's Repo Auctions" that 35 percent of SNB Swiss franc repo transactions are passed through Eurex Repo and 65 percent are handled by the interbank market. Market operations begin at 7:00 a.m. and end at 6:00 p.m. Swiss time.

During the crisis, the SNB established the Liquidity Shortage Facility but borrowers needed 110 percent of collateral plus payment 200 basis points above the prior day's overnight repo index. The overnight repo index has been replaced by the Swiss Average Index.

Swiss Repo and Spot Currency

Open-market operations are vitally important for any central bank because transactions determine not only funding costs but market size and liquidity levels. Success or failure of open-market operations connotes an economic expansion or contraction, up or down markets both long and short term that cover a wide range of financial instruments. The Swiss issue their final repo rate at the 6:00 p.m. close. This is the rate that will determine how the Swiss markets and the Swiss franc will react on their next day trading day, yet it sets a price for other overnight markets. It is the rate that sets the standard for swaps, forwards, fixed-rate instruments such as bond prices, yields, and yield curves. Yet the current rate will determine direction throughout the day as that rate is calculated every three minutes. Because Swiss repo markets allow for overnight, tom/next, Spot /next, and one week to 12 months out on the curve, Swiss francs will act in conjunction with these rates. Higher rates in the repo market will send the Swiss franc down as funding costs increase and up when rates fall as funding costs decrease. U.S. dollar/Swiss franc and Swiss franc/U.S. dollar must then be evaluated.

Eurex Zurich Clearing

Consistent with changes to major nation's repo markets, Eurex Zurich is the first exchange worldwide to institute changes to its risk data. As of March 15, 2010, interested parties can monitor margins, position information, cash flows, and margin requirements on any surplus or shortfall. All can be viewed in real time on the site (Eurex Zurich 2010).

Great Britain

The repurchase agreement market in England is governed by the Securities Lending and Repo Committee that was established in 1990 and the sterling Money Markets Liaison Group established in 1999. New changes were implemented in the repo market that began June 15, 2010.

Bids are accepted for two types of auctions, narrow collateral and wider collateral. Wider-collateral bids are accepted for high-quality debt and are longer lending terms. Narrow collateral bids are accepted for short-term repos. Bidders can bid on each or both sets of collateral.

After the bidding process, a clearing rate is issued for wide and narrow collateral. These auctions now occur once a month for a three-month and six-month operation. Repo rates are now indexed to the Bank of England's (BOE) Bank Rate, currently 0.5 percent. Great Britain's Bank Rate is like the

Fed funds rate in the United States. It is the price commercial banks pay on reserve balances held in banks overnight. The interest rate earned equals the bank rate at the close of the day.

The first repo auction saw 83.37 percent collateral allotted to the narrow set and 17.63 percent to the wider set of collateral. Changes in repo markets stem from the 2008 economic crisis.

For the BOE, a shortage of gilts was recognized in the repo market. This led to a shortage of liquidity. Because all central banks had liquidity shortages during the crisis, Central banks of England, Switzerland, Canada, and the ECB entered into swap agreements with the Federal Reserve to obtain U.S. dollars for central bank-funding operations. Central banks exchanged Treasury Bills for U.S. dollars. dollar-swap auctions began anew in May 2010 for the BOE, ECB, SNB, and the Canadian Central Bank. Every Wednesday, the BOE conducts seven-day repurchase agreements with the Federal Reserve as needed. The purpose of the new system, based on the 2010 *Quarterly Bulletin,* is to limit volatility and ensure yield curves remain at acceptable levels.

Canada

During the crisis, Canada established the Standing Liquidity Facility which is employed to supply liquidity to banks and the markets. Many changes occurred at the Bank of Canada (BOC).

The Bank either eliminated whole classes of securities used as collateral or implemented higher margin requirements to prevent collateralization. The pre-ferred list of collateral includes either Canadian dollar assets or U.S. Treasuries. Margin requirements for U.S. Treasuries are consistent with Canadian assets such as Canadian bonds, but a 4 percent rate is charged to account for FX risk. Yet margins were raised. For example, Canadian Government Securities are scheduled for 0.5 percent margin up to one-year maturities, 1.0 percent for one to three years, 1.5 percent for three-to-five years, and 2 percent for 5 to 10 years. For Canada guaranteed securities, 1.0 percent up to one year, 1.5 percent for one-to-three years, 2 percent for three-to-five years, and 2.5 percent for 5 to 10 years. These changes became effective in July 2010.

August 2010 saw a Bond Buy Back program implemented on most Tuesdays at 11:15 a.m. Up to 18-month maturities can be sold back where the total amount is greater than $5 billion. The Canadian overnight repo rate is a weighted average rate of overnight GC repo trades. The market is open from 6:00 a.m. to 4:00 p.m. eastern time. If $500 million is reported, the repo rate is set at the BOC overnight rate. This translates to the BOC LIBOR rate, termed OMMFR. Canadian repo trades settle through the Long Value Transfer System (LVTS).

The BOC maintains its target rate between CORRA and the Overnight Money Market Financing Rate, a weighted average of repo-funding costs of major money-market dealers. While swap lines are open from the Federal Reserve since it reopened, the BOC has not used this facility.

One method to track Canadian repo rates is by the overnight Repo Rate Futures contract traded on the Montreal Futures Exchange and called ONX. It is modeled after the Federal Funds Futures contract in the United States. The ONX contract determines what the CORRA rate is expected to average over one month's time (Johnson 2003). It is quoted as 100 minus the monthly average overnight repo rate for the contract month and priced as 0.005, which equals CAD 20.55 (1/2 of 1/100 of 1 percent of 5,000,000 on a 30-day basis). The Canadian dollar is priced within this context and represents the floor for rates.

Europe

GC trades go through Eurex Repo. Europe comprises a series of rates that govern their operations. Much has been written about the channel or corridor of rates that governs their markets. The Main Refinancing Operation (MRO) provides weekly liquidity based on minimum bid rates to the banking system. The current rate is 1 percent. This fixed rate has been higher than EURIBOR and GC rates for 2010 (ECB yearly report 2010). The Marginal Lending Facility provides overnight credit to banks. This rate is currently 1.75 percent and the Deposit Facility is 0.25. Factor in the base rate at 0.12 presently, and the corridor is established. Minimum bid rates normally establish Europe's Eurepo rate or deposit rate.

Australia

Australia's top Cash Rate is the same as the Prime Rate in the United States and is currently 4.50 percent. This rate hit a low of 3.00 percent in February 2009 and has been rising ever since. This says Australia's economy has weathered the financial storm since the Lehman Brothers collapse far better than its counterparts.

What further helped Australia was this quote from the March 2010 Financial Stability Report, "Six months to January 2010, total deposits in Australia increased by an annualized rate of 4 1/2 percent, 2008 to 2009 saw total deposits increase by 25 percent."

Australia's central bank, the Royal Bank of Australia (RBA), conducts open-market operations at 9:30 a.m. Bank repo bids and offers begin at 9:30 Australia time and end at 9:45. All bank operations conducted by repo transactions are incorporated by GC trades.

During the crisis, bank funding operations expanded to daily through the Intraday Liquidity Facility beginning at 7:30 Australia time and ending at 5:30 p.m. Sydney.

Repo rates begin at 0 and are determined by the market value of securities offered in the first leg of the repo transaction. The second leg determines first-leg monies plus transaction costs. Margin calls are made when the value of securities falls under 1 percent. If a security trades above the 1 percent threshold, a return is made. Trades settle on an Actual/360 basis through Austraclear on a delivery-versus-payment basis.

U.S. dollar Term Repo Operations rates are published at 10:15 a.m., settled on an Actual/360 basis and reported at 10:15 a.m. The minimum bid is $5 million. The RBA employs the 10:00 a.m. William Reuters Australian fix for Aussie dollar equivalents. Yet the RBA charges an additional 10 percent margin for foreign exchange risk.

The Guaranteed Scheme for Large Deposits and Wholesale Funding was employed during the crisis but closed in March 2010. Historic repurchase agreement totals in Australia-dollar terms forecasted a warning for market direction, then signaled an all-clear sign. In Australian billions of dollars, 2004 to 2005 saw 4,461 in repurchase agreement deals, 2005 to 2006 saw 4,421, 2006 to 2007 saw 4,415, 2007 to 2008 saw 3,885, and 2008 to 2009 saw 5,147 (2009 Australian Financial Markets Report).

For the Australian dollar, the OCR would always serve as the deposit rate in the Aussie market.

Repo Rates and Spot Currencies

Recognize that two repo rates and two different markets exist, one for an official government rate and one for the private interbank market. This was created by osmosis, by necessity due to market stress before and after Lehman, but proceeded further with other crisis announcements of bank failures, bank stress tests, and the Greek debt crisis. A crisis of confidence existed.

As important as this market is to inform other rates, all central banks had to review this market. Changes will occur. One obvious change is the renewed daily focus for central banks to guide market operations toward their target rates. This translates to guiding monetary policy toward the Consumer Price Index. This can only mean repo rates may be steered toward the target of inflation. Targets have a range but a small window. This may require a restriction to the repo market as higher margins and quality collateral may be the cost of business. Most important about this scenario is that repo rates establish a floor, the bottom of interest rates. Spot prices can't fall below this floor, regardless of the pair.

For spot-currency traders, the way to gauge this market is to monitor repurchase agreement rates, reverse-repurchase rates, and bid/ask spreads. Negative spreads mean the same masses of liquidity will only swirl around without direction in deflationary environments. Falling repo rates mean the same. Because repo rates are the shortest of rates, they can provide early signs toward recovery and higher policy rates or deflation and lower rates. Either way, this situation in turn will send currency pairs back to trends, up or down.

Another method is to gauge repo rates against deposit rates as deposit rates are the risk-free rate. The Japanese chart a trend line of repo rates against repo trades that range from overnight to one year to gauge market direction. The Bank of England charts an implied repo rate in two ways.

The first is to compare repo rates based on Government bond gilt yields because gilts were the preferred collateral. The second method is to calculate the implied three-month LIBOR rate. This is defined by the BOE as the average difference between the three month LIBOR rate and a bank repo rate. The difference between these two rates is both are the shortest of rates and repo rates are secured loans while LIBOR is the next open-market rate that is unsecured. Market circumstances dictate preferred methods of evaluation, yet market circumstances also dictate trends or ranges in spot currency prices.

Eurepo Charts

Provided in Exhibit 4.1 is a 12-month chart from the European Banking Federation's EURIBOR section that tracks repo rates. Trades and repo rates range from Tom/Next to 12 months.

EXHIBIT 4.1 12-Month Chart of Eurepo: 2008

Maturity	Today	Previous day
TN	0.354 (05/08/2010)	0.36 (04/08/2010)
1 Week	0.461 (05/08/2010)	0.433 (04/08/2010)
2 Weeks	0.474 (05/08/2010)	0.45 (04/08/2010)
3 Weeks	0.479 (05/08/2010)	0.459 (04/08/2010)
1 Month	0.488 (05/08/2010)	0.472 (04/08/2010)
2 Months	0.517 (05/08/2010)	0.506 (04/08/2010)
3 Months	0.547 (05/08/2010)	0.538 (04/08/2010)
6 Months	0.61 (05/08/2010)	0.599 (04/08/2010)
9 Months	0.662 (05/08/2010)	0.648 (04/08/2010)
12 Months	0.714 (05/08/2010)	0.696 (04/08/2010)

Source: European Banking Federation Note: Permission granted with attribution.

Intercapital

Intercapital (ICAP) touts itself as the world's premier voice and interdealer broker in spot foreign exchange, swaps, derivatives, credit, precious metals, and interest rates. This service in turn allows ICAP to be a premier information service to news providers around the world.

Each month ICAP provides average daily volume and historic reports in U.S. Treasuries, spot foreign exchange, and European and U.S. repo markets. More importantly, anyone can subscribe to the host of services and platforms ICAP offers and view streaming market information to allow informed trading decisions. For the repo market, to know what types of collateral are offered and accepted, and the direction of rates, can provide valuable insight to direction in swaps, derivatives, fixed income, and spot foreign exchange. For example, suppose last week or last month German Bonds were offered and accepted in the repo market at X rate. But this week, only U.S. Treasuries were offered and accepted at X rate. Does that scenario warn of a credit problem, either temporary or long term, and would the euro/U.S. dollar, British pound/U.S. dollar, Australian dollar/U.S. dollar, and New Zealand dollar/ U.S. dollar experience sell orders streaming? Absolutely.

Dollar Repos or Swap Lines

The proper name of these auctions is termed Reciprocal Currency Arrangements. When crisis grips the world or any associated financial problems, foreign central banks borrowing costs in their own currency in both LIBOR and Overnight Indexed Swaps rise, particularly those liabilities that are funded in U.S. dollars.

To meet these obligations, the U.S. Federal Reserve established currency swap lines to alleviate foreign central banks high borrowing costs. Throughout 2007 to 2009, swap lines were open every Tuesday for the BOE, BOJ, SNB, BOC, and ECB, with the results of auctions reported every Thursday on the Federal Reserve web site. This schedule remains the same. As of May 10, 2010, the Fed announced the reopening of swap lines until Jan 2011 but has since been extended to August 2011. It remains a monetary "tool" based on the Federal Reserve Act 1913, section 14 to be reopened if crisis again grips world banking systems.

Swaps entail each central bank to first sell their own currency to the Fed in exchange for U.S. dollars at current market rates and buy back their currency at a specified time at the agreed-upon rate in the first leg (Fleming 2009). These are periods of volatility for spot pairs, due first to market uncertainties then to a normalization of the market when LIBOR and other associated rates stabilize thanks to Fed auctions. Currency markets experience selloffs at the first sign of crisis but trend back up when the auctions materialize (Goldberg 2010 and 2011). Interesting is the recent development of the ECB and BOE to establish swap lines among each other, a first which deserves attention.

Chiang Mai Initiative Multilateralization

Chiang Mai was established from the Association of Southeast Asian Nations. Chiang Mai was adopted and signed by the ASEAN + 3 finance ministers and central banks that include China, Japan, and Korea. The purpose is to assist and address short-term liquidity needs and provide currency swap arrangements (EMEAP 2010 Report). Initial funding was considered at $80 billion U.S. dollars, but final funding was $120 billion U.S. dollars. Final agreements were reached at the May 2009 meeting, signed in December 2009, and became effective in March 2010. What this means in terms of currency funding is a guess. Consider Australia, Canada, New Zealand, Japan, the European Union, and the United States are all members of ASEAN. Where this agreement will lead is another question. Some speculate on an Asian Currency Unit such as the euro. Yet another swap line may be an open and viable vehicle that contrasts with the Fed's Swap Lines.

Conclusion

Provided in this chapter was a detailed nation-by-nation look into the repo market outlined by histories and parameters of the market from an overall perspective due to economic conditions that forced the market to halt. A detailed perspective on the operational parameters for each market was then provided. Each nation holds a vastly different view of their repo lending and borrowing activity with various methodologies that ensure the repo and reverse market function. Repo market participants vary from market to market as well and the times lending and borrowing occur, because a wide differentiation of time zones exist from nation to nation. Examples of repo trades were provided, as well as various calculations of interest. Formulas were provided that allow anyone to calculate the same interest as market participants. An insight into each nation's futures market as a guide to repo trades and market intelligence was provided. For the spot trade, repo markets provide the floor, the bottom of interest rates, and the bottom for a particular nation's currency price. To understand factors of interest will assist in the understanding of the next interest rate and the first open market tradeable rate, LIBOR.

CHAPTER 5

LIBOR

LIBOR is an imperative chapter because it represents the shortest-term open-market interest rate after a General Collateral (GC) repo rate that is widely anticipated, widely viewed, and widely traded every trading day. It is an open market rate and the first rate to inform other rates in all markets. Because LIBOR is priced to the currency, it is one of the most important of rates as a trading day begins. This chapter addresses the various types of LIBOR and the various interest rates associated with each rate in order to understand a spot price. LIBOR may begin in the United Kingdom but LIBOR interest travels to all markets and is informed by an internal LIBOR inside each nation's bank market. Two types of LIBOR are released and each are associated with a different interest rate. The chapter begins with details of the LIBOR process.

When major banks submit bids and offers through the British Bankers Association (BBA), what is represented is London banks that borrow and lend money in terms of various nations' currencies from their reserves to each other. Bank A may have more reserves due to daily transactions and is willing to lend, while Bank B found a deficit due to transactions and is willing to borrow. As lender, Bank A will submit a high offer to earn revenue while Bank B will submit low bids to cover their deficit at a low cost.

Banks must meet daily reserve requirements due to each nation's laws and regulations that address such issues as how much deficit is allowed and how much reserves can be lent, so what occurs at the BBA every day is the bid and offer for unsecured currencies in terms of a particular nation's deposit rates. The figure released is the day's interbank dealing rate, called LIBOR, a term to denote deposit rates.

LIBOR, the most sensitive of open-market rates, is the rate that allows other investment instruments the world over to be priced in the market for that day and over a term of 12 months such as spot currency prices, swaps, forwards, government bonds and yields, stock markets, options, and futures. It is the rate that allows day traders to profit, to hedge, and to trade their views on any investment instruments and it allows private banks to profit and central banks to fund their operations and manage their reserves. For consumers, this is the rate charged or at least considered for mortgages, student loans, and consumer credit.

For central bankers, it is the rate to understand their operational targets for their reserves, which in turn will facilitate the managing of reserves to properly fund their economies. BBA LIBOR sets the framework, the foundation. A typical example is the Swiss National Bank who employs a Swiss franc three-month BBA LIBOR as its target rate to manage the Swiss economy in terms of reserves and inflation.

The operational framework for the Swiss economy is zero to three months, priced in Swiss francs. Due to the wide band, central banks implemented an operational daily rate for protection to further manage the three-month target. This occurred for many central banks around the time of the introduction of the euro. The daily rate gives indication to economic direction and target ranges.

Central banks like to see daily rates in the middle of the overall three-month target so they know the three-month target will materialize without extra costs to their reserves. Above the target means inflation, an erosion of prices, and an unexpected cost to reserves if inflation grows too quickly. Below means economic under-performance and another cost to reserves. Both must be adjusted by reserves, but each has the potential to be more costly without daily rates as a guide to the target.

For exchange rates and spot currencies, daily rates led to the understanding of trends and ranges, entry and exits, profit and loss, and day trading versus swing trading as central banks better managed their economies. Some central banks are better than others in management but sometimes that led to more profits as currencies experienced larger swings in one instance and certain trends in another. But the daily rate actually led to more sophistication in the markets as the management function by central banks became a bit easier. Trends became real and much stronger.

The anomaly to LIBOR is U.S. SEC Rule 2a-7 that amends the Investment Company Act of 1940 that places regulations on tax exempt money market funds, a traditional source of funds for banks to borrow reserves. Beginning May 2010, final rules state that fund assets must be readily convertible to cash, report monthly holdings, limit portfolio holdings from a weighted average maturity of 90 to 60 days, and hold net asset values steady. The Committee of Securities Regulators in Europe are considering the adoption of the same rules. Rules stem from the Basel 3 Accord recommendations. Before we begin, notice another anomaly to LIBOR, SONIA and EURONIA Index rates.

SONIA and EURONIA Indices

SONIA and EURONIA Indices are the inventions of the Wholesale Market Brokers Association (WMBA) in London who are experts in not only all markets sterling but money markets in Great Britain and Europe. The SONIA Index was introduced in 1997 and it represents unsecured sterling cash transactions that occur only in the overnight market in London from midnight to 4:15 a.m., New York time. The WMBA brokers minimum deals of sterling 25 million by WMBA member firms to counter parties— other banks.

The proper name is sterling Overnight Index Average (SONIA). It is a weighted-average index with a weighted average rate at four decimal places. "Rates in the average are weighted by the principal amount of deposits on a particular day." (LWMBA site 2010)

EURONIA is the euro Overnight Index Average, a weighted average to four decimal places and introduced in January 1999 along with the euro. The WMBA brokers deals for their member firms to counter parties based on EURONIA rates in euros between midnight and 4:00 a.m., New York time. Both track overnight funding rates, better known as deposit rates and both are published by the WMBA at 1700 hours London time each day, 5:00 a.m. New York time. What occurs are swaps where short-term loans are funded by deposits against a rate in the index, a fixed rate as opposed to a floating-rate deal. Rates are based on deposit rates for a particular day. Sterling money-market trades all go through Clearing House Automated Payment System (CHAPS) sterling. CHAPS is operated and all trades recorded by the Bank of England (BOE).

SONIA, LIBOR, and British Pound Sterling/U.S. Dollar

The gauge for SONIA and British pound sterling LIBOR lies in the spread. The closer the spread in basis points, the more secure are money markets in terms of lending and borrowing with less risk. When spreads widen, it is an early warning sign to market risk as the cost of money increases. Would Bank B from the previous example be willing to cover reserve deficits in three-month LIBOR with wide spreads?

To track these rates, always look at the three-month LIBOR because that is the rate viewed by central banks to determine what their own cost will be in terms of their reserve target. Three-month rates give central banks operational direction, a rate that suggests confidence or disaster ahead. For major companies, conducting business in pounds sterling may not be affordable for costs in future three-month rates since they work on a quarterly basis in terms of their profit margins. Those companies may find another currency to conduct present business or repatriate in another currency if they are not domesticated in Great Britain. Both have huge interests in LIBOR and SONIA rates.

Widening spreads is a sell British pound sterling/U.S. dollar and a buy in euro/British pound sterling while narrow spreads is a buy British pound sterling/U.S. dollar and sell euro/British pound sterling due to opposite correlational differences. Correlational differences allow funding in either pair, and market rates dictate which pair.

For EURONIA, the same principles as for SONIA hold true. Widening spreads between EURONIA and BBA euro signal higher borrowing costs in the European money markets, so sell euro/U.S. dollar and consider buying U.S. dollar/Swiss franc as both are direct opposite pairs. For close spreads that distill confidence in borrowing costs, buy euro/U.S. dollar and sell U.S. dollar/Swiss franc. As shown in Exhibit 5.1, the SONIA rate released August 4, 2010 was 4906.

What transpired upon release was a number of interbank transactions along the interest-rate curve for that day that totaled more than $11 billion. Rates reflect the demand for money denominated in sterling at whatever agreed-upon rate. The majority transacted at the index rate says that bankers see a steady economic condition ahead. The key for the index is to determine the direction of money either in higher or lower rates. That will transpire into a British pound sterling/U.S. dollar price ahead. The same applies for EURONIA.

The rate released that day was 2790 and more than $17 billion in euros was transacted through the interbank market at various rates along the interest-rate curve. Once the rate is released, major banks post offers and bidders accept offers based on their need for capital. The factor for SONIA and EURONIA is it informs future LIBOR and determines the direction in the cost and supply of money, which will reflect the euro/U.S. dollar market price.

While these two examples represent overnight rates, the BBA releases LIBOR for 10 currencies with 15 maturities that range from overnight to 12 months. For currency traders, the questions must be where is the greatest demand for money, denominated in which currency, and where is the greatest demand along the interest rate curve?

Rising demand with higher rates can only mean a rising currency price, a trend. Trends through higher costs for money usually denote economic

EXHIBIT 5.1 SONIA and EURONIA Transaction Chart

EURONIA Index—Aug 04, 2010		SONIA Index—Aug 04, 2010	
Weighted Index (%)	Volume (£)	Weighted Index (%)	Volume (£)
0.2790	17,244,625,000	0.4906	11,973,571,871

EURONIA Index & Volume Bands—August 04, 2010		Volume Bands—August 04, 2010	
Rate (percent)	Volume (£)	Rate (percent)	Volume (£)
0.22	159,000,000	0.25	40,000,000
0.23	253,000,000	0.4	25,000,000
0.24	585,000,000	0.41	50,000,000
0.25	1,897,375,000	0.45	204,700,000
0.26	1,277,250,000	0.46	225,500,000
0.27	3,955,000,000	0.47	1,086,000,000
0.28	2,955,000,000	0.48	1,080,756,000
0.29	2,200,000,000	0.49	6,044,705,644
0.3	3,248,000,000	0.5	933,510,227
0.35	15,000,000	0.51	1,382,000,000
0.37	700,000,000	0.52	501,400,000
		0.53	80,000,000
		0.54	60,000,000
		0.55	200,000,000
TOTAL	17,244,625,000	TOTAL	11,913,571,871

Note: Permission with attribution by LWMBA.
Source: London Wholesale Market Brokers Association.

confidence and possibly higher policy rates later. This is the perfect growth and inflation scenario, where higher policy rates follow trends in higher costs for money because money multiplies through higher rates.

Falling demand with lower rates is a deflationary trend down and rates that are up one day and down the next is a range trade. This formula normally doesn't hold when crisis or uncertain economic times exist. During crisis situations the reverse scenario holds true; sell rates above target and buy dips when prices are below target. Because LIBOR is the start of market rates, LIBOR is considered the smart money because it is the largest world banks willing to spend reserves, deposit money on a specific rate.

A rising euro rate and a falling U.S. dollar may mean swap and forward interest-rate positioning changes, importers and exporters readjust, manufacturers adjust profit margins, banks earn profits through finance, central banks adjust to their target rates, and traders profit from a mismatch of rates.

During good economic times, LIBOR tends to rise for many nations and grouped currency pairs trend. This includes the euro/U.S. dollar British pound sterling/U.S. dollar, Australian dollar/U.S. dollar, and New Zealand dollar/U.S. dollar, while U.S. dollar/Swiss franc, U.S. dollar/Japanese yen, and U.S. dollar/Canadian dollar rates tend to fall due to opposite correlational differences between the pricing interplay of government bond prices and bond yields. It is the difference between safety and risky currencies.

One old method to gauge LIBOR is to plot LIBOR against any government-bond yields and draw a trend line to determine at what yield are LIBOR comfortable and where is the point where the majority of rates settle against yields? Higher LIBOR could mean higher yields, as both could directly correlate. The guiding principle is money must always seek its yield if that currency is a risk currency and tied to yield for its movement. But find the opposite correlations between government bond prices and LIBOR to determine where safe currencies are comfortable. But this scenario represents BBA LIBOR. These rates must transfer to each nation. A few examples follow.

To understand the importance of LIBOR and ramifications of a currency price, see Exhibit 5.2, the historic U.S. dollar LIBOR chart from the January 2007 high of 5.32 and the 0.23 low in January 2010.

As noted in Exhibit 5.3, from 2007 to 2008, U.S. dollar prices reflected the trend line fall in LIBOR, 2008 saw choppy rate releases, and 2010 saw the original 2007 dollar index 78 price to reflect the real trend. The 2007 fall didn't begin until October, but prior LIBOR prices and failures to rise was probably an early warning to U.S. dollar direction.

The caveat is LIBOR doesn't follow a tick-by-tick rise or fall in currency prices; rather it follows and alerts to trend direction. Small ranges may occur

EXHIBIT 5.2   Historic U.S. Dollar Libor

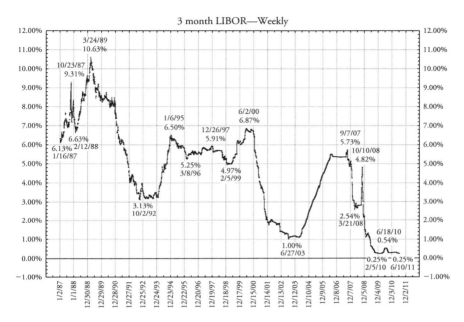

Source: The Chart Store, permission by attribution.

EXHIBIT 5.3   Historic Dollar Index Chart

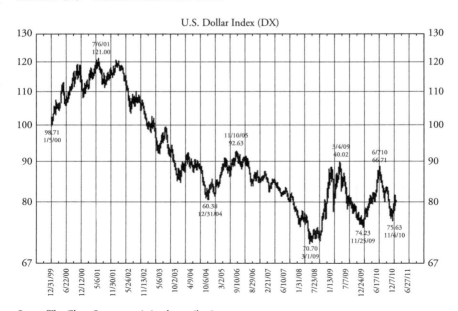

Source: The Chart Store, permission by attribution.

in currency prices as LIBOR ebbs and flows from day to day, but LIBOR can be the best alert to an overall trend.

For direction, plot a trend line, a moving average, or a standard deviation to determine where the mean of LIBOR lies. Markets and rates always normalize and always revert back to a mean. Look for the outliers, the place where LIBOR falls outside the mean. Those rates are anomalies. Direction can be ascertained based on a normalization and a currency pair such as the U.S. dollar or euro/U.S. dollar can be gauged due to opposite correlations and profit earned.

Seasonality and British Pound Sterling/U.S. Dollar

The U.K.'s Treasury Department in Great Britain presents a budget to the House of Commons to be voted in either March or April. Preliminary budgets are submitted traditionally in November, with the final budget submitted in March (House of Commons 2010). This period covers fiscal years for the British pound sterling and the U.K. Government. Interestingly, does the British pound sterling/U.S. dollar peak during this period along with British pound sterling LIBOR? The answer is no. The peak comes for the British pound sterling/U.S. dollar around the November/December period.

BBA and LIBOR

It should be noted the importance of the LIBOR. A LIBOR number is tied to a vast majority of the world's markets in terms of mortgages, consumer loans, student loans, investments, and savings that the release of LIBOR is so vital to the continued maintenance of the financial system. For this reason, the BBA guards this number jealously. It is important for market professionals to obtain a true number, a true release, so a valid financial decision can be rendered. The figure released is a tradeable rate in the interbank and money markets. The major data vendors around the world are the most reliable sources, such as Thomson Reuters and Bloomberg, because of their worldwide operations and their ability to report up-to-the-second events.

Seasonal Spot Currencies and LIBOR

For seasonal currency prices, see Exhibit 5.2, the historical monthly charts from 1999 to 2010 and notice that for most years, the highest LIBOR for the

U.S. dollar occurred in or around November. This trend held from 1999 to 2007 and for the most part will probably hold for future years.

My personal theory why this occurs surrounds the fact that U.S. government budgets are normally voted and passed in October due to fiscal year end. Major U.S. companies tend toward fiscal years in line with U.S. government fiscal years and write a budget the same time as the U.S. government. So both entities conduct their heaviest borrowing in November to fund new budgets and force dollar costs up due to demand for dollars.

The European Union, the U.S. dollar opposite to the euro, historically passes their budgets in November (Europa.eu 2010) so must borrow heavily in euros in December. Again see Exhibit 5.2. From 1999 to 2003, dollar LIBOR either dropped or remained the same in December. From 2004 to 2010, U.S. dollar LIBOR dropped in December 2004, remained close to November levels in 2005, dropped in 2006, 2008, and and 2009. At a December LIBOR of 5.24 in 2007 and a December 2008 rate of 1.90, 2007 is the outlier rate mentioned above.

Notice in December of Exhibit 5.4, the 2007 chart of the euro/U.S. dollar denoted by a rising trend line of higher LIBOR and further notice the December 2008 rise due to a reduction of U.S. dollar LIBOR.

EXHIBIT 5.4   2007 Chart of Euro/U.S. Dollar

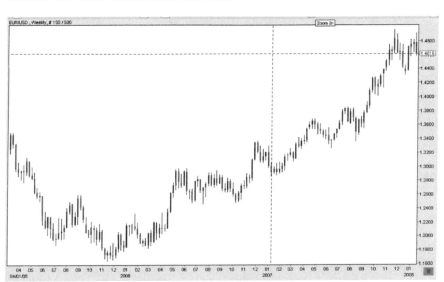

Note: Permission by attribution.

Source: Net Dania.

Historically, the euro/U.S. dollar peaks somewhere in the November/ December period. What may misalign rates is economic crisis, market uncertainties such as our present condition, or a central bank interest-rate change. Note rates may misalign, but they always normalize back to trend.

For traders to denote trends, compare overnight to three-month LIBOR to determine how far rates are predicted to rise or fall, where is the greatest rise or fall, and in what currency. Currency-pair prices fall within this range under normal conditions.

For the vast majority of central banks, the-three month LIBOR is their prime number of importance, but it is the overnight to three-month rate that is tracked for a whole host of reasons. The first is how much will borrowing cost be in three months and will that cost allow the central bank to meet its inflation-target rate. If not, central banks then adjust their reserves to bring that three-month rate in order. This scenario doesn't help trend traders and actually forced many to become day traders due to market uncertainties and central bank intervention of the three-month rate.

This present crisis really forced central banks to take a harder look at their operations. The trend in the last few years has been to limit volatility in overnight rates so a central bank can streamline its daily operations, meet its target rate, and not get caught by an unexpected outlier of a rate that will cost them more than expected and shock their economies. Explicit in central bank reports is limit volatility, flattening the yield curve, and getting to the next central bank meeting, to borrow the BOE approach. Yet this example holds true for all now.

Central banks are the money masters and in turn expert managers of their economies. If any institution sees trouble or good times ahead, it is the central banks, and they provide early warnings. For example, ever wonder why the Federal Reserve pays reserve interest on their Fed funds rate when that rate is presently 0.25?

Maintenance Periods

The Federal Reserve Board established in 2008 what it calls maintenance periods. These are weekly periods during which banks must maintain required reserves. Maintenance periods cover 14 consecutive days (Federal Reserve Manual 2010). Required reserves began as Regulation D that appeared first in the Federal Reserve Act of 1978 then carried forward to the 1980 Monetary Control Act that imposed mandatory reserve requirements (Federal Reserve Maintenance Manual 2010). All governments then imposed reserve laws and this gave rise to the need for the BBA, as reserves had to be priced and balanced in line with central bank target rates.

To pay interest on reserves was scheduled for 2011 with passage of the Financial Services Regulatory Relief Act of 2006 but moved forward by Congress to 2008 with passage of the Emergency Economic Stabilization Act of 2008 (Federal Reserve 2010).

Overdrafts are charged and reserves are credited an Effective Fed funds rate defined as a volume-weighted average rate of trades. Required reserves are credited an average targeted Fed funds rate minus 10 basis points, while excess reserves are credited the lowest targeted Fed funds rate minus 75 basis points (Federal Reserve 2010).

With a Fed funds target rate currently at 0.25, with hardly a possibility to sustain itself above due to crisis conditions, the Fed had to ensure this rate would never trade to zero or worse, trade a negative. Instead they had to shift reserves toward or in line with the target rate. See Exhibits 5.5 and 5.6 and notice that without required reserves, Fed fund rates would have traded to 0. Exhibit 5.7 provides actual Fed funds trades before, during, and after Maintenance Periods. Notice current Fed funds target rates are 0.00 to 0.25 so trading ranges will normally fall within this period unless crisis occurs or the market prices in an interest rate hike.

EXHIBIT 5.5 History of FED Funds Rates

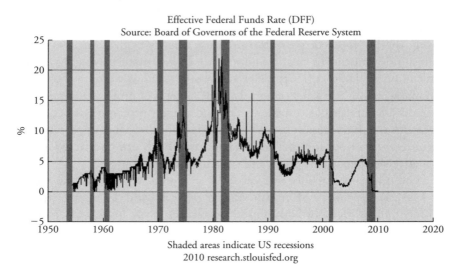

Effective Federal Funds Rate (DFF)
Source: Board of Governors of the Federal Reserve System

Shaded areas indicate US recessions
2010 research.stlouisfed.org

Source: Federal Reserve.

EXHIBIT 5.6 History of Maintenance Periods

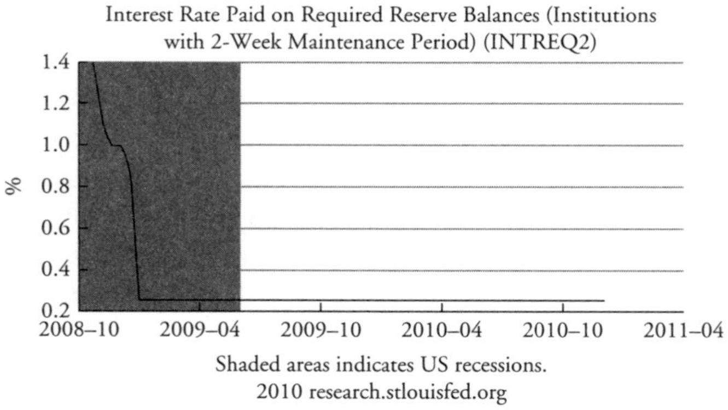
Interest Rate Paid on Required Reserve Balances (Institutions with 2-Week Maintenance Period) (INTREQ2)
1.4
1.2
1.0
%
0.8
0.6
0.4
0.2
2008–10
2009–04
2009–10
2010–04
2010–10
2011–04
Shaded areas indicates US recessions.
2010 research.stlouisfed.org

Source: Federal Reserve Bank of New York.

Mac Gorain in 2005 expertly outlined how the BOE maintains its 0.5 target by managing reserves so supply will equal demand to limit volatility until the next Monetary Policy Committee meeting. The central banks of Canada, Switzerland, and Japan, and the European Central Bank (ECB) all adopted some type of reserve policy and all have a unique way to achieve their desired target. See Exhibit 5.8. The number of maintenance periods changes based on the month. It's based on the demand and supply of euros. Did interest paid to reserves presage crisis times ahead?

Prior to maintenance periods, central banks borrowed for the next month during the last week of the prior month. Currency traders knew never to trade at this time due to volatile and sometimes wild market swings as central bank monies swung currency pairs wildly and without warning. For these and many reasons, the three-month LIBOR target is of profound importance to traders, central banks, private banks, and market professionals because it represents the prime cost of funds over a period of time. More important is to factor reserve periods for each central bank as LIBOR can be affected and in turn affects currency pair prices and movements.

The question possibly not yet fully answered is what are the effects to LIBOR in terms of maintenance periods and currency prices? Schlegel and Kraenzlin 2009 found that in the Swiss market after maintenance periods, a steeper demand curve was evident. This can only raise central bank borrowing costs along with LIBOR, and in turn affect currency prices in the context of economic conditions and trends as the demand for money increases once maintenance periods end each month.

EXHIBIT 5.7 Fed Funds Trades: Data

Date	Daily[1]	Range Low	Range High	Std. Dev.	Target Rate[2]
12/27/2010	0.19	0.05	0.5	0.05	0.00–0.25
12/24/2010	0.19	0.07	0.375	0.03	0.00–0.25
12/23/2010	0.19	0.1	0.375	0.03	0.00–0.25
12/22/2010	0.19	0.1	0.375	0.03	0.00–0.25
12/21/2010	0.2	0.12	0.375	0.03	0.00–0.25
12/20/2010	0.21	0.12	0.5	0.06	0.00–0.25
12/17/2010	0.2	0.12	0.375	0.03	0.00–0.25
12/16/2010	0.2	0.12	0.45	0.04	0.00–0.25
12/15/2010*	0.2	0.1	0.42	0.04	0.00–0.25
12/14/2010	0.19	0.12	0.375	0.04	0.00–0.25
12/13/2010	0.17	0.1	0.375	0.04	0.00–0.25
12/10/2010	0.16	0.1	0.375	0.03	0.00–0.25
12/09/2010	0.16	0.08	0.375	0.03	0.00–0.25
12/08/2010	0.17	0.1	0.375	0.03	0.00–0.25
12/07/2010	0.17	0.1	0.375	0.03	0.00–0.25
12/06/2010	0.18	0.125	0.375	0.04	0.00–0.25
12/03/2010	0.18	0.1	0.375	0.03	0.00–0.25
12/02/2010	0.19	0.125	0.375	0.03	0.00–0.25
12/01/2010*	0.2	0.125	0.4	0.03	0.00–0.25
11/30/2010	0.2	0.0625	0.4	0.04	0.00–0.25
11/29/2010	0.2	0.0625	0.375	0.04	0.00–0.25
11/26/2010	0.2	0.125	0.375	0.04	0.00–0.25
11/24/2010	0.2	0.11	0.375	0.03	0.00–0.25

*Indicates the last day of a maintenance period.

Source: New York Fed.

More important is what is the direction for a particular nation's money during maintenance periods? Another question that must be addressed is what is the payout in maintenance-period funds as opposed to market rates? This question addresses issues of supply and demand for money. This phenomenon sends currency pairs up toward weakness with increased

EXHIBIT 5.8 Indicative Calendar for Maintenance Periods in 2009

	Relevant Governing Council meeting	Start of maintenance period	End of maintenance period	Reserve base data for credit institutions reporting monthly	Reserve base data for credit institutions reporting quarterly	Length of the maintenance period (days)
1	15 January 2009	21 January 2009	10 February 2009	November 2008	September 2008	21
2	5 February 2009	11 February 2009	10 March 2009	December 2008	September 2008	28
3	5 March 2009	11 March 2009	7 April 2009	January 2009	December 2008	28
4	2 April 2009	8 April 2009	12 May 2009	February 2009	December 2008	35
5	7 May 2009	13 May 2009	9 June 2009	March 2009	December 2008	28
6	4 June 2009	10 June 2009	7 July 2009	April 2009	March 2009	28
7	2 July 2009	8 July 2009	11 August 2009	May 2009	March 2009	35
8	6 August 2009	12 August 2009	8 September 2009	June 2009	March 2009	28
9	3 September 2009	9 September 2009	13 October 2009	July 2009	June 2009	35
10	8 October 2009	14 October 2009	10 November 2009	August 2009	June 2009	28
11	5 November 2009	11 November 2009	7 December 2009	September 2009	June 2009	27
12	3 December 2009	8 December 2009	19 January 2010	October 2009	September 2009	43

Source: European Central Bank.

demand and lower with a decreased supply. After BBA LIBOR, rates must transfer within each nation. Provided is an example of each nation's internal LIBOR interest rates.

EURIBOR

The EURIBOR acronym is the European Interbank Offered Rate and is overseen by the European Banking Federation in Brussels. This rate, in 15 maturities from one week to 12 months, is the gauge for term deposits in the euro zone on a daily basis excluding holidays. Currently, 42 banks comprise the Steering Committee that bids and offers for euros and the Fix time is 11:00 CET. A closer view of rates inside the euro zone will help gauge the exact rates banks pay for euros and the movement of the euro.

See in Exhibit 5.9 the historical 12-month chart of EURIBOR and further see in Exhibit 5.10 historic euro/U.S. dollar charts, and notice how EURIBOR rates normally begin to ascend in the summer and peak in the fall, and a

EXHIBIT 5.9   Historic EURIBOR Charts and 2010 Rates

Graph EURIBOR rate development in 2010

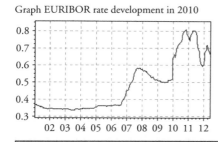

Graph of long-term EURIBOR rate development

EURIBOR rates 2010	first	last	highest	lowest	average
January	0.369%	0.344%	0.371%	0.344%	0.355%
February	0.347%	0.341%	0.348%	0.341%	0.345%
March	0.344%	0.340%	0.344%	0.336%	0.341%
April	0.344%	0.350%	0.350%	0.344%	0.346%
May	0.354%	0.363%	0.363%	0.354%	0.361%
June	0.361%	0.420%	0.420%	0.361%	0.375%
July	0.446%	0.577%	0.585%	0.446%	0.527%
August	0.577%	0.514%	0.577%	0.514%	0.544%
September	0.512%	0.520%	0.520%	0.500%	0.508%
October	0.640%	0.779%	0.813%	0.640%	0.736%
November	0.770%	0.602%	0.807%	0.595%	0.729%
December	0.606%	0.663%	0.722%	0.606%	0.679%

Note: Permission with attribution.

Source: EURIBOR-rates.eu.

EXHIBIT 5.10   Historic Euro/U.S. Dollar

Note: Permission granted by attribution.

Source: Market Scope 2.0.

rise in the euro/U.S. dollar normally follows the ascension. Also notice the euro/U.S. dollar traded its highest levels of the year in November/December every year since 1999.

From the 12-month EURIBOR chart, notice how EURIBOR rates rose during 2008 and 2009 and notice from the chart how the euro/U.S. dollar fell. From 2009 to 2010, EURIBOR rates fell and notice how the euro/U.S. dollar rose. Notice from the historical 12-month chart of EURIBOR and recognize in the first four years of the euro introduction, as EURIBOR rates rose, the euro/U.S. dollar fell and from 2003 to 2006, EURIBOR rates ranged along with the euro/U.S. dollar. Yet this pair followed EURIBOR rates up in 2006 and 2007. Crisis times occurred, and EURIBOR rates and the euro/U.S. dollar followed normal trends again from its early beginnings in 2008 and 2009. This is a typical example of a currency pair that must seek its yield. This means it must earn its highest rate. The answer to why can be found within EONIA.

EONIA

EONIA is the euro Overnight Index Average, a weighted average of all overnight unsecured lending deals. EONIA lending is for one-day to 24-month transactions and the fixing time is 19:00 CET. Look at EONIA as the Effective Funds rate for the United States. More importantly, it is the effective rate for EURIBOR simply due to its weight average factor against EURIBOR.

Notice Exhibit 5.11, the 12-month historical chart of EONIA rates and Exhibit 5.10 historic euro/U.S. dollar. From 1999 to 2004, the euro/U.S. dollar movements tracked opposite the EONIA rates. As EONIA rates went up, euro/U.S. dollar fell and vice versa. From 2003 to 2006 rates held steady, but 2006 to 2008 saw the euro/U.S. dollar track alongside EONIA rates with a normalization of original trend beginning in 2008 to 2010. The euro/U.S. dollar tracks EONIA rates up only when a demand for euros is evident such as in November/December when new budgets take effect or during good economic times when the euro zone economy is healthy and policy rates are expected to rise. Typically, EONIA and EURIBOR have an inverse relationship for most euro/U.S. dollar circumstances.

EXHIBIT 5.11   12-Month Chart of EONIA

EONIA - tables:

Current rate (by day)		Rate on first day of the month		Rate on first day of the year	
12-13-2010	0.588%	12-01-2010	0.468%	01-04-2010	0.341%
12-10-2010	0.627%	11-01-2010	0.683%	01-02-2009	2.221%
12-09-2010	0.646%	10-01-2010	0.721%	01-02-2008	3.782%
12-08-2010	0.721%	09-01-2010	0.370%	01-02-2007	3.600%
12-07-2010	0.738%	08-02-2010	0.399%	01-02-2006	2.350%
12-06-2010	0.386%	07-01-2010	0.480%	01-03-2005	2.090%
12-03-2010	0.414%	06-01-2010	0.329%	01-02-2004	2.060%
12-02-2010	0.462%	05-03-2010	0.339%	01-02-2003	2.900%
12-01-2010	0.468%	04-01-2010	0.325%	01-02-2002	3.350%
11-30-2010	0.539%	03-01-2010	0.314%	01-02-2001	4.830%

EONIA - charts:

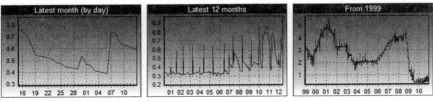

Source: EURIBOR-rates.eu.

Track EURIBOR and EONIA Rates

Euronext trades a EURIBOR/EONIA Swap Index futures contract. In this instance, EONIA is a mid-market rate that is calculated at 11:00 a.m. CET. Since 2008, the one-month EONIA contract and the three-month EONIA Swap Index aligned in terms of trade and settlement to central bank maintenance periods. The EONIA three-month contract tracks normal International Money Market dates while the one-month contract is aligned to European maintenance periods.

EONIA contract prices are quoted in percents to three decimal places and factored as 100 minus the traded average effective EONIA rate. Prices are quoted as 0.005 is equal to 12.50 euros.

EURIBOR prices are quoted in percents to three decimal places as 100 minus the rate of interest, 0.005 is equal to12.50 euros. Trades can be viewed almost in real time on the euronext site.

EURIBOR and EONIA are the determining factors that inform all European rates. They set the foundation, the floor.

Euro, EURIBOR, and EONIA

From an ECB and euro Governmental perspective, both would like to see cheaper borrowing costs to their currency to allow a greater demand for euro exports. Yet importers to the euro zone experience higher costs for their products due to a misalignment of rates that stems from EURIBOR and EONIA prices. EURIBOR and EONIA must be balanced against imports to exports yet all must be balanced against an ECB three-month target rate to allow inflation to remain sustained. This is Mundell-Fleming taken to the next level. The euro/U.S. dollar spot price can only fall between, above, or below these rates. Because the U.S. dollar has a direct opposite correlation to the euro, tracking the U.S. dollar for euro direction is paramount.

EURIBOR and EONIA rates will ebb and flow over any three-month time period as market and economic circumstances dictate so the euro/U.S. dollar will also ebb and flow. But as EURIBOR and EONIA rates rise, chances are good U.S. dollar rates will fall and vice versa over a three-month target period. This is the point of profit, the point of direction, the point of entry and exit, the point of decision as to which side of euro/U.S. dollar to go long or short. For example, what if U.S. dollar Fed funds rate hit a high of 2700? With a current 0.25 Fed funds target and no chance to raise rates in todays' economic conditions, chances are good 2700 is above target and the U.S. dollar should be sold against the euro because the cost for the U.S. dollar is too high. The Federal Reserve can't sustain finance costs at that level.

Yet what if rates at the three-month level came down? 2700 can be viewed in a much different light and could be the sign to go long the U.S. dollar against the euro due to signs that better economic conditions are ahead, as reflected by lower borrowing costs at the long end. This same scenario holds for the euro in terms of EURIBOR and EONIA; both U.S. dollar and euro rates ebb and flow in opposite movements to each other.

EURIBOR and EONIA rates can at times be difficult to gauge simply because those rates must be viewed within the context of economic conditions and because the euro is a currency that must seek and earn its yield. Notice the composition of the euro/U.S. dollar and notice this is exactly the order preferred by the ECB, while the U.S. dollar/euro is preferred by the U.S. Federal Reserve. The question always should be how much does one euro cost to one U.S. dollar and how much does one U.S. dollar cost to one euro? Viewed in this context with EURIBOR and EONIA, a euro/U.S. dollar spot determination can be better factored.

Australia and New Zealand

Why Australia and New Zealand run together is due to their historic and peaceful ties, their enormous cross-border trade, and their shared and similar market structure within their own economies and banking systems. The only difference is both are separate sovereigns and each has a separate currency. Yet both move in the markets almost in tandem as if they were the same currency. Both operate with a top prime rate called the Official Cash Rate (OCR), and both operate with issuance of Bank Bills.

Bank Bills are short-term bills, securities issued by trading banks to finance short-term financing from 30 to 180 days. For this reason, Australia and New Zealand are termed *cash economies* and Bank Bills are termed *Cash Rates* because Bank Bills are backed by bank reserves such as certificates of deposit and other deposits. Yet this is the rate that is of prime importance to both economies because it represents the shortest of open-market rates. Actual cash rates are factored by calculation of quarterly weighted-median-inflation rates. Bank Bills are to Australia and New Zealand what EURIBOR is to Europe. The difference is banks and markets decide rates in Australia and New Zealand rather than panel banks that bid and offer for money. Their in-nation LIBOR is different. Australia factors its overnight rate from the Interbank Overnight Cash Rate Survey, a survey of 25 Australian banks (Australia Central Bank). The overnight rate is a weighted average of funds lent and borrowed in the interbank market. For both economies, it is the 90-day Bank Bill rate of prime interest to bankers, central banks, and market professionals because that rate decides the cost of Australian and New Zealand dollars as well as determines good or bad economies. The current OCR rate in Australia is 4.50, and 3.00 for New Zealand.

See in Exhibit 5.12, the historic chart of the 90-day Bank Bill yield rate to cash rates in Australia. Also see Exhibit 5.13, the Australian dollar/U.S. dollar

EXHIBIT 5.12   Historic Chart of 90-Day Bank Bills and Chart of Cash Rates

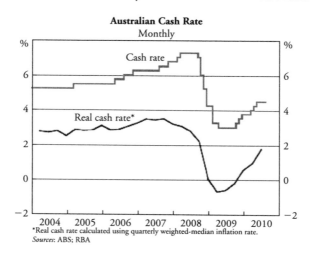

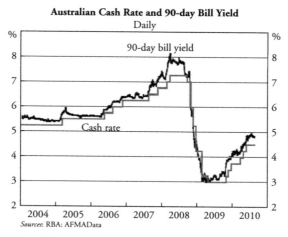

Source: Royal Bank of Australia.

EXHIBIT 5.13 Historic Chart Australian Dollar/U.S. Dollar

Note: Permission granted by attribution by FXCM.

Source: Market Scope 2.0.

historic chart. Notice how as Bank Bill yields rise, Australian dollar/U.S. dollar rises. Also notice how the cash rate serves as a buffer, an area of support.

The more telling story to an Australian dollar/U.S. dollar rise is the comparison to U.S. dollar cash rates. See Exhibit 5.14, Australian dollar versus U.S. cash rates. Australian dollar cash rates are far above U.S. rates. The question for traders should be where will money gain its greatest yield? In this instance, it is the buy Australian dollar and sell the U.S. dollar. This again is the typical carry trade as one currency is sold and the other is purchased to first gain yield then earn capital gains.

With an Australian OCR at 4.50 and U.S. rate of 0.25, a carry trader is selling the 0.25 U.S. dollar and buying Australian dollar at 4.50 minus U.S. dollar 0.25 with interest gained of 4.25 and paid daily in a rollover. Australian dollar/U.S. dollar will always out-pace New Zealand dollar/U.S. dollar in price and market movement because of the greater interest differential. Notice New Zealand's 3.00 OCR and U.S. dollar 0.25. New Zealand dollar/U.S. dollar carry trades earn 2.75 to Australia's 4.25. This interest differential is historic because Australian society is and has always been slightly

more progressive than New Zealand's. Yet no other central bank is more forward thinking than New Zealand's Royal Bank of New Zealand (RBNZ).

For New Zealand, the story remains the same. See Exhibit 5.15, historic
chart of Bank Bills and OCR rates and Exhibit 5.16, historic chart of New
Zealand dollar/U.S. dollar. As Bank Bill rates rise above OCR rates, the
New Zealand dollar/U.S. dollar rises, and in some years it trends and ranges

EXHIBIT 5.14   Australia versus U.S. Cash Rates Historical Chart

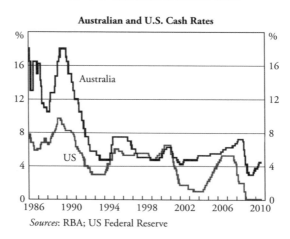

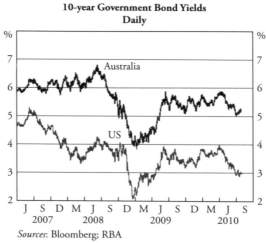

Source: Royal Bank of Australia.

EXHIBIT 5.15   Historic Chart of New Zealand Bank Bills and OCR Rates

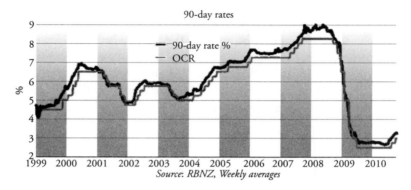

Source: Royal Bank of New Zealand.

EXHIBIT 5.16   New Zealand Dollar/U.S. Dollar Historic Chart

Note: Granted permission by FXCM with attribution.

Source: MarketScope 2.0.

when Bank Bills range. New Zealand reports Bank Bill yields daily at 11:10 as a mid-market rate, the same time as the TWI rates. Notice the real trend down in rates from 2008 to 2009 as the world crisis hit. Bank Bill rates still never broke OCR support. The story is the same when the New Zealand dollar is compared to U.S. rates. This is the typical carry trade as money must seek its yield, Australian dollar/U.S. dollar and New Zealand dollar/U.S. dollar is always a buy-the-dip strategy with focus on Bank Bills to determine entry and exit. The strategy should be: enter at OCR and let Bank Bills guide the trade.

Australian Dollar/New Zealand Dollar and Bank Bills

Notice Exhibit 5.17, the Australian dollar/New Zealand dollar historical chart and notice its opposite market movements to the Australian dollar/U.S. dollar and New Zealand dollar/U.S. dollar in Exhibits 5.14 and 5.16. For seasonality, one would recognize how many years Australian dollar/New Zealand dollar rose in the beginning months of the year and retraced at the end of the year while Australian dollar/U.S. dollar and New

EXHIBIT 5.17   Chart Australian Dollar/New Zealand Dollar

Source: MarketScope 2.0. Permission granted by FXCM with attribution.

Zealand dollar/U.S. dollar peak in the later months and reach lows in the beginning of the years. The reason for this scenario is the cost of trade between New Zealand and Australia. More important may be the fact that New Zealand governmental budgets are proposed in May. Further, summer months in the United States are winter months in New Zealand and Australia so the effects of trade are dramatic during these periods.

Australian Securities Exchange

The best method to track Australian and New Zealand Bank bills is through the futures contract traded on the Australian Securities Exchange (ASX). Each trade separately. Both 30- and 90-day New Zealand Bank Bills trade as a futures contract with the ability to also trade options on the contract. The ASX also trades a 30-day New Zealand OCR futures contract. Why? Because New Zealand doesn't trade futures and options, so any futures and option trading are conducted through the ASX.

Short-term Interest Rates (STIR) is the method to find short-term interest-rate instruments in Australia, New Zealand, Europe, and euronext in the United States.

OCR for both Australia and New Zealand represent deposit rates and bank bills as the measure of direction for economic and costs of funds.

In economic terms, the guide is the 30- and 90-day Interbank Cash Rate futures contracts. If the 90-day is above the 30 day, expect a rise in rates. If the 90-day is below the 30-day rate, it signals a decline.

Bank Bills are priced based on yield to maturity with a 365-day count. For example, a 90-day present value is determined as

Present value = Face value $\times$ 365/365 + (yield $\times$ days to maturity/100)

Face value = Future value at the end of the 90 days

From an ASX site example:

A 90 day Bank Bill, face value 100,000, yield to maturity trades 5.50 percent

where

$$P = 100,000 \times 365/365 + (5.5 \times 90/100) = 98.661.9$$

The 30-day Cash Rate Futures contract is settled at the cash-settlement rate that equals the monthly average of the interbank overnight cash rate divided by the number of days in a month and rounded to the nearest 0.001 percent. All are priced as 0.005 in basis point increments, 0.01 basis points is equal to Australian dollar 24.66.

The process is the same for New Zealand, with the only difference in the price of the contracts—Australian dollar is 5 million and New Zealand is 3 million.

Seasonality and Australian Dollar/U.S. Dollar, New Zealand Dollar/U.S. Dollar

Both governments present budgets to their respective parliaments in May to be voted on around the June/July period. And again, major companies pass budgets during this time to coincide with government budgets. As was the case for the British pound sterling/U.S. dollar, Australian dollar/U.S. dollar and New Zealand dollar/U.S. dollar, they don't necessarily peak during the June/July period. Rather both peak around the November/December time frame. What has occurred during July since 1999 for Australian dollar/U.S. dollar has actually been up months historically, while the majority of months for New Zealand dollar/U.S. dollar has actually been down. But both peak during the November/December period. The question of Bank Bills and BBA LIBOR cannot be a reliable indicator at the time of budget proposal and passage.

U.S. Dollar Pairs and LIBOR

An important point to note is the first four pairs addressed were the euro/U.S. dollar, British pound sterling/U.S. dollar, Australian dollar/U.S. dollar, and New Zealand dollar/U.S. dollar. In these examples, U.S. dollar was the base currency and it was sold with every rise of the quote currency and vice versa. The same principle holds for these pairs as was discussed for trade weight indices (TWIs).

Central banks and governments of these currency pairs want a rise in prices. They want their currency first in the quote position aligned with the U.S. dollar as the base. For example, the euro/U.S. dollar may trade at, for example, 1.2818 but the ECB and European governments would love to see 2.2818 or 3.2818. Under these circumstances, everybody associated with the euro gains. European governments receive a boost to their economies from increased export revenue that flows to them instead of the United States. Major companies earn revenue from increased exports and profits. Central banks earn foreign reserves that raise their balance sheets to better manage their economies. Jobs are created with rising wages, rising consumer spending, and rising interest rates that benefit all and allow this economy to flourish as long as the relationship holds. This relationship holds when the economic balance isn't so skewed in one direction, when interest rates to Gross Domestic Product (GDP) and other economic factors are balanced. Same with the British pound sterling/U.S. dollar, Australian dollar/U.S. dollar, and New Zealand dollar/ U.S. dollar since the United States is their largest and most-profitable market. Notice how U.S. dollar/euro, U.S. dollar/British pound sterling, U.S. dollar/ Australian dollar and U.S. dollar/New Zealand dollar won't work unless the U.S. dollar was shorted. So the factor of LIBOR to a currency pair must be viewed in the context of economic conditions. It is inflation versus deflation where only one side of a pair can benefit—one winner, one loser.

A rising LIBOR and a rising currency pair is good as long as conditions are sufficient as has been the case for Australian dollar/U.S. dollar and New Zealand dollar/U.S. dollar. When economic conditions turn for Australian dollar/U.S. dollar and New Zealand dollar/U.S. dollar, rising LIBOR will be a hindrance to business because the cost of those dollars will be too high.

The next three currency pairs, U.S. dollar/Japanese yen, U.S. dollar/Swiss franc, and U.S. dollar/Canadian dollar have quite different arrangements from their opposite counterparts due to the composition of the pairs. In this instance, U.S. dollar is the quote and Japanese yen, Swiss franc, and Canadian dollar are the base. LIBOR will work quite differently as we will see.

TIBOR and EUROYEN

The current Japanese top interest rate, termed the base rate, is 0.10 and their overnight rate is called the Call Rate, an unsecured loan market where rates are decided by bids and offers between 17 bankers inside Japan, with a 12:00 noon published Tokyo time release (Japanese Bankers Association). The actual rate is reported at 11:00 a.m. Tokyo time, 10:00 p.m. eastern time, and two hours after the Tokyo Stock Exchange opens (or one hour depending on daylight savings time) but the number filters through the world by 12:00 noon Tokyo time and is reported on the JBA site at 12:00 noon (Japanese Bankers Association).

This unsecured Call loan market is provided for TIBOR, the Tokyo Interbank Offered Rate, to factor unsecured loans denominated in Japanese yen. But TIBOR is a factor for Japanese loans inside Japan among Japanese bankers and has nothing to do with trade outside of Japan.

With a base rate so low and an economy in a deflationary downtrend for many years, where could these rates possibly trade? See Exhibit 5.18, the

EXHIBIT 5.18 Yen TIBOR for August

	One Week	One Month	Two Months	Three Months	Four Months	Five Months	Six Months	Seven Months	Eight Months	Nine Months	Ten Months	Eleven Months	Twelve Months
2010/08/16	0.15000	0.21000	0.29000	0.37923	0.41769	0.45692	0.49538	0.50692	0.51692	0.52077	0.52077	0.53077	0.53692
2010/08/13	0.15000	0.21000	0.29000	0.38000	0.41769	0.45692	0.49538	0.50692	0.51692	0.52077	0.52077	0.53077	0.53692
2010/08/12	0.15000	0.21000	0.29000	0.38000	0.41769	0.45692	0.49538	0.50692	0.51692	0.52077	0.52077	0.53077	0.53692
2010/08/11	0.15000	0.21000	0.29000	0.38000	0.41769	0.45692	0.49538	0.50692	0.51692	0.52077	0.52077	0.53077	0.53692
2010/08/10	0.15000	0.21000	0.29000	0.38000	0.41769	0.45692	0.49538	0.50692	0.51692	0.52077	0.52077	0.53077	0.53692
2010/08/09	0.15000	0.21000	0.29000	0.38000	0.41769	0.45692	0.49538	0.50692	0.51692	0.52077	0.52077	0.53077	0.53692
2010/08/06	0.15000	0.21000	0.29000	0.38000	0.41769	0.45692	0.49538	0.50692	0.51692	0.52154	0.52154	0.53077	0.53692
2010/08/05	0.15000	0.21000	0.29000	0.38000	0.41769	0.45692	0.49538	0.50692	0.51692	0.52154	0.52154	0.53077	0.53692
2010/08/04	0.15000	0.21000	0.29000	0.38000	0.41769	0.45692	0.49615	0.50692	0.51692	0.52154	0.52154	0.53077	0.53692
2010/08/03	0.15000	0.21000	0.29000	0.38000	0.41769	0.45692	0.49615	0.50692	0.51692	0.52154	0.52462	0.53077	0.53692
2010/08/02	0.15000	0.21000	0.29000	0.38000	0.41769	0.45692	0.49615	0.50692	0.51692	0.52231	0.52615	0.53077	0.53692

Source: Japanese Bankers Association.

EXHIBIT 5.19 Historic Chart EUROYEN TIBOR

(1) Short-Term Interest Rates

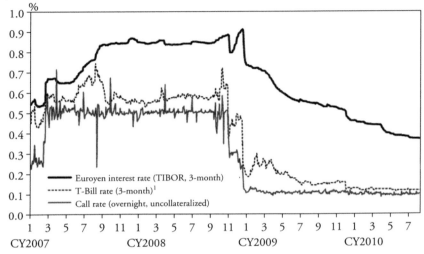

Source: Bank of Japan.

TIBOR chart for the month of August and notice the settlement of rates. yen becomes expensive as borrowing occurs past the one-week rate.

Further notice Exhibit 5.19, the historic chart of EUROYEN TIBOR against Exhibit 5.20, the historic chart of U.S. dollar/Japanese yen and notice how little the U.S. dollar/Japanese yen moves in line with EUROYEN TIBOR rates.

When the U.S. dollar/Japanese yen becomes too expensive, it aligns with TIBOR. This occurred in August 2008, but the remainder of the world's currencies during that time suffered the same effects as during the month the U.S. housing crisis was announced. Any spikes up or down in TIBOR were a reflection of world crisis rather than normal market movements, because the Japanese can't afford to have rates deviate too far from a norm due to deflationary environments.

TIBOR has leveled since 2009, yet the U.S. dollar/Japanese yen ebbed and flowed. For the most part, the U.S. dollar/Japanese yen has been in a long-term downtrend that was never forecast nor reflected through TIBOR. What this means is TIBOR can't be relied upon to trade the U.S. dollar/Japanese yen inside or outside of Japan unless it is traded another way.

As was discussed with central banks and TWIs and interested pairs to a central bank, look at U.S. dollar/Japanese yen differently. What if the order

EXHIBIT 5.20   Historic Chart of U.S. Dollar/Japanese Yen

Note: Permission granted by FXCM with attribution.

Source: MarketScope 2.0.

was reversed to Japanese yen/U.S. dollar? This says TIBOR now reflects this relationship, as can be evident from early 2007 and the uptrend in Japanese yen/U.S. dollar. TIBOR not only reflects Japanese yen/U.S. dollar but Japanese yen has actually been in an uptrend. In this instance, the U.S. dollar was actually sold against the Japanese yen and led to an enormous uptrend for Japanese yen. Because this is the order the Bank of Japan (BOJ) and the Japanese government actually want, the uptrend has earned enormous foreign reserves for the Japanese against the U.S. dollar. Looked upon another way, why would the Japanese care about U.S. dollar conversions into Japanese yen, U.S. dollar/Japanese yen? This composition doesn't help initially until it is time to repatriate. They need to know Japanese yen conversions into U.S. dollars. This answers the question how much will it cost, how many Japanese yen will it take to ship and sell its products in the United States and how much will they earn in profits?

An even further way to look at this relationship is to factor exchange rates. On August 11, 2009, U.S. dollar/Japanese yen was trading about 90.37 in the spot price and on August 17, 2010, U.S. dollar/Japanese yen was trading at about 85.23. In exchange rate terms, August 2009 began 0.70530 and ended August 2001 at 0.78020. It took many more U.S. dollars to convert to Japanese yen, which was not good for a U.S. exporter. Conversely, Japanese yen/U.S. dollar began August 11, 2009 at 0.01028 and ended August 17, 2010 at 0.0116920, good for the Japanese because they earn more yen against the U.S. dollar and they earn their desired yield and foreign reserves.

For traders, it is good to track spot against exchange rates and TIBOR because while Japanese bankers may have a desired level for TIBOR, it is the prevailing economic conditions that dictate TIBOR. Caution is always advised when betting against a central bank with a financial interest in market prices, especially the Japanese who are smart traders. Also be aware that this discussion concerns Japanese and American market trading arrangements. How this pair will trade in other markets, such as Europe, may be different.

Repatriation and the Yen

For repatriation purposes, let's look at the U.S. dollar/Japanese yen and Japanese yen/U.S. dollar relationships. Notice the historic TIBOR chart and notice the Japanese central bank tracks U.S. Treasury bills and their own T-Bill rates and again further notice Treasury-bill rates are always above TIBOR. According to the August 2009 Treasury International Capital report that tracks foreign investment in the United States, the Japanese are and have been number two in purchases of U.S. Treasury securities for a number of years (TIC Data 2011). As the Japanese earn profits in Japanese yen/U.S. dollars, they purchase Treasuries with profits and wait for favorable exchange rates in U.S. dollar/Japanese yen and transfer the money back to Japan. Exchange rates and spot prices for U.S. dollar/Japanese yen and Japanese yen/U.S. dollar ebb and flow, so the Japanese wait until the price is acceptable then repatriate. Notice the Japanese government never complains about Japanese yen/U.S. dollars but they speak volumes when U.S. dollar/Japanese yen is not sufficient a price.

EUROYEN

The EUROYEN is another Call market rate used to gauge rates in offshore markets (Japanese Bankers Association). The term *offshore market* has many variables, with arrangements that changed dramatically since the inception of the EUROYEN in 1998. A whole host of academic literature exists that explains the many connections of EUROYEN to Eurobonds to Eurodollars and now directly to the money markets.

World governments assisted the yen to become internationalized with the introduction of TIBOR in 1995 and EUROYEN in 1998 (Japanese Bankers Association). EUROYEN's introduction was enhanced by the introduction of currency cross pairs during this period. Recognize TIBOR covered U.S. markets and EUROYEN assisted the yen in euro markets that further sealed the goal of internationalization because both are Japan's largest export markets.

Notice in Exhibit 5.21 the historical charts of euro/Japanese yen since 2007 and further notice Exhibit 5.22, historical charts of EUROYEN TIBOR. The relationship has nearly perfect correlations, so EUROYEN can be absolutely employed as a tool to forecast euro/Japanese yen movements.

Notice Exhibit 5.22, the August charts of EUROYEN, and recognize higher rates as borrowings occur in later months. This can be viewed as a possible early warning indicator of trouble ahead. Notice then the euro/

EXHIBIT 5.21   Historic Chart of Euro/Japanese Yen

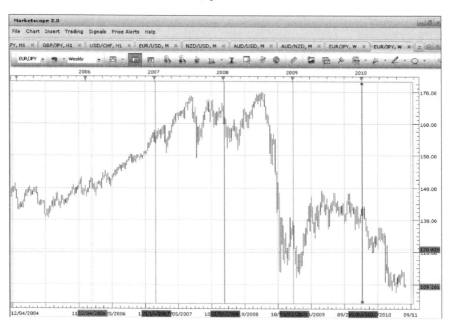

Note: Permission granted with attribution by FXCM.

Source: MarketScope 2.0.

EXHIBIT 5.22 August Chart EUROYEN

	One Week	One Month	Two Months	Three Months	Four Months	Five Months	Six Months	Seven Months	Eight Months	Nine Months	Ten Months	Eleven Months	Twelve Months
2010/08/16	0.14923	0.20385	0.28308	0.37154	0.41077	0.45154	0.49000	0.50615	0.51846	0.52538	0.53231	0.54385	0.55231
2010/08/13	0.14923	0.20462	0.28385	0.37231	0.41077	0.45154	0.49000	0.50615	0.51846	0.52538	0.53231	0.54385	0.55231
2010/08/12	0.14923	0.20462	0.28385	0.37231	0.41077	0.45154	0.49000	0.50615	0.51846	0.52538	0.53231	0.54385	0.55231
2010/08/11	0.14923	0.20462	0.28385	0.37231	0.41077	0.45154	0.49000	0.50615	0.51846	0.52538	0.53231	0.54385	0.55231
2010/08/10	0.14923	0.20462	0.28385	0.37231	0.41077	0.45154	0.49000	0.50615	0.51846	0.52538	0.53231	0.54385	0.55231
2010/08/09	0.14923	0.20462	0.28385	0.37231	0.41077	0.45154	0.49000	0.50615	0.51846	0.52538	0.53231	0.54385	0.55231
2010/08/06	0.14923	0.20462	0.28385	0.37231	0.41077	0.45154	0.49000	0.50615	0.51846	0.52538	0.53231	0.54385	0.55231
2010/08/05	0.14923	0.20462	0.28385	0.37231	0.41077	0.45154	0.49000	0.50615	0.51846	0.52615	0.53308	0.54385	0.55231
2010/08/04	0.14923	0.20462	0.28462	0.37308	0.41154	0.45231	0.49077	0.50615	0.51846	0.52615	0.53308	0.54385	0.55231
2010/08/03	0.14923	0.20462	0.28462	0.37308	0.41154	0.45231	0.49077	0.50615	0.51846	0.52615	0.53462	0.54385	0.55231
2010/08/02	0.14923	0.20462	0.28462	0.37308	0.41154	0.45231	0.49077	0.50615	0.51846	0.52692	0.53538	0.54385	0.55231

Source: Japanese Bankers Association.

Japanese yen charts and notice the down month of August 2010. Further, notice the relationship euro/Japanese yen has with U.S. dollar/Japanese yen from Exhibit 5.20. Both correlate in market movements. Further notice Exhibit 5.23 euro/Japanese yen trading on Euronext in Europe.

Notice how much cheaper EUROYEN rates are when compared to TIBOR. This is the difference between an offshore and an onshore rate as well as TIBOR quoted as 1 percent with a 365 day count and EUROYEN with a U.S. and European 360 day count. The Japanese would actually like to see EUROYEN rates low in deflationary environments and high when economic conditions improve. But each rate serves a different function. The best method to trade these pairs together is to watch EUROYEN rates. If short-term rates stream higher, chances are good trouble may be ahead due to a deflationary Japanese economy or detrimental economic condition outside Japan that affects the cost of money. This would serve for trading in Japanese, American, and Asian markets.

Yet if longer-dated rates edge down, this is an all-clear sign to go long euro/Japanese yen because it says to the markets that no trouble is expected. The euro/Japanese yen would take off in all markets, especially European and U.S. markets. It is a question of confidence.

EXHIBIT 5.23   Euro/Japanese Yen chart

Note: Permission granted upon attribution.

Source: Euronext.

Longer-dated rates on the way down say bankers are not worried about defaults. Yet look at EUROYEN as a LIBOR. A high daily number normally means a down day while a low number may signal an up day in American and European markets. Rates will ebb and flow and euro/Japanese yen will coincide with those flows. Finally, the pair of interest to the Japanese is the Japanese yen/euro and the pair of interest to the Europeans is the euro/Japanese yen. These pairs may trade quite differently in their respective markets so both combinations should confirm each other before a trade decision.

For example, notice Exhibit 5.24, the three-month futures chart of EUROYEN that trades on the Tokyo Futures Exchange and compare that chart to Exhibit 5.25 euro/Japanese yen in May, June, and July 2010. EUROYEN futures were up for the three-month period, yet euro/Japanese yen was down. The caveat is that the three months includes all markets. EUROYEN released as one rate only means the start of trading of that rate in the Japanese interbank market. For the Japanese, Japanese yen/euro was actually up during Tokyo trade from May to July. For traders, Japanese yen/euro should always be looked upon as the long trade or short euro/Japanese yen in Asian trading while Japanese yen/euro should be looked upon as the short trade and long euro/Japanese yen in European and American markets as market conditions

EXHIBIT 5.24   EUROYEN Three-Month Futures Chart

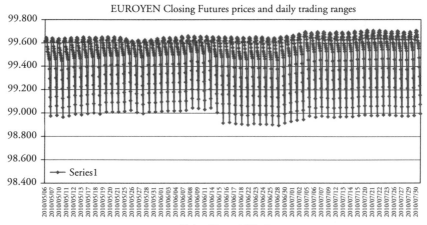

Note: Permission granted upon attribution.

Source: Tokyo Futures Exchange.

EXHIBIT 5.25 Euro/Japanese Yen, May through August 2010

Note: Permission granted by FXCM with attribution.
Source: MarketScope 2.0.

represent themselves. To trade Japanese yen/U.S. dollar in Japanese markets, enter at TIBOR and allow Japanese Treasury Bills to guide the trade.

Euronext and EUROYEN

While the Tokyo Futures Exchange trades EUROYEN futures, Euronext in Europe also trades EUROYEN futures contracts, the Chicago Mercantile Exchange (CME) trades futures contracts so anyone can track EUROYEN from market to market and gauge euro/Japanese yen prices and direction. The preferred method to trade Japanese yen/U.S. dollar is to measure the spread between EUROYEN and Eurodollar futures because both have the same day counts. EUROYEN is priced in yen and represents deposits in offshore markets while Eurodollars represents U.S. dollar deposits in Europe. Spreads will determine direction as no better gauge exists as an early-warning sign to measure interest rates between these two pair arrangements. What is measured is the cost of money—borrowing costs —so wider spreads say trouble exists.

Euro/Japanese Yen as a Risk Indicator

For U.S. markets, EUROYEN TIBOR trades in the money markets on the CME. Research suggests that euro/Japanese yen is the only pair of this type ever traded directly in the money markets. Many currency pairs trade as futures contracts on the CME, but none trade directly in the money markets. Because U.S. money markets are so sensitive due to the short-term nature of many varied rates and varied financial instruments, euro/Japanese yen is classified as a market-risk indicator by market convention.

euro/Japanese yen as a risk indicator measures risk for carry trades and provides overall direction for all other currency pairs because of direct opposite correlations of this pair. When risk grips the markets, euro/Japanese yen TIBOR will soar, so carry trades will be the first instrument sold and euro/Japanese yen will be the first instrument to feel the market effects. Early-warning or all-clear signs for American market trading can occur during European market trading, as continuity for the most part exists from market to market, continent to continent for euro/Japanese yen.

When trouble grips the markets, money finds safety in non-risk assets and non-risk currency pairs. Risky markets means money flows into U.S. dollar/Swiss franc, U.S. dollar/Japanese yen, U.S. dollar/Canadian dollar, euro/British pound sterling, Australian dollar/New Zealand dollar, and British pound sterling/New Zealand dollar. This sends these pairs toward weakness, so go long these pairs in times of market stress and short euro/U.S. dollar, British pound sterling/U.S. dollar, Australian dollar/U.S. dollar, and New Zealand dollar/U.S. dollar. Stress means short carry trades such as euro/Japanese yen, British pound sterling/Japanese yen, British pound sterling/Swiss franc, Australian dollar/Japanese yen, and New Zealand dollar/Japanese yen. In nonrisk markets when EUROYEN TIBOR are acceptable, go long euro/U.S. dollar, British pound sterling/U.S. dollar, Australian dollar/U.S. dollar, and New Zealand dollar/U.S. dollar, and short U.S. dollar/Japanese yen, U.S. dollar/Swiss franc, U.S. dollar/Canadian dollar, Australian dollar/New Zealand dollar, euro/British pound sterling, and British pound sterling/New Zealand dollar as market conditions dictate.

While market convention may suggest euro/Japanese yen is the premier measure of risk, I suggest euro/Swiss franc as a better indicator for many reasons. The first is euro, Swiss franc, and U.S. dollar markets trade together part of any trading day, while Japanese yen does not. The response from any three markets will be felt immediately through euro/Swiss franc so strategy can be factored much quicker. The question of euro/Japanese yen is how will U.S. dollar react? Swiss franc will be seen much faster than a Japanese yen response because Japanese yen responses to markets can at times be slow. euro/Swiss franc can be classified in this instance as a forward indicator. It's not only euro to measure risk but Swiss franc is the premier measure of safety. euro/Swiss franc serves a more perfect balance because the euro is more widely traded, as is Swiss franc, more so than Japanese yen. Further euro/Swiss franc futures contracts trade in Europe, so a market response will be felt much faster.

For U.S. and European markets, another method to measure risk directly from money markets is the Overnight Indexed Swap (OIS)–Eurodollar spread. This trade is essentially U.S. dollar/euro, but it could easily be euro/U.S. dollar depending which way the spreads move. OIS represents U.S. OIS and Eurodollars represent the euro. As OIS rates increase, Eurodollars will fall and vice versa. The question is will OIS–Eurodollar rates translate fast enough to be reflected in the currency markets? The answer is yes, because sell offs will occur simultaneously.

Seasonality and U.S. Dollar/Japanese Yen

Traditionally, the U.S. dollar/Japanese yen peaks during the year around April or May along with LIBOR. The answer is believed to be due to Japanese governments who pass and vote budgets during this time. The Ministry of Finance in Japan writes initial budgets in December, adjusts the budget in February due to supplementary requests by Japanese Ministries, and a vote is held around the April/May period in the Japanese Diet (Ministry of Finance2010). Japanese companies pass budgets in line with government budgets for purposes of business planning and taxes. If U.S. dollar/Japanese yen peaks, Japanese yen/U.S. dollar bottoms and allows Japanese yen to be borrowed to fund the new year.

Canada

Canada's overnight rate is termed the Overnight Money Market Financing Rate (OMMFR), a rate determined as an estimate based on an end of day survey by the Bank of Canada (BOC) banks. The OMMFR is a weighted average of repo funding costs by money dealers (Reid 2007). It is a one-day rate that measures the cost for securities dealers to finance their operations.

The Canadian Overnight Repo Rate is a weighted average of GC rates of repo transactions between 6:00 a.m. and 4:00 p.m. and is employed to measure intraday and end-of-day levels of the OMMFR (Reid 2007). The reason for using the OMMFR is it is not as volatile as the CORRA rate, plus many more transactions occur in Canada's interbank market (Reid 2007).

One would note from Exhibit 5.26, the chart comparison of the CORRA and OMMFR, that not much volatility exists between the two rates but both travel together. Ironically, 145 instances have occurred since 2005 where daily Canadian dollar transactions reached below the $500-million threshold in the repo market so CORRA was employed as the overnight rate (Reid 2007). Notice Exhibit 5.27, the chart of U.S. dollar/Canadian dollar from 2009 to 2010 and notice the spike in CORRA and OMMFR.

The spike was caused by the June 1, 2010, hike in Canada's target rate from 0.25 to 0.50. This raised Canada's borrowing costs and in turn raised

EXHIBIT 5.26   CORRA and OMMFR Chart Comparison

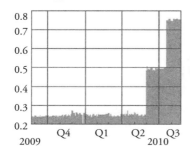

Overnight money market financing[1]
Previous data ▶

23 Aug 2010:	**0.7500**
20 Aug 2010:	**0.7480**
19 Aug 2010:	**0.7482**
18 Aug 2010:	**0.7501**
17 Aug 2010:	**0.7477**

GRAPH PERIOD:
21 Aug 2009–23 Aug 2010

Overnight repo rate (CORRA)[2]
Previous data ▶

23 Aug 2010:	**0.7508**
20 Aug 2010:	**0.7532**
19 Aug 2010:	**0.7543**
18 Aug 2010:	**0.7533**
17 Aug 2010:	**0.7500**

Source: Bank of Canada.

EXHIBIT 5.27   U.S. Dollar/Canadian Dollar, 2009 to 2010

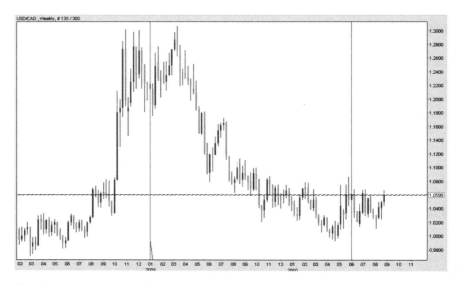

Note: Permission granted by attribution.
Source: Net Dania.

the Canadian dollar side of U.S. dollar/Canadian dollar pair. If future raises occur, Canadian dollar will rise further in the U.S. dollar/Canadian dollar combination. Further notice the downtrend from 2009 to 2010. This was caused by rate decreases that began in 2007. U.S. dollar/Canadian dollar has actually been in a long-term downtrend when rates began to descend. To understand the relationship further, view Exhibit 5.28 of the Canadian CORRA rate minus the target in basis points.

Seasonality and U.S. Dollar/Canadian Dollar

The Canadian Parliament normally votes and passes a government budget during March/April. Fiscal years in Canada begin April 1, so normally a budget is already in place from the traditional March introduction (Canada Department of Finance 2010). Major Canadian companies also write their own budgets in line with government budgets. Look for Canadian LIBOR and the OMMFR to reach its peak of the year during this period and also look for U.S. dollar/Canadian dollar to peak, Canadian dollar/U.S. dollar to bottom.

EXHIBIT 5.28   CORRA Rate Minus Overnight Rate

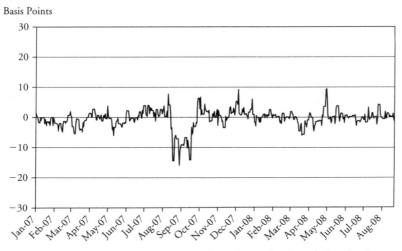

The Overnight Rate is me asured by CORRA, which is the Canadian Overnight Repo Rate Average.

Source: Bank of Canada.

Switzerland

The Swiss National Bank's (SNB) overnight rate is termed SARON, Swiss Average Rate Overnight, and is employed as the rate to achieve the BBA Swiss franc LIBOR three-month target. It is a volume-weighted average and is calculated every 10 minutes with noon and 4:00 p.m. end-of-day Swiss Fixing times (SIX Swiss Exchange). To ensure accuracy of the target, the Swiss employ three more indicators to oversee SARON.

SCRON is the Swiss Current Rate Overnight and is employed to view current interbank market trades. SCRON is calculated every three minutes throughout any trading day by the SIX Swiss Exchange, the Swiss Stock Market where these various rates trade.

SAION is the Swiss Average Index Overnight and SCION is the Swiss Current Index Overnight. What determines these various rates is the importance of Swiss franc repo, since the SNB adds or subtracts liquidity based on Swiss franc BBA LIBOR through Swiss franc repo. Repo rates hold dominance in the SNB's target, because liquidity is added or subtracted to support repo trades, repo rates establish a floor for rates. The repo floor translates to a Swiss franc/U.S. dollar floor, U.S. dollar/Swiss franc peak.

The SNB likes to hold their three-month target in the middle of the range to allow for any outside economic developments and prevent them from sidetracking their target structure. SARON is the preferred indicator because that is the rate that establishes and defines the all-important Swiss yield curve. The Swiss economy is heavily monitored by these rates.

Seasonality and U.S. Dollar/Swiss Franc

The Federal Finance Administration prepares and submits a budget to the Swiss Parliament to be voted on, usually by December. Swiss companies, like their governmental counterparts, write their own budgets in line with Swiss calendar years. Look for Swiss franc LIBOR and SARON rates to peak during the December/January period. Yet U.S. dollar/Swiss franc will begin its ascent and Swiss franc/U.S. dollar to bottom at that time.

Target Rates Defined

Monetary policy for Canada and most of the world's economies are found in the target for the overnight rate. That establishes borrow and lend rates, bid and ask, buy and sell. Canada operates monetary policy based on an operating band. The band is one half of a percentage point wide and the overnight is the target. If the operating band is 2.25 to 2.75 percent, the overnight target -2.50 percent. The top band is the top bank rate and establishes interest for one day. The bottom band is the deposit rate and the rate banks pay on surplus funds.

The repo rate for Canada is important because it establishes the overnight rate. The OMMFR is a mystery rate and will always remain that way. The markets then decide if the overnight rate should be tied to the repo rate or a market rate such as a T-bill.

Canadian borrowing costs are factored as

$$\text{Interest} \times (90/365)$$

Now convert to U.S. dollar for a Canadian dollar/U.S. dollar price.

Canada's inflation-control target is the midpoint of the control. The operational guide is equal to core CPI. If the target is equal to 1 to 3 percent, 2 percent is the midpoint.

Notice Exhibit 5.29, the chart of the key indicators of the Bank of Canada. These are indicators that define the Canadian financial system during the

EXHIBIT 5.29   Canada Key Indicators

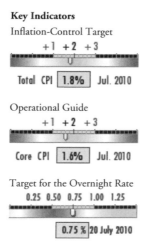

Key Indicators

Inflation-Control Target

+1 +2 +3

Total CPI 1.8%   Jul. 2010

Operational Guide

+1 +2 +3

Core CPI 1.6%   Jul. 2010

Target for the Overnight Rate

0.25 0.50 0.75 1.00 1.25

0.75 % 20 July 2010

Source: Bank of Canada.

three-month target period, but they could easily serve for any central bank. Total for the CPI falls perfectly within the middle of the range at 1.8 percent for July 2010. Consumer prices define inflation.

If the target was 1 percent and the actual number was 3 percent, adjustments in reserves would be implemented because the remaining figures couldn't support such a high erosion of prices and such an erosion of the currency. Stated differently, the amount of reserves targeted for the three-month period cannot support prices in the 3 percent range. The purchasing power of the Canadian dollar would erode. This is a buy Canadian dollar/U.S. dollar and sell U.S. dollar/Canadian dollar situation and an easy, profitable trade when an economic CPI release occurs.

Core CPI is a measure of prices minus food and energy. It defines further the overall CPI target. More importantly, it is the defining factor to measure monetary policy. The 1.6 percent core is perfect and correctly in line with not only overall CPI but the overall 0.50 target. The caveat to this scenario is the BOC raised its top rate from 0.25 to 0.50 in June 2010. So the 0.75 OMMFR is on the high side and would probably come down unless the market is factoring another rate increase. This is a buy Canadian dollar/ U.S. dollar and sell U.S. dollar/Canadian dollar if an actual rate increase occurs because BOC borrowing costs will be raised and the Canadian dollar must be priced to reflect that new rate. The next CPI report will determine this answer.

EXHIBIT 5.30   Inflation Curve for U.S. Dollar, Expected Inflation Curve

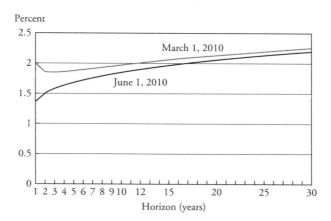

Source: Cleveland Fed.

If CPI is above target, chances are good a rate increase will occur and the Canadian dollar will be reflected in its price in terms of its new purchasing power. The outline here is a potential trend situation for U.S. dollar/Canadian dollar and a total outline of the implications of LIBOR and Canada's OMMFR.

Further notice Exhibit 5.30, the inflation curve for the U.S. dollar and notice how inflation is factored in terms of various rates. This again could be a trend implication for the U.S. dollar if economic conditions warrant. Yet it should be measured against U.S. dollar/Canadian dollar and Canadian dollar/U.S. dollar.

The next question to consider is where do LIBOR and currency prices go from here? The answer is rates fan out like a Fibonacci arc priced into other financial instruments such as swaps, forwards, stock markets, bonds, and yields. A one-day rate is a one-day trade, but a one-day rate determines direction for trends.

Conclusion

Now that monetary policy, short-term interest rates, and spot prices are established, the next juncture is to price interest rates in terms of open-market instruments. Deposit rates, the understanding of the floor, and the bid in interest rates were established in this chapter. But that is only one side of the currency pair equation. The next question is how far will rates travel and what instruments to employ to gauge the spot price?

CHAPTER 6

Government Bonds, Yields, Yield Curves, and Currency Prices

A yield-curve chapter is imperative to understand a currency pair and its price because a yield curve represents an interest rate priced to the market at a specified maturity. But one yield curve and one interest rate only prices one side of a currency pair. A two-nation yield curve must be understood in order to understand the other side of a currency pair. From a two-nation perspective, a true currency-pair price can be factored and traded. How to denote trends and ranges as it relates to yield curves will be fully highlighted as well as the necessary formulas and conditions to trade currencies against the U.S. dollar. Cross pairs should only be traded under certain circumstances, and they will be equally highlighted. The other side of a yield is a sovereign bond, and bonds must be understood in terms of not just their yields but under what circumstances currency pairs can be traded against a bond. Many examples are offered to ensure a full understanding of how to trade currency pairs against yield curves. The chapter surveys each nation and highlights its yield curve, bond prices, and movements, with operation explanations provided.

Yield Curves

After LIBOR and daily internal nation rates are released, curves are plotted such as LIBOR curves, bond-yield curves, treasury-yield curves, swap curves, and forward curves. Each nation will have a different yield curve to represent the disparity of interest rates, yet all curves for the most part are represented by the official government bond-yield curve.

A yield curve is called the term structure of interest rates because it forecasts interest rates, affirms present market rates, inflation, and expected inflation. Lending and borrowing, investments, trading, and financing all are traded along the curve. The shape of the curve and the price of yields will determine where activity will be traded. For example, if the long end of the yield curve crosses below the shorter end, this predicts recession because yields will be out of sync on the long end. Recognizing this, market professionals will act accordingly for down economic times ahead. If a yield curve is perfectly sloped where all yields fall into a smooth trend line up from the short to the long end, market professionals will again act accordingly based on good times ahead.

Yield curves have predictive powers. Market professionals will look at U.S. three-month Treasuries against the two-year note to determine direction of yields while others will look at the two-year against the 10-year note to determine longer-term direction. Still others will view the 10-year against the 30-year note. But all will look at the entire slope of the curve in its entirety in basis-point terms to determine how slopes and shapes align to determine changing economic activity. Flattened curves at the long end could mean economic trouble ahead, while humps in the middle of a curve could be derived from an economic shock.

Central banks and economists determine and predict economic activity by the slope, price of yields, and spreads between maturities. For example, Haubrich and Bianco at the Cleveland Federal Reserve determine Gross Domestic Product (GDP) based on the difference of spreads between the three-month treasury, 10-year note, and slope of the curve in basis points. Slopes are measured as the difference between long- and short-term yields measured in percents. Predictions were perfectly on target. Others employ yield curves to predict Consumer Price Index (CPI) and interest rates. Inflation can be found in any nation's yield curve by subtracting the 10 year from the 3 month domestic interest rate, Bank Bills in Australia and New Zealand, EONIA swap index in Europe, BBA LIBOR minus SONIA in the UK. The determination is the difference between nominal and real yields where nominal yields are unadjusted for inflation while real yields relates a true rate of return in relation to taxes as just one example of unadustments. Still others use yield curves between nations to determine economic direction between nations. Spot prices can be viewed from two nations' yield curves. Three variations occur. Yield curves can either widen, narrow, or remain flat based on the yield spreads, and all have important implications for the spot trade.

The U.S. example says that as yields fall, yield curves steepen or widen; when yields rise yield curves flatten.

Currency Trading and Yield Curves

Currency traders determine trades based on yield curves between two nations. This historic development apparently began in 2007 with Arnaud Mehl in

Open Economies Journal when he looked at the yield curve as a predictor of industrial production and inflation in emerging market economies based on the euro and U.S. yield curve. Building on decades and piles of previous research, Mehl found prediction factors compelling. Mehl's findings allowed nation-to-nation research to continue into yield curve comparisons, and this phenomenon gave currency traders an opportunity to trade the curve and trade various comparisons of the curve slope. Further, Mehl's research allowed deeper comprehension of yield-curve slopes. As euro and U.S. yield curves predicted inflation and industrial production in emerging-market economies, so can emerging-market economies predict inflation in the United States and the euro zone. Traders began to measure slopes in percents in relation to Regression using R2.

Market professionals factored this phenomenon and used it to their trading advantage. From Mehl, Exhibit 6.1 is an historic comparison of the downward slope of yield curves between South Africa and Taiwan. Notice Exhibit 6.2 and the downslope of the U.S. and upslope of the euro yield curve. The measure is gold as the best predictor of inflation. Gold is fixed twice daily by the London Bullion Market Association at 10:30 a.m. and 3:00 p.m. London time, 5:30 a.m. and 10:00 a.m. New York time for the U.S. dollar, euro, and British pound. This means gold is priced in euros, British pounds and U.S. dollars, and each has a different price due to different economies and different inflation rates. A gold trade is measured by the price of gold between and among each currency.

In Exhibit 6.3, view the historic chart of the same period of Gold/U.S. dollar. Predictions were forecasted about gold's rise to yields between the United States and South Africa. The final analysis is that Mehl may be on track in his inflation prediction, as gold is the best measure of inflation.

For currency traders, what if one nation's short-end yields were rising and another falling, or what if one nation's long-end yields were falling and another nation's long-end yields were rising? These are perfect trades and occur all the time. The best determination is to know each nation's yield curve in its

EXHIBIT 6.1   South Africa and Taiwan Yield Curve

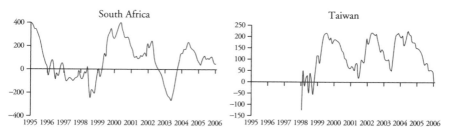

Source: Open Economics Journal 2007.

EXHIBIT 6.2   U.S. and Euro Yield Curve

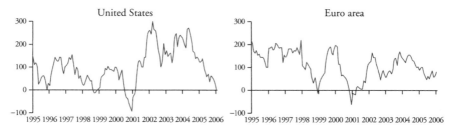

Source: Open Economies Journal 2007.

EXHIBIT 6.3   Historic Chart XAU/U.S. Dollar

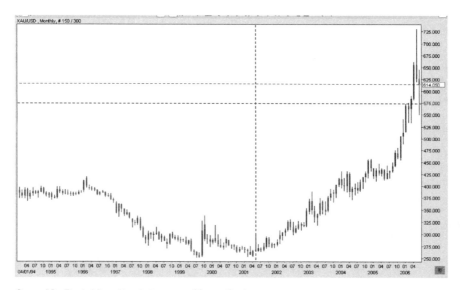

Source: Net Dania Note: Permission granted by attribution.

entirety for all maturities to determine where to profit. A yield curve can be drawn by a list of yields on the left and maturities listed on the bottom. Then plot the yields and measure slopes.

The best determination is to view the slope, yields, and where on the curve is the majority of activity. The spread between yields is the most important aspect to determine slope and curves. Take, for example, a two-year comparison of any nation's yield curve and divide the yields to determine a spread. What occurs is spreads ebb and flow over time to reflect the different prices between maturities. Each maturity is attached to a price, and that price is factored into the markets. The question for any trader must be which side of the currency pair is expensive and which side is less expensive in terms of the yield. It is the price of money in the traded markets. The less expensive side of a pair will be bought and the expensive side sold. Trends are denoted by following slopes to yields.

Notice Exhibit 6.4, the U.S. Treasury Yield Curve chart from February 2010 to June 2010, and notice the difference from month to month of how yields in various maturities rise and fall. This represents profits for currency and other traders of various instruments.

What to surmise is where is a mismatch of rates and how is profit earned? Suppose LIBOR rates were expensive in U.S. dollars one day but cheap in British sterling. Would it make sense to swap U.S. dollars for British sterling to either profit or arrange financing for business conducted in Great Britain? Would it further make sense to buy British pound/U.S. dollar? Yet curves have three junctures: long, middle, and short. Where a rate may fall on the long, middle, or short end would better determine how to arrange strategic investments and trades. After a brief historic walk, we will look at the relationship between government bonds, yields, and currency prices.

Historically, yield curves are not a new phenomenon. With the introduction of LIBOR in the late 1980s, research was under way to factor LIBOR against bond yields. The swap market's introduction in the late 1990s introduced a new point along the curve that had to be factored. All central banks adopted various yield-curve methodologies to account for this new phenomenon. The rise of the forward market was the last factor that added still another point along the curve. By the late 1990s, an abundance of literature already existed in many forms regarding the yield curve.

Throughout the early 2000s, yield-curve literature grew again that added newer methodologies to the 1990s research. One factor that changed yield curves for many nations during this period was the introduction of the euro. Yield curves had to synchronize to euro bond trading, so accrued interest as well as yield-curve calculations were refactored. All nations engaged in this new methodology. Today, so many variations, computations, methodologies, and factors of the yield curve exist they are too numerous to list here. Yet so many similarities now exist nation to nation due to bond-issuance terms that are similar nation to nation in maturities and coupon payments. It actually helped to understand currency pairs and movements in a clearer light and took away the market guesses.

Central banks and market professionals began to look at the yield curve with its abundance of factors represented either as a rate of return or a measure of risk. A yield is factored in the United States by dividing the coupon payment by the bond price, and a coupon payment is divided by yield to equal a price. Most bonds in many nations offer semi-annual payments. This had to be factored according to the new yield curve.

EXHIBIT 6.4 Four-Month Chart of U.S. Treasury Yield Curve

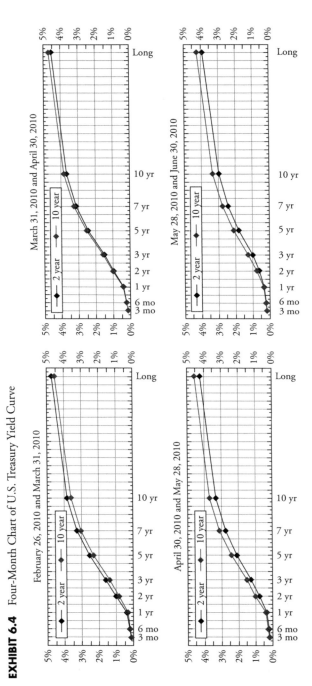

February 26, 2010 and March 31, 2010

March 31, 2010 and April 30, 2010

April 30, 2010 and May 28, 2010

May 28, 2010 and June 30, 2010

Source: The Chart Store, Permission by attribution.

Index-linked bonds vastly changed yield-curve calculations. By the early 2000s, all nations offered some type of bond indexed mostly to inflation, except for the Bank of England (BOE), which indexed to retail prices.

The real reason to follow yield curves is due to their changing nature on a daily basis. Short-term interest rates are tied to bond prices and bond prices are tied to spot-currency prices. And all factor into a yield curve. This requires a regular calculation to determine changes to slopes, yields, and bond prices to yields. But the short end was much easier for computation and investment purposes due to the many instruments offered. Longer-term bonds required an iteration, an estimate of price compared to yield. It is an assumption, a best-guess scenario. This is why market professionals obtain daily bond closing prices and draw a new curve every day.

One would recognize from the Bank of International Settlements (BIS) Triennial Surveys in Chapter 1 the historic rise in the swap and forward markets from 2000 and beyond. Yield-curve methodologies allowed for the rise of both instruments. A few examples of the most popular employed by central banks follow.

Central Banks and Yield Curves

The U.S. Treasury employs a "Quasi Cubic Hermite Spline function", a calculation the Treasury doesn't make public. Yet the St Louis Federal Reserve provides a few clear examples. Because the Treasury releases daily yield rates, many hedge funds, bank research departments, and trading firms approximate almost an exact Treasury Yield Curve.

The Japanese employ a type of Gaussian Affine rate-term structure for their yield curve's predictive powers. From mathematics, Carl Friedrich Gauss gave the world in 1809 the normal distribution with a probability function—the Gaussian approach to mathematics called standard deviation. The difference between the Japanese and other central banks and market professionals is the Japanese always employ any calculations to determine an error term, a measure to determine risk. The normal distribution was also termed the Law of Errors, so the Japanese follow Gauss to his last calculation. This is traditional Japanese methodology, yet a method employed by only a few central banks.

The Bank of England is forthright in its yield-curve calculations and methodologies in every aspect, rare for a central bank. A special department called Yield Curves exists within the Bank of England. The BOE employs a version of the Cubic Spline model to calculate its yield curves. The ECB publishes an actual spot-rate yield curve, instantaneous forwards, and par yields along with maturities from three-months to 30-year bonds. The ECB yield curve is published every trading day, with an interactive device offered for comparison of slopes and shapes among the various maturities.

Bonds and Yields

The bond interplay has two sides, the bond price and the bond yield. Both have an inverse relationship. As bond prices rise, yields decrease and vice versa. This scenario factors for all government bonds. The choice of which side is the best investment angle depends not only on the day's LIBOR but the trend in LIBOR in terms of the three-month target.

A yield investment is a risk trade while the bond purchase is the safe trade due to backing by government revenues. What drives either side of the bond/yield interplay is interest rates, and what drives interest rates is economic conditions short and long term. In market terms, it is bond cash flows that determine a currency-pair price in nations whose bonds are tied to economic performance.

Market professionals' interest lies in yields because yields are the focus for central banks due to focus on their own yield curves as a measure of risk in both target and inflation. Yield curves measured against maturities and yields determine for central banks how to better manage their reserves. Central banks release daily tables of yields for maturities of their bonds. For currency pairs, each pair follows a different side of the bond/yield interplay.

In U.S. markets, the euro/U.S. dollar, British pound/U.S. dollar, Australian dollar/U.S. dollar, and New Zealand dollar/U.S. dollar follow yields while U.S. dollar/Swiss franc, U.S. dollar/Canadian dollar, and U.S. dollar/Japanese yen follow the safety of the bond price. For currency cross pairs, U.S. dollar cross pairs follow bond prices and opposing U.S. dollar cross pairs follow yields. Yet this scenario is not perfect, as will be seen.

In European markets, the scenario works quite differently. The British pound/U.S. dollar follows the safety of its own bond price and actually despises yields while euro/U.S. dollar is attached to yields. The reason for this is borrowing costs and an easier relationship to manage between the euro and British pound. Any two-nation relationship, for the most part, follows a bond/yield relationship. What if yield spreads widen between British pound gilts and German bunds in European trading? Higher borrowing costs will force the British pound into a sell position, as the British pound must reflect higher costs.

It is a different scenario for Australian dollar/U.S. dollar and New Zealand dollar/U.S. dollar and far from the norm. Both abhor yields in their own markets and rely on the bond price. Higher yields force both pairs into a sell position in their respective markets.

Canadian dollar/U.S. dollar, U.S. dollar/Japanese yen, and U.S. dollar/ Swiss franc follow the same principles. All love U.S. bond prices. A few examples will clarify this explanation.

Euro/U.S. Dollar and U.S. Treasury Bond Yields

Notice Exhibit 6.5, the chart of the three-month Treasury Bill and two-year Treasury Note along with spreads of each, and further notice Exhibit 6.6, the historic euro/U.S. dollar chart marked exactly as the Treasury chart.

From 2000 to 2002, yields for both were down but so were the spreads and the euro/U.S. dollar hardly moved. Yet notice the almost 7 percent yield payout for the two-year note and three-month bill. This explains the no-movement aspect. The payout is too expensive for the short end of this curve, especially if present interest rates and reserve requirements aren't in sync to the 7 percent yield.

From 2002 to 2003, yields and spreads were down and the euro/U.S. dollar began its ascent. From 2003 to 2006, yields were up, spreads were down and the euro/U.S. dollar trended. In 2007 to 2008, the euro/U.S. dollar followed the yields of both, but the spreads rose as well. This set the euro/U.S. dollar up for the 2008 to 2009 fall. Notice further how the spreads leveled and caused uncertainty of direction.

The perfect scenario to trade the three-month Bill against the two-year note occurs when yields are low and trending up and spreads between both decrease, such as the 2003 to 2006 example. For the euro/U.S. dollar, this represents a trend on autopilot. A leveling of spreads says indecision and market uncertainty. Notice the low present yield of both Treasury instruments and leveled spreads. Market uncertainty says either a small trend will occur or yields and spreads will remain low over time due to economic conditions and the uncertainty of future rates. Present economic conditions do not give a reason for the euro/U.S. dollar to move. This is a no-trade condition. Yet here is the point to now look at the middle or long end of the curve for directional guidance.

British Pound/U.S. Dollar and Bond Yields

Notice Exhibit 6.7, the monthly chart of the British pound/U.S. dollar and notice the exact directional movements to the euro/U.S. dollar. The difference is the British pound/U.S. dollar moved farther and faster up, yet its fall was greater. This is typical of this relationship, as the British pound/U.S. dollar always has and probably always will out pace the euro/U.S. dollar in up trends and down trends. Why?

Recall repurchase agreements and the mention of the corridor of rates. The euro is locked into a EURIBOR, EONIA, EURONIA, deposit rate, Minimum

EXHIBIT 6.5 Three-Month, Two-Year Treasury Yield Curve

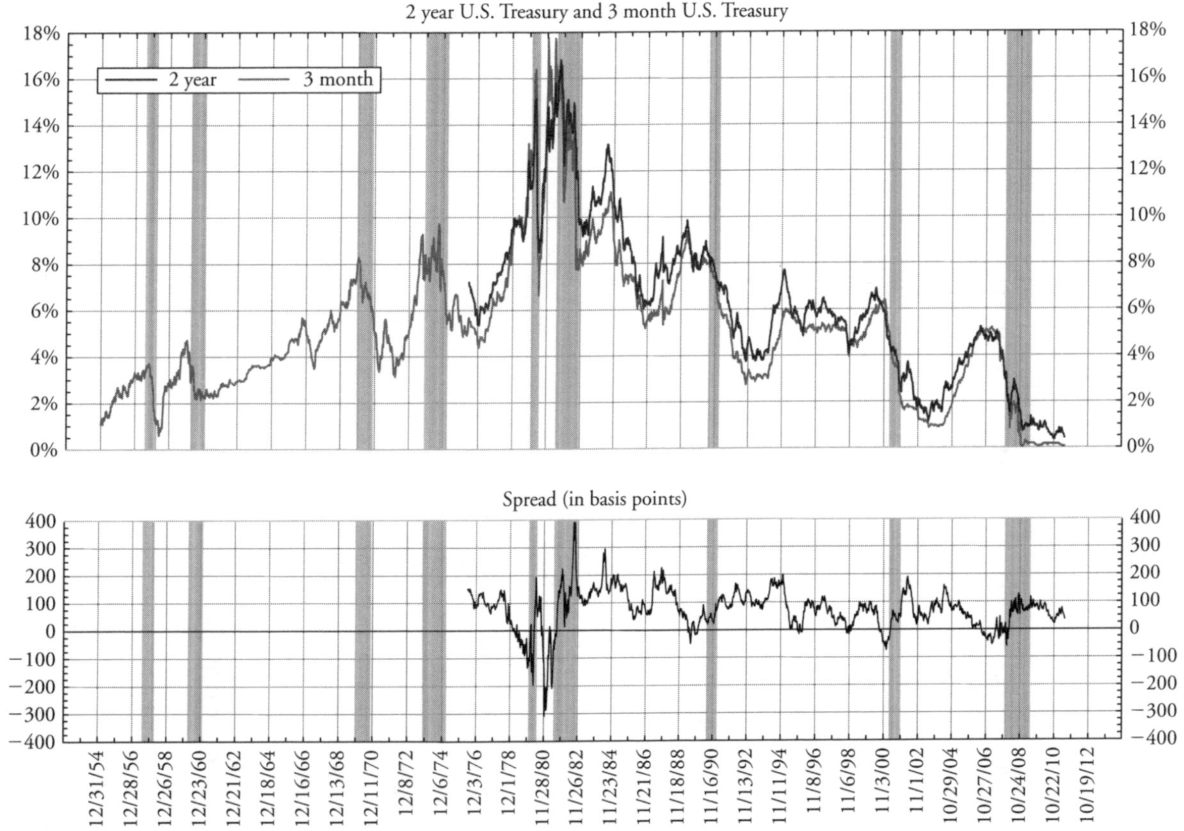

2 year U.S. Treasury and 3 month U.S. Treasury

Spread (in basis points)

Source: The Chart Store, permission by attribution.

156

EXHIBIT 6.6 Historic Euro/U.S. Dollar Chart

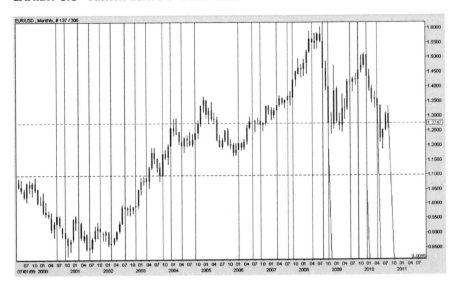

Source: Net Dania, permission with attribution.

EXHIBIT 6.7 Monthly Chart British Pound/U.S. Dollar

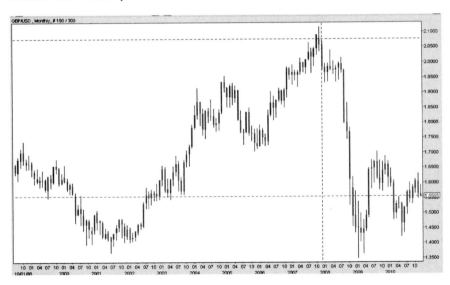

Source: Net Dania, permission by attribution.

EXHIBIT 6.8   Central Bank Rates, Interest Rate Control

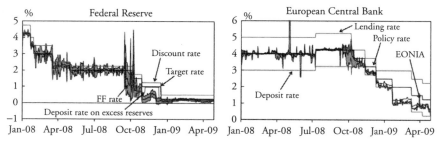

Source: Bank of Japan.

EXHIBIT 6.9   Bank of England and Bank of Japan Rates

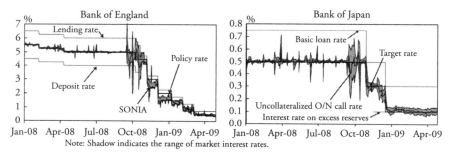

Note: Shadow indicates the range of market interest rates.

Source: Bank of Japan.

Bid Rate for Refinancing Facility and rates in the Marginal Lending Facility. See Exhibits 6.8 and 6.9 from the Bank of Japan's (BOJ) annual report of important interest rates and how nations align currencies into various rate channels. The euro/U.S. dollar must be priced between or against this corridor while the British pound/U.S. dollar is not locked into such a series of rates and is allowed a freer movement in the markets. Yet the exact same scenario holds for this pair as the euro/U.S. dollar. It is a no-trade condition until the economic situation changes or the middle or longer end of the curve can reveal direction. In this instance, it is the Treasury curve that may provide U.S. market information.

U.S. Dollar/Swiss Franc, U.S. Dollar/Canadian Dollar, U.S. Dollar/Japanese Yen and Bond Yields

The opposite scenario holds for the U.S. dollar/Swiss franc and U.S. dollar/Canadian dollar as both follow not yields but the actual bond price. When U.S. bond prices rise, both pairs rise and vice versa. See Exhibits 6.10 and 6.11.

EXHIBIT 6.10 Historic Chart of U.S. Dollar/Swiss Franc

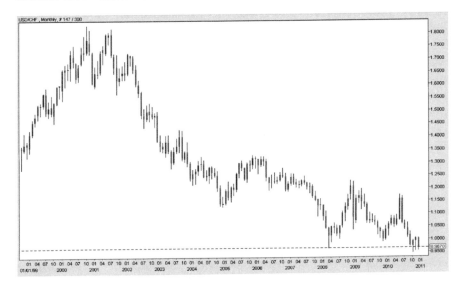

Source: Net Dania, permission by attribution.

EXHIBIT 6.11 Historic Chart U.S. Dollar/Canadian Dollar

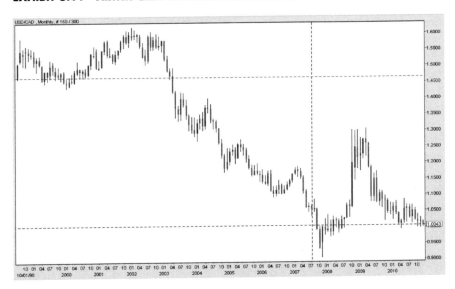

Source: Net Dania, permission by attribution.

In this instance, as the British pound/U.S. dollar and euro/U.S. dollar trended up between 2003 and 2006, U.S. dollar/Canadian dollar and U.S. dollar/Swiss franc trended down to follow the bond price and Treasury Bill. The difference was more pronounced for U.S. dollar/Canadian dollar than it was for U.S. dollar/Swiss franc. This difference lies between the two economies, as the Swiss economy is more controlled, more guarded by a series of locked rates like the euro, while the Canadian economic system is less controlled and allows for U.S. dollar/Canadian dollar to move more freely. No two pairs will ever move in exact pips because no two economies are the same.

What separates economies are reserve requirements, interest rates, target rates, LIBOR, bond prices, growth targets, rate channels, and the methodology to measure each. Some central banks heavily control and monitor economies, others do not. U.S. dollar/Japanese yen movements are reflective of U.S. dollar/Swiss franc and U.S. dollar/Canadian dollar, exact movements, exact times of movements, and varying amounts of pips. U.S. dollar/Japanese yen is not a controlled currency by the Japanese government or locked into various rate channels. Instead, other market instruments hold the U.S. dollar/Japanese yen pair from movement, and this will be addressed in future chapters.

Carry Trades and Bond Yields

See Exhibit 6.12, the chart of euro/Japanese yen from 2003 to 2006. What is evident is that within a three-year period, euro/Japanese yen moved about 2000 pips. This reflects not only a stable economic environment that is conducive for carry trades to earn its yield, but carry trades won't have the same volatile movements as the euro/U.S. dollar and opposite dollar pairs.

Carry trades follow the underlying pairs rather than the straight connection to bonds and yields. That connection of movements can only reflect in economic conditions and interest rates. Stable economic environments bring with it slow but certain trends for carry trades. Uncertain or erratic economic conditions and interest rates bring market volatility. Volatility is reflective of a market out of sync and not normal because direction is uncertain. Employed correctly and in certain economic times, carry trades can be not only a perfect investment vehicle but a profitable investment. All cross pairs acted the same as euro/Japanese yen whether it be British pound/Japanese yen, British pound/Swiss franc, euro/British pound, or British pound/New Zealand dollar. Between 2003 and 2006, volatility was low and trends progressed.

EXHIBIT 6.12   Euro/Japanese Yen Chart, 2003 to 2006

Source: Net Dania, Permission by attribution.

U.S. Treasury Yield Curves and 2- and 10-Year Notes

Yield curves can be viewed in their entirety to observe trades. See Exhibit 6.13, the four-month chart of the Treasury yield curve shown earlier in the chapter, and notice the difference between the two- and 10-year bond yields. Notice Exhibit 6.14, a monthly chart of British pound/U.S. dollar. As spreads between the two- and 10-year yields widened from February to March, the euro/U.S. dollar and British pound/U.S. dollar trended down. March to April saw a compression of spreads and a rally occurred. April to May witnessed long-end, 10-year, and two-year yields retreat that again caused a trend down. May to June witnessed another compression of spreads at the two-year and higher yields at the 10-year plateau that caused a trend up for the British pound/U.S. dollar and euro/U.S. dollar. It is the compression of spreads that lends confidence and is paramount to any higher yield strategy.

The question to employ spread and yield methods is why should a pair be bought or sold. A currency pair won't move unless a reason exists for it to move. A currency pair must have value in terms of yields and bond prices or

EXHIBIT 6.13 Four-Month Chart of U.S. Treasury Yield Curve

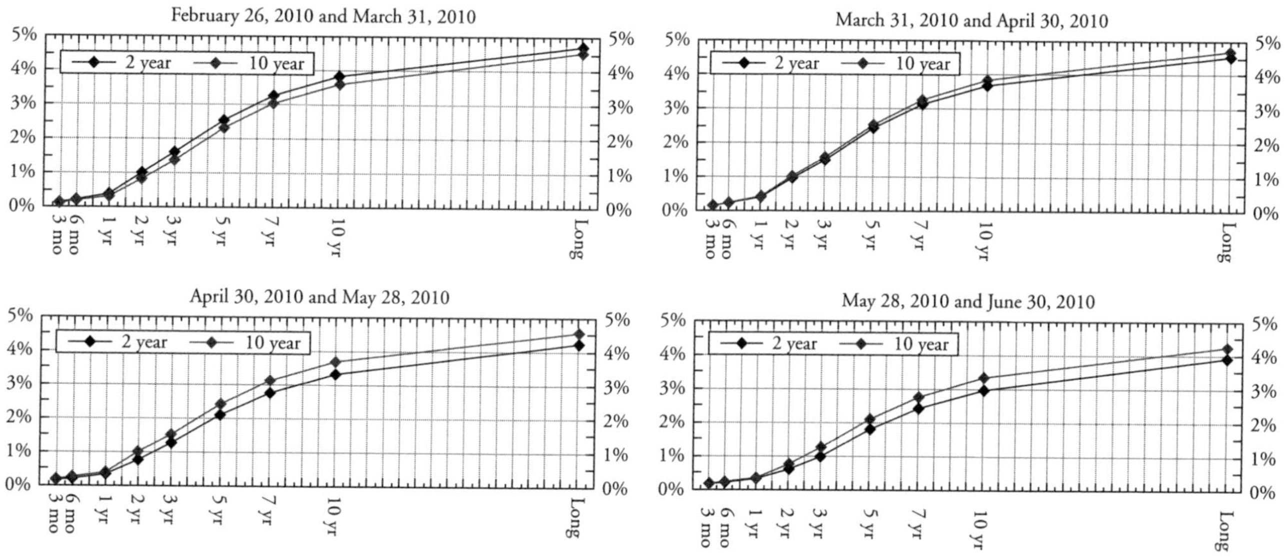
February 26, 2010 and March 31, 2010
March 31, 2010 and April 30, 2010
April 30, 2010 and May 28, 2010
May 28, 2010 and June 30, 2010
2 year
10 year
5%
4%
3%
2%
1%
0%
3 mo
6 mo
1 yr
2 yr
3 yr
5 yr
7 yr
10 yr
Long

Source: The Chart Store, Permission by attribution.

EXHIBIT 6.14 British Pound/U.S. Dollar Monthly Chart

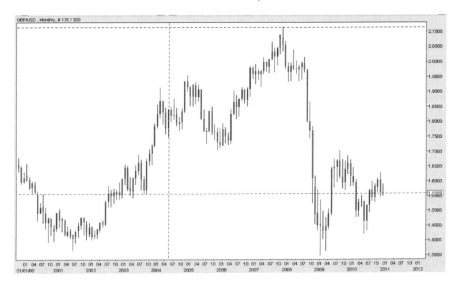

Source: Net Dania, permission by attribution.

a mismatch of both in order for traders and the market to force movements and profit. Yet a currency pair must be priced correctly in terms of yields and spreads. How much is always questionable because so many factors of yields, bonds, and economic conditions exist in this equation. Many times spot prices can be ahead or behind a yield play. Examples of this will be in future chapters.

Yet others may anticipate movements such as the present euro/U.S. dollar example of the three-month and two-year bond. It is evident that the euro/U.S. dollar will move, as both the three-month and two-year note yields are low as well as the spreads. But where will it move and is it worth the risk? In terms of the yield curve, any shape can materialize that would change quickly any anticipation of a price move such as inversion of the curve or a flattening or steepening at the short or long end. Yet any shape can occur between two yield curves. To gauge any movements, look at each currency pair in relation to its exact counterpart as well as its exact opposite.

U.S. Dollar/Swiss Franc, U.S. Dollar/Japanese Yen, and U.S. Dollar/Canadian Dollar

Evident within the U.S. dollar/Swiss franc and U.S. dollar/Japanese yen charts is the opposite movements to the euro/U.S. dollar and British pound/U.S.

dollar caused by the movement of bond prices rather than yields, the safe trade. Opposite to the euro/U.S. dollar and British pound/U.S. dollar compression of spreads with higher yields is U.S. dollar/Swiss franc and U.S. dollar/Japanese yen that react more confidently when spreads widen and yields head lower. This distills confidence of movement and secures trends. How much each pair moves in relation to each other can only be guessed based on the above factors. An example will follow.

Notice U.S. dollar/Canadian dollar and notice the disjointed moves. This raises two factors for consideration. Canada raised its top rate in June 2010. One can say the market was undergoing a repricing in anticipation of the hike. In this instance, Canadian bond yields would far surpass U.S. yields and cause the disjointed movement. The gauge for this bond/yield strategy focused on the U.S. market and U.S. bonds and yields.

A rate hike in Canada raises Canadian borrowing costs. This sends LIBOR, CORRA, and OMMFR higher, and in turn Canadian yields also move higher. Canada's economic situation took precedence. This is obvious, as a nation will always defend its currency and economic system above others. But it is a market-pricing factor in terms of the pair rather than a defense of a currency in this instance.

Amongst the three pairs, the yield strategy is buy U.S. dollar against Swiss franc, Japanese yen, and Canadian dollar. U.S. dollar/Canadian dollar reacted as sell Canadian dollar against U.S. dollar. Under normal circumstances, U.S. dollar/Canadian dollar's movements would have reflected exactly as U.S. dollar/Swiss franc and U.S. dollar/Japanese yen.

Secondly, U.S. dollar/Canadian dollar is never a sure bet. For the most part, U.S. dollar/Canadian dollar can be trusted, other times it cannot. This is typical for this pair, as the relationship to U.S. dollar is a yield/yield. The nickname for the Canadian dollar is the Loonie, and it lives up to its reputation at times, simply because of its funny movements due to its yield relationship between the United States and its own market. U.S. dollar/Swiss franc and U.S. dollar/Japanese yen are better gauges against each other and against its counterparts and between the two, U.S. dollar/Swiss franc is the best gauge.

Canada Yield Curve and Bond Issuance

Canada issues Canadian Treasury bills every two weeks with maturities of three and six months and one year. The terms to maturities are 98 days, 168 days, 182 days, 350 days, and 364 days. T-Bills are priced at a discount and have been issued in book-entry form since 2008 (Bank of Canada). Canadian tradeable bonds include maturities of two years, three years, five years, seven years, 10 years, and 30 years.

Maturities of two-, five-, 10-, and 30-year Government of Canada bond futures contracts trade on the Montreal Exchange, Canada's premier futures and options exchange. The two-year bond contract is termed the CGZ, the five-year is the CGF, the 10-year is the CGB, and the 30-year is the LGB. Direct bond trading is conducted through Candeal, Canada's premier online debt-trading network.

Canada issues foreign currency bonds termed Canada Notes and Canada Bills. Canada Bills are promissory notes denominated in U.S. dollars that are issued in book-entry form with a maturity of 270 days (BOC).

Canada Notes are promissory notes denominated in U.S. dollars and issued in book-entry form. Denominations of $1000 accompany maturities of nine months or longer with a fixed or floating coupon. Principal and interest is paid in U.S. dollars (BOC). Canada also issues Indexed Bonds called real Return Bonds with various maturities and indexed to Canada's CPI.

Calculate Canada Bonds and Yields

Treasury Bills are calculated as simple interest using actual/365. The price per $100 par value of a T-Bill yielding Y calculates as:

$$p = 100/(1 + Y \times T/365)$$
$$\text{Yield} = (365/T)(100 - p)/p)$$

Short Canada bond—sum of the quoted price plus accrued interest paid on actual/365 basis. Interest accrues at the rate of 1/365th of annual coupon rate per day. Accrued interest for a bond that pays interest semiannually at an annual rate of C as a percent of par is calculated as:

$$A = C(D/365)$$

where
D = number of days to settlement date.

For a Canada bond with one coupon remaining, the price of a bond with T days remaining to maturity to yield y,

$$\text{price} = (100 + C/2)/(1 + y \times T/365) - A \text{ Yield}$$
$$= (365/T)((100 + C/2)/(P + A) - 1)$$

More than one coupon payment until maturity factors as actual/actual because it depends on the number of days of the actual accrual period. Canada never factors for bad days. The formula:

$$A = (C/2) \, (D/E)$$

where
> D = number of accrued days to the settlement date, and
> E = number of days in the coupon period.

With more than one coupon remaining to maturity where yield is calculated semi annually and compounded on an actual/actual basis. Canada bond with N semiannual coupon payments remaining to maturity to yield y as a percent of par.

$$P = C1(1 + Y/2) - t1 + (C/2) \, N \, \Sigma \, k$$
$$= 2(1 + y/2) \, Tk + 100 \, (1 + y/2) - Tn - A$$

> Tk = fraction of a payment period to Kth payment date and C1 next coupon payment amount as a percent of par.

The first coupon payment is usually just half of the annual payment rate ($C1 = C/2$), but when the next coupon payment is short

$$C1 = (C/2) \, (D/C/E)$$

where
> D/C = number of days from, but excluding, the issue date to the first coupon payment date

Real Return Bonds nominal yields depend on inflation with a three-month lag in the calculation, as is the norm for nations with index issuance. The formula is:

$$\text{Index Ratio date} = (\text{Ref CPI date}/\text{Ref CPI base})$$

CPI factors as the third preceding month.

$$\text{Ref CPI date} = \text{Ref CPIm} + t - 1/ \, D \, (\text{Ref CPI } m + 1 - \text{Ref CPIm})$$

D = number of days in calendar month where date falls,

t = calendar date corresponding to the date,

Ref CPIm = reference CPI first day of calendar month where date falls,

Ref CPI m+1 = reference CPI for first day of calendar month immediately following the date, and

Interest = Inflation compensation date = (Principal × index ratio date) – Principal.

Yield Curve and U.S. Dollar/Canadian Dollar

The U.S. dollar/Canadian dollar relationship in U.S. markets is supposed to factor as the Canadian dollar is the U.S. Treasury Bond follower, while the U.S. dollar is the Canadian Bond yield seeker in Canadian markets. Sometimes this relationship holds for Canadian dollar, sometimes not. The BOC's interest lies in Canadian dollar/U.S. dollar. This relationship is quite different and it leaves the Canadian dollar in a particular place. This is why the Canadian dollar can be a tricky trading vehicle in U.S. markets and this is also why it is known in market terms as the Loonie.

Canadian dollar/U.S. dollar allows the Canadian dollar to weaken and rise at the expense of the U.S. dollar. Yet the pair accepted for trading purposes the world over is the standard U.S. dollar/Canadian dollar configuration. For U.S. market trading, it is imperative to evaluate this relationship before a trade is implemented. The methodology to do this lies in the short end of the Treasury and Canadian yield curves, as both are abundant with short maturities. The question within this relationship is how much are borrowing costs for the Canadian Government, business interests, and investors. The answer will provide U.S. dollar/Canadian dollar direction and which side of the pair to trade.

Australian Dollar/U.S. Dollar and New Zealand Dollar/U.S. Dollar

Both pairs are unique and not highlighted due to their interest rate disparity between all industrialized nations. Yet both pairs follow the exact patterns as the euro/U.S. dollar and British pound/U.S. dollar. When U.S. Treasury yields go up, Australian dollar/U.S. dollar and New Zealand dollar/U.S. dollar will also travel up. Australian dollar/U.S. dollar will always outpace New Zealand dollar/U.S. dollar on the way up due to higher paying interest, but neither will outpace the British pound/U.S. dollar due to interest in trade of the British pound/U.S. dollar.

British Pound Yield Curve

Notice Exhibit 6.15, the yield-curve chart of British gilt bonds. This is from the three month to two year, and further notice the earlier two- and 10-year Treasury yield spread. Further, refer to the Treasury Yield Curve chart and notice the difference in yields.

Notice Exhibit 6.16, gilt yields from 2005 to 2010 and notice Exhibit 6.17, monthly chart of British pound/U.S. dollar. Under good economic conditions between the United States and United Kingdom, it is a buy British pound/U.S. dollar. When conditions turn down, it is a sell British pound/U.S. dollar.

The gilt Yield Curve differs from Japan and the United States on the long end of the curve. The Debt Management Office in Great Britain issues

EXHIBIT 6.15   Three-Month and Two-Year Gilts

Source: Bloomberg Finance, LP.

EXHIBIT 6.16   Gilt Yields from 2005 to 2010

Source: Bloomberg Finance, LP.

EXHIBIT 6.17   Monthly Chart British Pound/U.S. Dollar

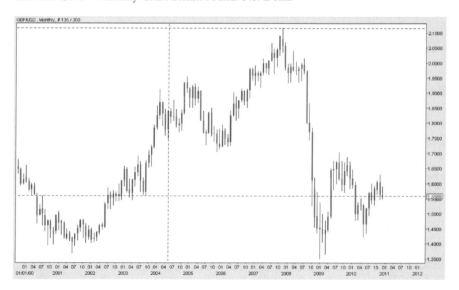

Source: Net Dania, permission by attribution.

50-year gilts as opposed to the U.S. 30 year and the Japanese 40 year. This changes the long end of the curve for all three and should be monitored.

View the British pound yield curve as a complete opposite scenario to the United States.

Gilt Issuance

Two types of gilts are issued by the Debt Management Office in Great Britain—conventional and index-linked gilts. Conventional gilts reflect the liability of the U.K. government, while index-linked gilts reflect the borrowing rate of the government. Therefore, Index-Linked gilts have smaller variations in yields.

The linked variation reflects coupon and principal payment links to the United Kingdom's Retail Price Index. Beginning in 2011, the Retail Price Index was supposed to change to a CPI link. This at least has been the prevailing proposal, but the House of Commons has yet to address this issue directly. Plus the DMO must reprice past and future issuances, which will take time. The real purpose for issuance of Index-Linked gilts is coverage of various pension liabilities. Both indices are reported in yields and maturities by FTSE, an index company.

The DMO issues sterling Treasury Bills once a week. One-month or 28-day Bills, three-month or 91-day Bills, and six-month or 182-day Bills are wholesale money-market instruments that trade in lots of 500,000 pounds sterling. This structure ensures the importance of the short end of the British pound yield curve and can provide vital direction to the British pound/U.S. dollar.

British Pound/U.S. Dollar

In U.S. markets, British pound is the yield seeker against Treasury Bonds and the U.S. dollar is the bond follower. In London trading, U.S. dollar is the yield seeker to British gilts and the British pound is the gilt bond follower. In European trading, U.S. dollar is again the yield seeker to German Bonds while British pound holds a static position. That static position is derived from London and German stock market trading that overlaps from the open to close. Yet the latter part of European and London trading rolls into U.S. trading. The British pound will always take precedence in U.S. markets because it must seek its yield, and no better market exists where yield can be earned. As we view trading strategies in later chapters, we will see the exact positions of the U.S. dollar, as these positions don't always hold.

Japanese Yield Curves

For the Japanese Central Bank and Government, the focus is the benchmark 10-year bond, called the Japanese Government Bond (JGB). Why this is so can only be surmised. Consider the first-ever futures contract traded on the Tokyo Stock Exchange (TSE) was the 10-year JGB bond in 1985 (Tokyo Stock Exchange 2010).

As time progressed, a mini 10-year futures contract that was one tenth the size of a regular JGB 10-year contract began trading. The TSE offered an option contract on the JGB five-year bond in 2000, but stopped in 2002 when no interest in the contract materialized (Tokyo Stock Exchange 2010).

Consider further that 63.9 percent of all JGBs are owned by Japanese banks and insurance companies, 0.3 percent are owned by the BOJ, and 4.6 percent are owned by foreigners (Ministry of Finance 2010). The Japanese do not provide an actively traded bond market in JGBs. JGBs are issued and bought by insiders such as banks and insurance companies, premier companies in Japan. Instead, the only measure for JGBs is the futures contract.

Interest in the 10-year JGB is due to the 10-year JGB as an inflation-indexed bond where the principal fluctuates with Japan's CPI. It is essentially a floating-rate bond and the only one of its type employed in Japan and traded on the Tokyo Stock Exchange. The Japanese issue a 15-year Floating Rate JGB but it is not tied to inflation. Both reflect a difference of trade. Refer to Exhibit 6.18, the chart of the compound interest rate between the

EXHIBIT 6.18 Interest Rate Difference between 10-year JGB and 10-Year Inflation Indexed Bond

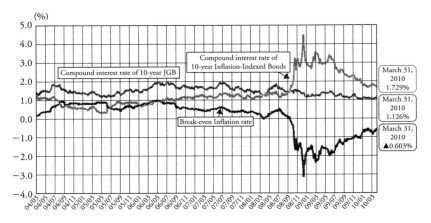

Source: Japanese Ministry of Finance.

EXHIBIT 6.19   Historic 10-Year JGB Yields from 1989 to Present

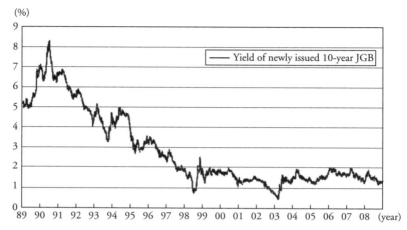

Source: Japanese Ministry of Finance.

10-year bond and the 10-year inflation-indexed bond. Refer to Exhibit 6.19, the 10-year JGB difference in yields.

Japanese Yield Curve and U.S. Dollar/Japanese Yen

There are two factors for consideration regarding the Japanese yield curve and the U.S. dollar/Japanese yen. The Japanese issue 40-year JGBs. This time frame is longer than the United States, which issues 30-year Treasuries at the longest end of their curve. This must be factored in any long-term U.S. dollar/ Japanese yen investment strategy.

Secondly, the Japanese Ministry of Finance just issued, for the first time, in July 2010 a three-year fixed-rate bond. Sales and longevity of this issue is anyone's guess at this stage, but what this does to the short end of the Japanese/ U.S. curve is interesting. Refer to Exhibit 6.20, the chart from the September 1 and 2, 2010, auction of JGBs and notice the difference between interest rates from the one-year to the 40-year bond between auction days. Further notice the inclusion of the three-year maturity.

Prior to the one-year JGB maturity, the Japanese issue Treasury Discount Bills with maturities of three and six months. The vast majority of all trading along the curve will occur at the short end of the Japanese yield curve simply because interest rates are 0.10 and not expected to rise to any prominence and because the Japanese are always concerned with issues of liquidity, as is evident in Ministry of Finance reports.

EXHIBIT 6.20   September 2010 Auction of JGBs

Date	1Y	2Y	3Y	4Y	5Y	6Y	7Y	8Y	9Y	10Y	15Y	20Y	25Y	30Y	40Y
9/01/10	0.108	0.119	0.138	0.218	0.291	0.403	0.535	0.704	0.892	1.051	1.482	1.740	1.840	1.854	1.880
9/02/10	0.107	0.124	0.146	0.236	0.319	0.436	0.571	0.739	0.933	1.099	1.544	1.804	1.911	1.924	1.947

Source: Japanese Ministry of Finance.

For example, the Japanese have a 48 percent bond dependency ratio to match 2010 liquidity needs. For these reasons, the three- and six-month Treasury Bill should always be compared to the two-year and 10-year Inflation Indexed JGB in order to derive a U.S. dollar/Japanese yen trading plan. The reason is that shaky economies must be measured in terms of longer-term trades due to risk.

Suppose growth and inflation occurs in Japan and interest rates rise. Where will the majority of trades occur and where will early warnings occur? Predominantly at the short end of the yield curve. Why? This is the confidence interval. Stated succinctly, with a high bond-dependency ratio who would buy the long bond and who would tie up money for 40 years on an unknown interest rate in an unknown economic situation?

The Samurai Bond is not an issuance of the Ministry of Finance, but should be viewed in the bond and yield-curve context. The Samurai Bond is yen denominated, issued in Japan by non-Japanese companies, with maturities that range from one to 30 years and used for investment purposes inside Japan. Central bank reports would call this phenomenon foreign direct investment. It is a measure of non Japanese companies' confidence in Japan's economy, because those investments are long term.

U.S. Dollar/Japanese Yen, Bonds, and Yields

The most interesting pair is the U.S. dollar/Japanese yen. In U.S. markets, the arrangement is supposed to work as the Japanese yen is the Treasury-bond price follower and the U.S. dollar is the JGB yield seeker in Japanese trading. This correlation doesn't always hold on the Japanese yen side. Remember interested pairs for the BOJ in terms of their TWI. That arrangement was Japanese yen/U.S. dollar. This arrangement changes the bond/yield correlation in U.S. trading.

Japanese yen/U.S. dollar allows the U.S. dollar to be the bond-price follower and the Japanese yen to be the yield seeker. In this manner, the

Japanese earn yen in terms of yield against the U.S. dollar, especially as the Japanese yen/U.S. dollar price rises. Japanese yen/U.S. dollar should always be the focus in U.S. trading, as the Japanese not only need this arrangement to earn yen against Treasury Bond yields but U.S. dollar/Japanese yen as a combination for U.S. trade would defeat the purpose of this arrangement as a pair on Japanese terms. It is a very mixed arrangement, but an arrangement instituted long ago with the introduction of the yen as a currency accepted by all nations and markets. The true conundrum of the Japanese yen is it is well connected to the U.S. Treasury bond.

The mixed aspect came into focus as the Japanese mix and match both currency-pair arrangements as it satisfies their needs. Yet both pairs should be carefully evaluated before a trading plan is implemented. The questions for consideration should always be what is in the interest of the Japanese central bank and how can they profit? In Japanese markets, Japanese yen/U.S. dollar must be the arrangement. This is constructed by convention, and the Japanese are almost forced into this arrangement. A closer look in later chapters will fully outline trading arrangements, as sometimes this outlines only one side of the currency-pair equation.

Australia Yield Curve

The Australia Office of Financial Management offers a Treasury Bond, a Treasury Indexed Bond, and a short-term Treasury Note. The proper term for all is Commonwealth Government securities.

Short-term notes are issued only to meet liquidity needs of Australia's Government but are not issued routinely. Treasury Bonds are issued for the medium to long term with fixed interest every Wednesday and Friday.

Treasury Indexed Bonds are issued with capital that adjusts to Australia's CPI Index. Payments are made quarterly based on a fixed rate, with tenders that occur every Tuesday.

The best method to gauge Australia's yield curve for Australian dollar/U.S. dollar trades is to watch the three- and 10-year bond futures contracts that trade on the ASX. This is also the indicator watched by the Office of Financial Management and is highlighted in Royal Bank of Australia (RBA) reports routinely. The RBA publishes a daily yield curve for Australia's debt instruments.

The Australian economy has far outperformed the vast majority of all industrialized economies, so its present debt-issuance schedule is able to easily meet the finance needs of the Australian economy. Consider Australia's top present OCR rate is 4.50 percent, so bonds issued further out along the yield curve pay far more than 4.50 percent. Australia debt management is just not a problem presently. With an OCR at 4.50 percent, it is a buy-the-dip strategy for Australian dollar/U.S. dollar.

Factor Australia Yield Curve

Australia factors yield curves based on half years. The basic formula is:

$$P = v^{f/d} \left(g(1 + a_n) + 100v^n \right)$$

$$\text{Ex interest} = P = v^{f/d} (ga_n + 100v^n)$$

Near maturity (purchaser final coupon and principal).

$$P = \frac{100 + g}{1 + \left(\dfrac{f}{365} \right)i}$$

Between record date and final coupon.

$$P = \frac{100}{1 + \left(\dfrac{f}{365} \right)i}$$

P = Price per \$100 rounded three decimal places,
$v = 1/1+i$,
f = number of days from settlement to next interest payment,
d = number of days in the half year ending on next interest payment date,
g = half yearly rate of coupon payment per \$100 face value,
n = term in half years from next interest payment date to maturity, and
$a_n = v + v^2 + \ldots + v^n = 1 - v^n/i$.

Treasury Capital Indexed Bonds:

$$P = v^{f/d}\left(g(1+a_n)+100v^n\right)\times \frac{K_t\left(1+\dfrac{P}{100}\right)^{-f/d}}{100}$$

where

$v = 1/1 + i$

$100i$ = quarterly real yield in percent to maturity,

f = number of days from date of settlement to next interest payment,

d = number of days in quarter ending on next interest payment date,

g = rate of quarterly coupon payment per \$10 face value,

n = term in quarters from next interest payment date to maturity,

$a_n = v + v^2 + \ldots + v^n = 1 - v^n/i$, K_{t-1} = indexation of previous interest payment date,

K_t = indexation at next interest payment date,

$K_t = K_{t-1}(1 + P/100)$,

p = semi-annual change in CPI over two quarters example if next interest payment is Nov, and

p = movement of CPI over two quarters ending the preceding June quarter = $100/2(CPI_t/CPI_{t-2}) - 1$ two decimal places.

Australian Dollar/U.S. Dollar and Australia Yield Curves

This pair has opposing configurations, therefore as Australian dollar/U.S. dollar rises along with U.S. bond yields, it drops as Australia's bonds fall. In this instance, Australian dollar is tied to U.S. yields during U.S. market trading and the U.S. dollar is tied to Australia's bond yield during Australia trading. For further confirmation, one only has to look at LIBOR or Bank Bills. We follow yields in the United States and bond prices in Australia for direction and continuity as Australia trading ends and trade shifts to the next market. What to look for in yield curves is a widening and narrowing of spreads.

Track Australian Dollar/U.S. Dollar

A comparative indicator is a "first of its type" bond-spread futures contract. The ASX offers a 10-year Australia Bond against a 10-year U.S. Treasury

On-the-Run Note. The contract price is determined as "the difference between forward rates of each asset" (ASX).

The spread is the "quoted price of the ASX 10-year bond futures contract yield minus the forward yield for the On-the-Run Treasury" (ASX). A widening of spreads denotes Australia bond yields are up and Treasury yields are down, while a narrowing of spreads denotes Australia yields decreasing as Treasury yields increase. The price of the contract is denominated in Australian dollars. "The price of the contract began as 1000 Aussie dollars plus the yield differential in basis points to allow for negative spreads to be traded and quoted" (ASX).

Interest-rate futures are priced based on yield to maturity, so contracts trade on the basis of yield. Prices are quoted based as 100 minus yield to maturity. Because contracts trade based on a fixed-tick system, longer-term bonds may be a measure to gauge economic conditions. Fixed-tick values decrease as interest rates rise and increase as interest rates fall. For the 30-day ASX interbank cash-rate futures, multiply price movements by fixed-tick dollar value of Australian dollar—24.66 per 0.01 move by number of contracts. An interest-rate measure is the ASX Target Rate Tracker based on the 30-day contract, and can be monitored on the ASX web site (ASX).

New Zealand

New Zealand yield curves are fairly simple, as this is another economy that currently outperforms all industrialized economies. New Zealand's current OCR is 2.75 percent, so debt issuance is not a problem to fund New Zealand's economy, nor are buyers for New Zealand's debt. New Zealand's debt-to-GDP ratio is currently 23.1 percent. In comparative European terms, 23.1 percent is low.

New Zealand's Debt Management Office currently issues three-month, six-month, and one-year Treasury Bills weekly (NZDMO). The one-year Treasury issuance began in April 2010.

Kiwi Bonds denominated in New Zealand dollars are offered to domiciled residents in denominations of six-month, one-year, and two-year maturities. The two-year Kiwi bond pays 3.75 as of August 2010. Remaining bond issuance has maturities of 3, 5, 7 and 10 years.

Kauri Bonds are not issued by the New Zealand Debt Management Office, but their importance to New Zealand yield curves can be constructive. Kauri Bonds are New Zealand dollar denominated and registered in New Zealand, but issued by a foreign issuer (Groom 2008). This method allows companies and institutions with overall funding programs in other currencies to fund only their New Zealand investments. The Kauri bond issuance began in 2004 and grew due to its acceptance as collateral in the New Zealand repurchase-agreement markets (Groom 2008). Since acceptance, issuance has grown steadily (Groom 2008). Prior to its formal acceptance, the euro-KIWI bond held dominance (Groom 2008).

The NZDMO will issue inflation-indexed bonds in 15-year maturities that are indexed to New Zealand's CPI. The first issuance is proposed for late 2010, early 2011 but hasn't materialized yet.

Treasury Securities are factored as a settlement price per New Zealand dollars. The formula is:

$$N/1 + (i \times n/365)$$

N = principal of Treasury Bill,
I = Yield divided by 100, and
n = number of full days from settlement date until maturity.

Government bonds with more than one coupon to maturity factor as a settlement price per New Zealand dollar as principal.

$$\left[\frac{\dfrac{1}{(1+i)^n} + r\left[c + \dfrac{1 - \dfrac{1}{(1+i)^n}}{i} \right]}{(1+i)^{\frac{a}{b}}} \right] N$$

where
    N = principal of bond;
    r = annual coupon interest rate divided by 200, semiannual coupon interest rate percent;
    i = yield divided by 200, semi annual yield percent;
    c = where settlement date is after the record date and up to, not including, the next coupon interest payment date where c has the value of 0 otherwise c has the value of 1;
    n = number of full half years between the next coupon interest payment date and maturity date;
    a = number of days from the settlement date to the next coupon interest payment date; and
    b = number of days in the half year ending on the next coupon interest payment date.

Short-dated government bonds with one coupon to run factored as a settlement price per NZ dollars as principal.

$$N(1 + r)/1 + (I \times n/365)$$

where

N = principal of bond;

r = annual coupon interest rate divided by 200, semiannual coupon interest rate percent;

1 = yield divided by 100; and

n = number of full days from the settlement date until maturity.

Inflation-Indexed Bonds Factored as a Settlement Price per New Zealand Dollar as Principal

$$\left[\frac{\frac{1}{(1+i)^n} + r\left[c + \frac{1 - \frac{1}{(1+i)^n}}{i}\right]}{(1+i)^{\frac{a}{b}}}\right]\left[\frac{K_t\left(1 + \frac{P}{100}\right)^{-\frac{a}{b}}}{100}\right] \times N$$

where

n = principal of indexed bond;

r = annual coupon interest rate divided by 400, quarterly coupon interest rate percent;

i = annual yield divided by 400, quarterly yield percent;

c = where settlement date is after record date and up to, not including, next coupon interest payment date c has value of 0 otherwise c has value of 1;

n = number of full quarter years between the next coupon interest payment date and maturity date;

a = number of days from the settlement date to the next coupon interest payment date;

b = number of years in the quarter year ending on next coupon interest payment date; and

K_t = total value of principal and index component at the next coupon interest payment date whether or not interest payment is due.

On coupon interest payment date, next refers to the following coupon interest payment date.

$$K_{t-1} (1 + p/100)$$

where

K_{t-1} = total value of principal and the index component at the previous coupon interest payment date;

K_{t-1} = 100.00 at the coupon interest payment date on or prior to the earliest date on which the bond may be settled at their first issue. K_t and K_{t-1} are rounded to two decimal places;

p = average percentage change in CPI index over the two quarters ending the quarter which is two quarters prior to that in which the next interest payment falls. If interest payment in February p is based on the average movement in CPI over the two quarters ended in the September quarter preceding factored $100/2 (CPI_t/CPI_{t-2}) - 1$; and

CPI_t = CPI for the second quarter of the relevant two quarter period, CPI_{t-2} = CPI for the quarter immediately prior to the relevant two quarter period.

New Zealand Dollar/U.S. Dollar and New Zealand Yield Curves

What if we know New Zealand dollar/U.S. dollar rises in U.S. markets with the rise of U.S. bond yields? The question of what direction will New Zealand dollar/U.S. dollar take when New Zealand bond yields rise during New Zealand trading is another issue.

Because New Zealand dollar/U.S. dollar are opposing pairs in this form, New Zealand dollar/U.S. dollar will follow its own bond price up or down rather than New Zealand bond yields. Stated differently, when New Zealand bond prices are down, New Zealand dollar/U.S. dollar will fall, and rise when bond prices rise.

Both markets have opposite effects due to the opposite alignment of the New Zealand dollar/U.S. dollar configuration. If the alignment were configured as U.S. dollar/New Zealand dollar, then a completely opposite effect would occur. The Royal Bank of New Zealand (RBNZ) would rather see a rise in New Zealand dollar/U.S. dollar more than any currency pair in their TWI.

The only method to obtain a weakening or rise in New Zealand dollar/U.S. dollar is for U.S. bond yields to rise to levels acceptable to the RBNZ.

New Zealand dollar/U.S. dollar rises only on the basis of good U.S. economic conditions. So if U.S. and New Zealand yield curves were compared against each other, what would be the factors to go long or short? If yields rose in the United States during U.S. trading hours and trading shifts to New Zealand, chances are good New Zealand bond prices will rise and New Zealand dollar/U.S. dollar will rise along with those bonds. This is so because many nations and their currencies are dependent on a healthy U.S. economy for their own healthy economies. Further, continuity normally exists from U.S. to NZ markets as all take their cues from the United States. A down U.S. market may easily see a down New Zealand market. It is the question of the business of trade that New Zealand transacts in the United States more so than any dependency factor. Yet if the U.S. economy falls, so does New Zealand dollar/U.S. dollar. Continuity of markets holds as long as political or economic news doesn't disrupt the balance between markets.

Track New Zealand Dollar/U.S. Dollar

On the ASX, New Zealand trades the 30-day Official Cash Rate Futures and the 90-day Bank Bill Futures contract. Margin requirements were lowered in May 2010 to a tier structure that enhances trading in these contracts. The 30-day contract is quoted in yield percent per annum in multiples of 0.005, it is yield − 100. 1 basis point = New Zealand dollar 24.66. New Zealand, like Australia, works on a fixed-tick arrangement. Multiply price movements by the fixed-tick dollar value of New Zealand dollar—24.66 per 0.01 move by number of contracts (ASX).

Australian Dollar/New Zealand Dollar and Yield Curves

If New Zealand dollar/U.S. dollar and Australian dollar/U.S. dollar follow their own bond prices during New Zealand and Australia trading, which way will Australian dollar/New Zealand dollar move? This pair is the yield seeker.

Currency pairs must be viewed as not only trading mechanisms to profit, but mechanisms for finance. Currency pairs configured as New Zealand dollar/U.S. dollar and Australian dollar/U.S. dollar only satisfy one side of the finance equation. This was the reason for inventing these cross pairs. Australian dollar/New Zealand dollar allowed for the flow of funds to travel either inside Australia or New Zealand from abroad or it was used as a cheaper mechanism to finance outflows. For this reason, Australian dollar/New Zealand dollar will always move opposite to its counterparts in terms of yields and bond prices.

Think about the current economic conditions in Australia and New Zealand. Both economies are growing in GDP and OCR. And both economies are earning enormous revenues from the Australian dollar/U.S. dollar and New Zealand dollar/U.S. dollar configuration from the U.S. dollar side. This allows both currency-pair prices to rise, good for both nations. But what about the U.S. dollar side of this equation? How does the U.S. dollar side finance Australia and New Zealand operations against a high Australian dollar/U.S. dollar and New Zealand dollar/U.S. dollar currency price? The price is prohibitive in terms of Australian dollar/U.S. dollar and New Zealand dollar/U.S. dollar. Australian dollar/New Zealand dollar satisfies the U.S. dollar side by following yields, and is used as the finance aspect for U.S. dollar operations.

As Australian dollar/U.S. dollar and New Zealand dollar/U.S. dollar prices continue to rise, Australian dollar/New Zealand dollar continues to fall. These pairs are called U.S. dollar pairs because they allow the U.S. dollar to seek yield outside of the United States. Or it allows financing in Australian dollar/New Zealand dollar to occur in yields at a preferable cost. So Australian dollar/New Zealand dollar can also be viewed as a finance mechanism as it is cheaper to finance in terms of yields than it is to finance in terms of a high currency price.

In terms of the yield curve, Australian dollar/New Zealand dollar will follow U.S. bond prices during U.S. trading, while Australian dollar/U.S. dollar and New Zealand dollar/U.S. dollar will follow U.S. bond yields. The U.S. dollar will follow Australian dollar/New Zealand dollar and Australia and New Zealand bond yields in Australia and New Zealand trading.

Euro Yield Curve

The yield curve for the euro comprises four nations: france, Germany, Italy, and Spain (German Finance Agency). Of the four, German bonds, called bunds, comprise 21 percent of the European debt market, Italian bonds called BTPs are 29 percent, French bonds called OATs are 20 percent, and Spanish bonds called Letras del Tesoro comprise 7 percent (Investinginbondseurope.org).

The focus to trade the euro/U.S. dollar will be granted to German bonds due to Germany's powerful and always leading economic position in the euro zone, its low debt compared to the others—euro 1.043 billion—and its close proximity to the Frankfurt Stock Exchange. Plus the ECB is housed in Frankfurt and the German Bundesbank.

Prior to the euro, the German Deutsche mark was the leading currency of Europe, so it is only natural that the Germans help steer the economic policy process in Europe to secure their legacy from the Deutsche mark to the euro. The last important consideration is that bunds are quoted and traded in euros.

The Germans issue two types of bonds, tradeable and non-tradeable. By doing this, the Germans track two yield curves, one for tradeable bonds, and the other for non-tradeable debt. The tradeable bonds with an interest rate exposure comprise the two-year German Federal Treasury Schaetze Note, the five-year Federal Treasury Note, and the 10-year Federal Treasury Note. Federal Bonds or bunds comprise the 30-year note and determine the long end of the curve.

Non-tradeable Bonds include the German Government Day Bond that currently pays a rate per day of 0.21 percent (German Finance Agency). This rate is managed by the German Finance Agency and represents an important indicator. Purchasers receive par value plus interest to determine yields.

Federal Treasury Financing Paper offers maturities from 12 to 24 months. Yields are determined by offering paper at a discount and redemption at maturity. BuBills or bund Bills are discount paper offered for maturities of six months and one year. Currently the Germans are negotiating the offer of three- and nine-month BuBills.

Federal Savings Notes comprise a six-year note for type-A issues and a seven-year note for type-B issues. Inflation-indexed bonds include the 5- and 10-year note. Inflation is tied to the interest rate at maturity.

Yield Calculations for German Federal Securities with Fixed Interest

Compound interest formula, yield for fixed interest securities with annual interest payment and maturity N years is equal to:

$$C = p/g + p/g_2 + \ldots p/g_n + r/g_n$$

where

$\quad$ C = purchase price including accrued interest in percent,

$\quad$ p = coupon rate in percent,

$\quad$ n = maturity in years,

$\quad$ r = redemption price in percent,

$\quad$ 1/g = conversion factor in compound discounting, discount factor, $(1/g = 1/1 + p/100)$, and

$\quad$ p = yield in percent.

$p/g \times p/g_2$ gave discount interest payments (cash value of interest payments).

Simplified as:

$$C = p \times (1/g + 1/g_2 + \cdots + 1/g_n) + r/g_n$$
$$= p \times g_n - 1/ g_n \times (g - 1) + r/g_n$$
$$g_n - 1/g_n \times (g - 1)$$
$$= \text{annuity value factor}$$

Using an annuity value factor rewritten as:

$$C = p \times a_n + r/g_n$$

P yields are not possible after four years, determined iteratively—estimate yield value and insert into equations.

Track the Euro Yield Curve

The German Bundesbank reports daily yield curves on its web site. Eurex trades a 10- and 30-year bund Futures contract and Markit has an index called the iBoxx that reports cash bond-market transactions for the euro.

Markit is many things in Europe: a data vendor, a market analysis provider, and, through a host of indices that calculate within seconds, a market reporter of up-to-the-minute market information. The information materializes quickly, but it is reliable so any trade decision can be instituted with reliability.

The key for EURO/USD in European trade is once German yields are up, the majority of European nations normally follow. At times the peripheral nations can drag down EUR/USD prices such as the Greek crisis, Ireland crisis, Italy, Portugal, and Spain termed the Pigs in market parlance. Peripherals are other European nations.

Euro/British Pound and Yield Curve

Euro/British pound satisfies the same scenario as Australian dollar/New Zealand dollar. As euro/U.S. dollar and British pound/U.S. dollar seek their yield from U.S. bonds and Bills in U.S. trading, euro/British pound as the U.S. dollar pair follows U.S. Bond prices.

Euro/British pound and Australian dollar/New Zealand dollar are the safe trades in U.S. trading as they like the safety backing of U.S. Bonds. In European trading, the opposite scenario holds.

Euro/British pound loves yields while euro/U.S. dollar likes bund yields and British pound/U.S. dollar likes the safety of the bond price. This says that

U.S. dollars seek yields in Europe through euro/British pound. Yet euro/British pound is the finance mechanism for trade and other operations from the United States to Europe and the United Kingdom to Europe. It is a pair of vital importance and monitored continuously by the United Kingdom and Europe.

Swiss Franc Yield Curve

Between the SIX Swiss Exchange and Eurex, the Swiss offer up-to-the-minute comparisons of not only their own yield curve as their bonds trade but an interactive assortment of yields can be monitored to compare Swiss franc bonds against other nations' bonds.

Eurex trades derivatives and option contracts on bonds and various investment instruments while SIX Swiss Exchange trades Swiss Sovereign bonds through the Swiss Domestic Bond Index, termed the SBI. Any bond in the SBI can be compared to 26 nations bonds so yield curves can be viewed on a chart. This can be viewed from the interactive yield-curve tool directly on the SIX Swiss Exchange web site. It is useful and reliable.

Because the Swiss so heavily monitor their economy and calculate every transaction as it occurs, a trading decision based on yield curve comparisons is very reliable. For example, Swiss franc yield curves can be compared to U.S. dollar curves, euro to U.S. dollar, or euro to Swiss franc. Any combination of the 26 nations can be viewed within seconds. This interactive device serves well for European trading but is employable in any market.

The Swiss offer fixed SNB Bills formally known as Debt Register Claims that are tradable money market instruments. SNB Bills are issued at a discount in denominations of 28, 84, 168, and 336 days. Swiss Government Confederate Bonds are offered in maturities of 1, 2, 3, 4, 5, 6, 7, 8, 9, 10, 20, and 30 years.

To further measure Swiss Yield Curves, Scoach Schweiz introduced a Yield Enhancement Index developed by Derivative Partners Research in February 2009. Scoach Schweiz is an exchange that trades cash and forward transactions in securities traded on the SIX Swiss Exchange.

The index comprises four products that offer coupons or discounts: Discount Certificates, Barrier Discount Certificates, Reverse Convertibles, and Barrier Reverse Convertibles. All are equal weighted with clean prices as are the vast majority of Swiss financial instruments. The index is calculated once daily by Derivative Partners, but plans to calculate the index every three minutes will materialize in the future.

Index calculations are derived from market mid prices that include the mean of the best bid and ask price. The index is benchmarked against a synthetic index that comprises 60 percent of SMI equities and a bond component that comprises 40 percent of the Total Return Index of all Swiss bonds (Scoach). The formula is:

$$I_t = I_{t-1} + I_{t-1} \times \sum_{i=1}^{M} \left[\left(\frac{P_{i,s} + \alpha_{i,t} \times C_i}{P_{i,t-1} + \alpha_{i,t-1} \times C_i} - 1 \right) / M \right]$$

where

I_t = Current Index level,

I_{t-1} = Closing value of index on previous day,

$P_{i,s}$ = Last mid price of security I at times,

$P_{i,t-1}$ = Last mid price of security I on previous day,

$\alpha_{i,t}$ = Current fraction of an interest period since the last coupon for security i fell due prior to inclusion in the index (calculated 30/360),

$\alpha_{i,t-1}$ = Current fraction of an interest period on the previous day since the last coupon for security I fell due prior to inclusion in the index,

C_i = Coupon of security I per annum in percent,

s = current time on day t, and

m = number of securities in the index.

The Swiss offer three variations of the SBI: SBI Domestic T with one- to three-year maturities, SBI Government with three- to seven-year maturities, and Domestic Government with 7-to 15-year maturities. Swiss yield curves are factored based on accrued interest with yield variations based on each index. The yield curve is factored as yield-to-worst-case scenario which is a Value as Risk calculation and duration is factored based on a worst-case scenario.

Swiss Yield Curve

$$\text{Yield} = g + (cc - cp)/L$$

g = annual coupon in percent,

cp = clean price,

c = redemption value at maturity date or earliest redemption in percent, and

L = life to maturity/earliest redemption in years = d/y.

Accrued interest is factored as coupon amount $\times$ (N/360). Swiss bonds are factored the same as the German 30/360 day-count convention, where 30 equates to number of interest-bearing days to 360 days per year. The formula is:

$$N = (D2 - D1) + 30 \times (M2 - M1) + 360 \times (Y2 - Y1)$$

where

   N = Start date,
   D1, M1, Y1 = date from which accrued interest is calculated (Exclusive),
   D2, M2, Y2 = date accrued interest is calculated (Inclusive), and
   D3, M3, Y3 factored as n + 1 = date of next interest payment.

Between D1 and D2, factor number of interest-bearing days to determine proportion of next coupon equal to accrued interest.

where

   day count methods = A = accrued interest amount,
   F = annual coupon frequency,
   N = number of interest bearing days,
   Swiss bond interest payments = P = coupon/F, and
   P = coupon amount × (N/360).

U.S. Dollar/Swiss Franc

During New York trading hours, U.S. dollar/Swiss franc loves U.S. bond prices, Swiss franc/U.S. dollar loves bond yields. The opposite holds for Swiss trading. Swiss franc/U.S. dollar is the confederate bond follower, U.S. dollar/Swiss franc the yield seeker. It is important to remember that the Swiss Central Bank much prefer the Swiss franc/U.S. dollar configuration. This principle is just like the U.S. dollar/Japanese yen example. The Swiss would much prefer to earn Swiss francs against the U.S. dollar. U.S. dollar/Swiss franc almost defeats the purpose for the Swiss due to their enormous trade with the United States.

U.S. Yield Curve

The Office of Debt Management offers T-Bills with maturities of one, three, and six months and one year. Treasury Notes are offered in maturities of 2, 3, 5, 7, and 10 years. Treasury Bonds are offered with maturities of 20 and 30 years. The 30-year bond was reissued in 2006 (Treasury Department).

   The following information was derived from Treasury Direct: Four-week bills are issued every week, auctions occur on Tuesdays. Thirteen- and 26-week bills are issued weekly, and auctions occur on Mondays. Fifty-two-week bills are issued every four weeks, and auctions occur on Tuesdays. Two-year notes are auctioned somewhere in the latter part of the month. Three-year notes are issued on the fifteenth of each month, with auctions around the middle of the month. Five-year-note auctions occur somewhere in the middle of the month. Seven-year notes are announced in the second half of the month, and auctions occur in the middle of the month. Ten-year notes are announced in the first part of February, May, August, and November, and auctions occur in the second week of that month. Thirty-year bonds are announced, issued, and auctioned with the 10-year note.

The U.S. Treasury offers Treasury Inflation Protected Securities (TIPS) with maturities of 5, 10, and 30 years. Inflation protected ties these securities to the U.S. CPI. Five-year auctions occur the last week of April, 10-year TIPS are auctioned in the second weeks of January and July, and 30-year TIPS are auctioned in the last week of February.

The U.S. factors yield curves by two methods, the discount yield and the investment yield. The discount yield is employed to factor three- and six-month T-Bills and calculates as:

$$(FV - PP)/FV) \times (360/M)$$

where

      FV = Face Value,
      PP = Purchase Price, and
      M = Maturity.
For three-month T-Bills, use 91 and use 182 for six month.
      360 = Bank calculation to determine interest rates.

The Investment yield relates the return to the purchase price of notes and bonds. To factor:

$$R + (FV - PP)/M)/(FV + PP)/2$$

where

      R = Coupon Rate,
      FV = Face Value,
      PP = Purchase Price, and
      M = Years to maturity.

Dollar Pairs and Yield Curves

The following pairs are cross pairs that are considered U.S. dollar pairs due to their movements in terms of U.S. bond prices and yields. U.S. dollar/South African rand is considered a dollar pair because it follows U.S. bond prices in U.S. markets, but the U.S. dollar side of the equation follows yields of South African bonds when trading in South Africa. The time difference is six hours ahead when compared to New York Eastern Standard Time.

The Johannesburg Stock Exchange opens for trading in Bond Futures, currencies and other stocks and derivatives at 3:00 a.m. EST and closes at 11:00 a.m. EST, so part of a New York morning will have duality of trading between both markets. Yet U.S. dollar/South African rand should and normally does hold precedence in U.S. markets. This pair has large swing tendencies that derive from the South African side for the U.S. dollar more so than South African rand in U.S. trading. Look for the London gold fix before the Johannesburg close to swing this pair.

British pound/New Zealand dollar, euro/Australian dollar, British pound/Australian dollar, and euro/New Zealand dollar are dollar pairs, but the tendencies for all pairs are very volatile. Remember that neither pairs are among the list of large interest in the central bank scheme of interested pairs. The euro/New Zealand dollar was once an interested pair when euro-Kiwi bonds were issued by New Zealand. Consider these pairs as a sort of outlier arrangement. Sometimes they follow Treasury Bonds or yields, other times they follow the U.S. dollar underlying pair. At times, movements may confound a trader. Overall they revert to trend, so wild swings may be market gifts. So while these pairs are dollar pairs, volatility can be high and caution is advised in any market.

Reserve Requirements and Bonds

Why the opposite scenario holds for currency pairs can be related to funding requirements. Suppose a government passes a budget. Outside of tax revenues, budgets are financed by the sale of bonds. Because the budget is a known figure, bonds will be sold to equal the number. This ties the particular nation's currency into the budget figure. The currency now rises and falls based on revenue earned or lost from bond sales and the direction it takes in the marketplace. Past issuance means nothing unless large redemptions occur in short time frames.

A home currency can't always be tied to yield because yield can't be a guarantee since it is costly and risky due to the many unknown market and economic variables. Now suppose this nation can match its currency pair with another nation's currency. Suppose the second nation had a rising economy and its bond yields or bond prices were rising. This allows revenue to be earned by the first nation by rising yields or bond prices. It is the method to offset its own budget requirements. Stated differently, suppose Australia passes a budget and sells its bonds. They will also know in advance what their currency price will be at the start and end of the budget year, at least in terms of the target. What if the price was, say, 9100 at the beginning and they planned for 9200 at the end of the year. Now Australia ties its currency to U.S. dollar bond yields. U.S. dollar bond yields rise and Australian dollar/U.S. dollar trades to, say, 9500 and completes the year at 9700 Australian dollar/U.S. dollar. Australia offsets its budget and bond sales from 9200 to 9700. It is a basic example, but one that holds. Nations share the economic services of each other and are tied together by currency-pair arrangements.

The same scenario holds for the United States, Great Britain, New Zealand, Japan, Switzerland, euro Land, and Canada. One side of a currency pair is a yield seeker while the other side is a bond follower. It is an economic relationship, a relationship that has held since currency pairs became two-sided equations.

Reserve requirements form the basis of the bond sales. It is the target, the rate that must be managed throughout the year, as bond sales are conducted and revenue is earned from yields or bonds and economic conditions. All dictate the imperatives of the bond sales in terms of issuance, prices, and maturities. The quarter-to-quarter LIBOR and in-nation rates help to manage the yearly target on a quarterly basis.

As currency pairs became connected, it created a dependency—an interdependency—that linked the world together. As new tax rules, cross pairs, and issues of open borders for trade were created, the interdependency aspect became tighter. Add the ability to communicate nation to nation through technology, and we found the world not to be the wide-open spaces we once thought. Suddenly we found New Zealand not to be such a distant and unknown land. Further add the ability to find advantage in each nation's economies, and the interdependency link became tighter.

Technology allowed us to know and understand New Zealand's economic structure in terms of merchandise trade, financing mechanisms, central bank operations, debt management, and stock and bond markets. The most important aspect was to allow the world to evaluate the second part of the currency-pair trade in an instant. It was found that smaller economies were dependent on larger economies and all were dependent on the United States, so their currencies aligned with the U.S. dollar with the hope of appreciation to offset their own nation's economic budgets. Up-to-the-second information allowed a certainty of a trade, a confidence feature.

Yet the United States offers nations the opportunity to sell their goods, finance operations, and enjoy currency appreciation. This scenario describes the vast majority of nations and their currencies, not just the major currencies addressed in this text. To align with the United States presupposes that the U.S. economy continues its historic winning ways in stable political and economic growth. If the U.S. dollar falls, all will fall due to the many varied investments that nations maintain in the United States.

As this text progresses, one would notice the uniqueness of a government that helped to create an economic system that was designed not for its own benefit but for the benefit of a world that could profit and grow off its kindness, open markets, political stability, and low regulatory structure. The U.S. system is the complete opposite to other nations, and that is what gives this economic system its uniqueness, a uniqueness that hasn't been replicated nor may ever be replicated again.

The relationship between other nations is not a dependency, rather it is an opportunity that must be respected and appreciated the world over. Without a stable United States, the world would literally be a very different place under rules that would be quite harsh in terms of economic gain. The United States is chosen as the destination for goods simply because it is one of the world's largest consumer markets with a rule of law and stable political system.

Cross Pairs, Bonds, and Yields

The question of how will British pound/Japanese yen and Australian dollar/Japanese yen trade in relation to bonds and yields is constructive. The answer depends on which market.

In each respective market, both pairs will follow bond prices up and down. The British pound will follow gilts and Australian dollar follows Commonwealth bonds. This allows for stability of these pairs and allows carry traders to safely earn their yields over time by the difference of interest rates between their respective nations. In Tokyo trading, British pound and Australian dollar will seek yields. In Australia and London trading, the Japanese yen will seek yields. In U.S. markets, the answer is quite different.

In U.S. markets, both pairs seek yield. For the granddaddy of cross pairs, the British pound/Japanese yen seeks the most yield and finds it in U.S. markets. The British pound/Japanese yen moves almost six pips to every one-pip movement in the respective U.S. dollar pairs. This specifically applies to the British pound/U.S. dollar, as the U.S. dollar/Japanese yen can be a laggard at times. The British pound/Japanese yen in U.S. markets is a free floater, and all advantage is taken to this free-float movement. This movement can only be explained by the enormous opportunities the United Kingdom and Japan have for U.S. markets in terms of trade and interests. Issues of finance can be conducted in any currency pair at any time. The price of any pair will determine which one to employ. Moreover, because this and other cross pairs like Australian dollar/Japanese yen seek yield, it is the fast moving U.S. Treasury market that explains the fast movement of these pairs. Bond prices fluctuate, therefore yields fluctuate.

Trade Strategies

The currency-pair code of yield-seeker versus bond-price follower says much for trades and trade strategies. Suppose the euro/U.S. dollar is in a trend in U.S. markets. Based on the currency-pair code, it doesn't mean the same pair will trend in European trading. Yet it may trend.

As currency pairs change markets, new factors of consideration must be contemplated from market to market. Factors such as economic conditions, economic announcements, interest-rate decisions, bond issuance, and overall market conditions are just a small part of contemplation of what type of market will trade.

The same trend in U.S. trading could easily become a range trade during European market hours. This would require new strategic tactics to trade that market. Those that expected a trend that never materialized are locked into the position until trading shifts to the next market. Sometimes it is better to trade in one market, take profits at closing, and evaluate market conditions in the next market before employing a trade strategy.

For example, suppose the U.S. dollar/Japanese yen trended during U.S. trading. Who would want to bank on the fact that this pair would trend in Japanese trading, knowing the economic conditions of Japan? A range trade may be the better consideration, or even a no-trade strategy. In this instance, it may be a better arrangement to wait until European trading to evaluate a trade in U.S. dollar/Japanese yen. The same applies for markets that shift from Europe to the United States. A trending European market may result as a range trade or a down market in U.S. trading that would require new trade tactics.

So the question is will a trending currency pair trend in all markets, and the answer is no, absolutely not. A correction of trend must come from a market somewhere, but it doesn't have to occur in the same market. Currency pairs must be viewed within the context of every respective market it trades in, because no two markets are the same nor will any two markets result in the same effects. Profits in one market do not mean, nor do they guarantee, profits in another market. A short in one market may be a long in another or a range trade.

For major currencies, Wellington, New Zealand, and Sydney, Australia, represent one market. Asia is the second with Tokyo the main, Europe is the third, and the United States and Canada is the fourth.

The idea that one can trade based on Fibonacci numbers is a losing proposition. Fibonacci numbers may signal where a pair currently trades at one moment in time, but don't guarantee in what market a continued trend, correction, or range may occur.

The proposition by certain central banks to align with the idea to flatten yield curves purposefully until the next central bank meeting is constructive in many respects. Will their markets be flooded with bond issuance at a certain maturity? This is economic weakness to flatten a curve. Will central banks buy bonds from the market at another certain maturity is more economic weakness to flatten a curve. Control the currency price—more economic weakness to flatten the curve.

Or will these nations whose economic situations are dire regulate the relationship of a currency pair by the regulation of movements? This is worse than debasement of a currency because it wrecks the purpose, intent, meaning, and economic relationship a currency has to the world economic order, an order established and recognized since World War I. To regulate a free market can only mean a forceful limit of a currency-pair's movement and admitted economic weakness to flatten the curve.

Yield Curves and Currency Prices

Yield curves can now be drawn and plotted and a trading strategy planned. How this is done depends on the trade strategy, which pair to trade, which market to trade, which side of the yield/ bond strategy traders wish to follow, and duration of the trade.

Short-term traders should look at the short end of any single nation yield curve, or two curves if a trade runs into another market under another time frame. Longer-term trades should be monitored specifically in terms of each nation's yield curves. The question should always be the relationship of the spread and its narrowing, widening, or flattening in relationship to bond maturities.

Any yield-curve strategy should account for BBA LIBOR, in-nation LIBOR rates, and CPI within both nations, as all will correlate. For example, suppose the United States released its CPI number at 2 percent, and 3 percent was expected when three-month T-Bills traded at a yield of, say, 5 percent. What would occur to the euro/U.S. dollar if a trader was long the euro/U.S. dollar at the time of release? The euro/U.S. dollar would crash faster than he or she could bail out because the three-month T-Bill would reflect this new CPI price and in turn the euro/U.S. dollar would also reflect its new price. LIBOR, CPI, and yields possibly anticipated the event but another scenario occurred. Markets prices again always normalize and reflect the new price.

Yields and bonds have tendencies to trade outside of their respective central bank target ranges. This is not unusual, as markets have tendencies of anticipation or over-anticipations of events. Uncertain economic times may be to blame, overanticipation of an economy may be as well. Many reasons exist as to why.

One major reason is central banks are remiss in regular release of their overall money supply M1 numbers that outline money stocks. Instead of weekly releases, central banks release monthly M2 and M3 figures that are in ranges to highlight money stock, credit, and lending conditions rather than specific currency amounts. If we knew the money supply number along with the new budget in terms of spending and anticipated bond sales, we could know almost exactly the central bank target number for their currency price. Absent the money supply figure leaves market professionals to make educated guesses for a currency-price target. So economic events are best guesses. Instead of best guesses, currencies will price in yield and bond prices in relation to economic data. Either way, markets will always normalize to the release and revert to trend. How long that takes is always questionable. Normalization may take anywhere from minutes to months to years.

An over anticipation may mean for example the euro/U.S. dollar rises in price without the backing of yields to rise in price. This scenario is a false move, so the euro/U.S. dollar will be sold to reflect its true market price that aligns to a yield. It is an opportunity for profit and a market gift.

Suppose a LIBOR curve was plotted against a yield curve for any nation's bonds. Specifically, what if we plotted U.S. dollar LIBOR against a Treasury yield curve or British pound LIBOR against a gilt yield curve? Exactly what would we learn? Remember LIBOR and in-nation LIBOR have overnight to 12-month maturities, and bond yield curves extend 30 years for Treasuries and 50 years for gilts.

The shorter end of each bond yield curve can provide vital answers to currency direction when compared to the shorter end of a LIBOR curve, especially in uncertain economic times because cash won't be committed at the long end due to economic uncertainty. Yet no two curves will look exactly alike. Australia and New Zealand LIBOR and bond yield curves will look very different than, say, U.S. dollar LIBOR and Treasury curves.

Yield curves as a forecast for trading currency pairs is contained within one nation's bonds and maturities with the view to look at other markets for yield curve, yields, and bond direction. Here the focus is on inter-nation spreads between maturities. Australia's issuance of comparable bonds as a formally listed trading vehicle is instructive of future events.

A main factor to measure spot prices in relation to yield curves is the cash markets and the U.S. example will be employed, yet it may serve for almost any nation.

The difference between the cash market and the yield curve in the United States is bond auctions. Bond auctions represent the cash rate, the price investors are willing to pay. The yield curve is the measure that reflects this new price as auctions occur in various maturities, so yield curves will shift with new bond auction prices. The U.S. Treasury schedules bond-maturity auctions on a routine schedule rather than based on need in terms of economic conditions. This method allows an economy and the yield curve to hold fairly steady. The spot-currency price will factor within this matrix. A number of measures exist with the assumption to measure a Treasury bond price to interest-rate changes in yield curves.

Dollar Value of Basis Point and Modified Duration

The CME factors DV01, dollar Value of a Basis point, as the average absolute price changes of Treasury securities to a 1 basis point increase and decrease in yield to maturity by:

$$((\text{change in absolute value with 1 bp}) + (\text{change in absolute value with 1 bp}))/2$$

The idea is that it captures the bond/yield inverse within small increments by when interest rates rise, bond price falls and vice versa. The purpose of DV01 is to hedge, but it may serve for small currency price moves. It locks one bond price against one small yield. The caveat is DV01 is not fixed, it can move as bonds and yields move.

Modified duration is a weighted average maturity of Treasury security cash flows. As yields fall, modified duration increases and vice versa. The formula

$$D = 1/P \times \text{change in P/Change in Y}$$

This formula captures small changes in yield to maturity that affect the bond price. It is a measure of interest-rate sensitivities of a financial instrument. If modified duration is high, it says an instrument is more interest-rate sensitive and vice versa. The Dow Jones Bond Index incorporates modified duration in its index calculation. While modified duration is a few years old, it is still widely employed by banks, as new methodologies haven't been adopted as standard practice. On the CME web site is an Empirical Duration tool that calculates inputs for duration and DV01.

An important feature and wide use of modified duration is to measure a nation's bond indices.

Traders in yield-seeking nations such as the United States, Europe, and Canada must establish a cash rate in relation to the yield curve to determine currency-pair prices. The iBoxx bond market in Europe is a cash index, and can be compared to the same maturity in the futures contract.

For the United States, one measure of the cash rate in terms of yield curves is the Treasury On-the-Run futures contract. It is a one-month contract that changes with each new bond auction. It is the best measure of cash prices in relation to yield curves, and contracts are offered for all U.S. government maturities so yield curves can be measured against any maturity. The recommendation is to focus on the various one- to five-year contracts for short-term measures of spot prices. On the Run can also be measured against the concomitant futures maturity.

For nations whose bonds are tied to performance, such as England, Switzerland, Australia, and New Zealand, the focus must be on the bond price, particularly the short term. Yield curves operate as measures of risk rather than measures of performance, so the bond indices and bond futures will be the measure for spot prices in these nations. The actual methodology for professional traders is to connect the bond price to cash flows to factor a spot price.

Conclusion

The bond/yield interplay is useful and a vital tool to determine not only the cost of money, but how money is priced in the markets within each side of a currency pair. Two nations' yield curves constantly ebb and flow as well as a single nation's curve along the various maturities. The vital determination to measure yield curves is in the slopes, but slopes must be measured in basis-point terms in order to understand the insight into direction of a curve. Currency pairs move based on this scenario due to the cost of each currency priced in the markets. It is a market-driven rate rather than a controlled rate. How each side of a currency pair is priced in terms of an interest rate is found in the yield curve.

CHAPTER 7

Swaps and Forwards

Swaps and forwards are priced in the market as an interest rate and as an interest-rate differential. How to price swaps and how they are traded in many of their various forms will be outlined in depth in this chapter. The interest-rate differential as it relates to forward points is not only discussed but an example is presented. The chapter begins with a discussion of swaps and forwards and their many types are detailed as examples. The various types of interest rate swaps, their types, examples, and how they relate to the markets and currency pairs in particular will be discussed and explained in detail on a step-by-step basis. This chapter begins with an explanation of swaps and forwards along with examples. Swaps comprise many types and all will be highlighted. Next, the discussion will progress to each nation and their swap rates and/or index.

After internal-nation LIBOR are released and the price is settled for the respective currency, the next rate for consideration is the swap rate. The swap rate is constructive for many reasons.

It closely resembles a more truly priced currency on any given day within the respective nation so the rate is vitally important to any trade strategy. On a local level, swap rates are employed to price mortgages. For example, mortgages in Singapore are factored either in terms of the three-month swap rate or the three-month Singapore Overnight Rate (HSBC Singapore). England factors five-year fixed rate mortgages against five-year swaps. For this reason, the five-year credit default swap (CDS) is a priority indicator for the Bank of England (BOE). These examples serve many nations' mortgage markets, but all employ these rates in various ways. *Swap rate* is a market term.

In Europe, view a swap rate as an effective rate as part of the overnight rate. It is shorter, more sensitive, moves with volatility within small ranges as it trades, and explains currency and currency-pair movements and volatility better than an overnight rate. This example deviates from standard definitions but the euro is strictly a yield seeking currency and it will find its best movement when swap and internal LIBOR align properly. Does a swap rate move bond prices and yields or do bond prices and yields move swap rates is a debatable question, because different markets hold different answers. Market events, economic events and projections, and risk versus non-risk are a few factors for consideration. Swap rates can move quickly with events and cause market volatility for currency pairs, so it is imperative to understand movements in order to understand the relationship between the two investment vehicles.

Secondly, the swap-rate spread can distill vital importance to future-priced currencies because it closely resembles the direction and price of future internal-nation LIBOR rates as well as Government bond prices and yields. This is the Overnight Index Swap (OIS)-LIBOR connection. Finally, swap rates provide a check, a further confirmation of in-nation LIBOR, bonds, and yields, and in turn provide affirmation of the direction of a currency and currency pair.

The swap-rate curve extends 30 years into the future because it represents the long, short, and middle of any government-bond yield curve. For the United States, it is 30 years, for the United Kingdom it is 50 years, and it is 40 years in Japan. For our purpose, it is the zero-to-three-month target range that is of interest because it closely aligns to central bank interest in its own three-month target period and because it aligns with government-bond yield curves. Look at the swap curve as the guide between the interplay of government bonds and yields and overall nation rates. It provides answers to government-bond yield direction and in turn spot-currency prices because of its risk nature. Government-bond yield curves are considered the risk-free rate due to government backing, while swap curves represent risk because borrowing and trading in swap rates occur at higher rates than bond-yield curves. It is a measure of the health of banks since banks are the main traders of swaps. So swap curves will always be higher than bond-yield curves. Normally this represents a positive development when measured against each other. Yet if bond-yield curves were ever higher than swap curves, that represents a negative curve and an economy in trouble.

For spot trades, it is the Interest Rate Swap, Currency Swap, and Cross Currency Basis Swap that are of prime importance because they lend credence to direction of currency prices. A few examples follow.

An interest-rate swap. "Suppose Firm A invests in a bond that pays a coupon of 5 percent yearly while Firm B invests in a floating-rate bond. The two firms enter into a swap to exchange interest payments. An interest-rate swap is defined as a fixed versus floating arrangement. The purpose is to hedge and/or manage funding risks" (Haubrich 2001).

A foreign-exchange (FX) swap. "A borrows X minus the spot rate U.S. dollars from and lends X euros to B. At contract expiration, A returns X U.S. dollars minus the forward rate to B and B returns X euros to A. FX swaps are employed as a hedge against speculative trading and used by importers and exporters" (Baba 2008). Yet central banks are heavily involved in the FX-swap market, as will be seen in the New Zealand example.

An FX cross-currency basis swap. "A borrows X minus the spot U.S. dollars from B and lends X euros to B. During the contract term, A receives the euro three-month LIBOR and pays the U.S. dollar three-month LIBOR to B every three months. At expiration, A returns X minus spot U.S. dollars to B and B returns X euros to A" (Baba 2008). More specifically, what if, for example, British pound/U.S. dollar basis swap spreads fall, then U.S. dollar funding in terms of the cross-currency swaps would also fall. This is negative for cross pairs and the British pound/U.S. dollar, and says sell both.

The Overnight Indexed Swap Rate on a derivative contract measures the overnight rate for a particular nation (Sengupta 2008). This rate has a different reference point from nation to nation. The swap spread is the difference between the swap rate and government bond yield at any point along the yield curve. Swap spreads in basis points measures the spread between 3 month FX implied dollar rates and 3 month LIBOR. It's a measure to determine if risk exists in the market. The swap curve is defined as swap rates across maturities. Swap rates can be defined as forward expectations of LIBOR. So a forward LIBOR curve represents future LIBOR that determines future benchmark interest rates as well as future inflation and Consumer Price Index (CPI). Yet currency forward implied rates can gauge an expectation of future spot prices. Interest rates are the gauge.

Simple interest equals Interest $\times$ principal $\times$ rate $\times$ time. Future value of simple interest $= p\,(I + rt)$, Compound interest $FV = P\,(1 = r/n)\,nt$, continuous compound $p =$ amount ert where r equals interest rate expressed as a fraction, n equals the number of compound periods, $t =$ time in days, months or years, $e =$ natural logarithm. Simple forward interest $Fv1\,(1 + rt) = fv2$, compound $fv1\,(1 + r/n)\,n = fv2$ and continuous interest $= fv1\,ert = fv2$.

Interest rates are arranged to imply forward expectations. For example,

$$\text{Forward interest} = FI1(1 + rt) = F12$$

Future spot price curves and future interest rate priced in interest rate instruments are then constructed.

Armed with this basic information, we can move to a nation-by-nation look at swap rates and currency prices.

EONIA Swap Index

EURIBOR may be the overnight rate established for the price of the euro, but it is the EONIA Swap Index that more closely resembles the actual euro market price since EONIA is offered as a mid-market rate on any given day by banks in the money market.

The EONIA Swap Index rate should not be confused with the EONIA rate. The EONIA rate is like the Effective Funds rate in the United States, while the EONIA Swap Index rate is quite different. The EONIA Swap Index rate will always be above the EONIA rate, because borrowing costs will always be higher at this level. EONIA sets the foundation for the EONIA Swap Index rate and it is employed for trading swaps along the yield curve. The EONIA fixing time is 19:00 CET, while the EONIA Swap Index Fixing time is 11:00 CET. Both should be monitored carefully.

Swap rates in the EONIA Index are offered from overnight to one, two, and three weeks, monthly from 1 to 12 months, and yearly from one to two years. The EONIA Swap Index rate is employed for interest rate and other types of swaps and forwards. Twenty-five banks comprise the Panel Committee at the European Banking Federation (EBF) in Brussels that bid and offer for euros, but all banks in the euro zone are involved in the swap market and all have an interest in the EONIA Index (European Banking Federation).

Normally swap and forward traders follow the OIS rates and enter into swap and forward deals based on the OIS. That's fine. For the spot trade and the euro/U.S. dollar in particular, the EONIA Swap Index is a much better, much tighter index rate that tracks the euro much more closely than the OIS.

Notice Exhibit 7.1, the euro/U.S. dollar chart, then refer to Exhibit 7.2, the one-, two-, and three-month charts of the EONIA Index and notice the period from January to May. Spreads and swap rates barely moved, yet as spreads and swap rates widened between the one-and three-month period, the euro/U.S. dollar trended down, but trended up when spreads decreased and swap rates turned up in May. Further notice the upward pressure on the three-to-nine-month swap rates as well as EURIBOR in Exhibit 7.3. This scenario denotes a trend due again to the compression of spreads and resulted in another trend on autopilot. All European rates can be viewed along with various charts and historical rates on the EBF web site.

EXHIBIT 7.1 Euro/U.S. Dollar Chart, March to September, 2010

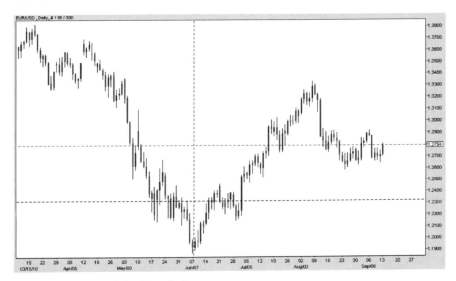

Source: Net Dania, permission by attribution.

EXHIBIT 7.2 EONIA Chart, One, Two, and Three Month

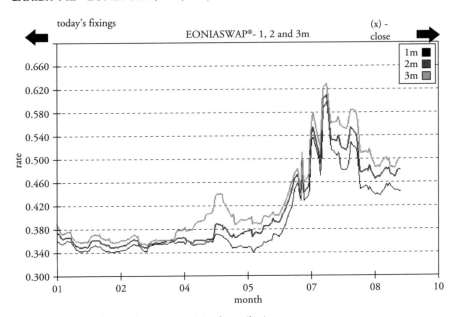

Source: European Banking Federation, permission by attribution.

EXHIBIT 7.3   EURIBOR Chart of Three- and Six-Month Rates

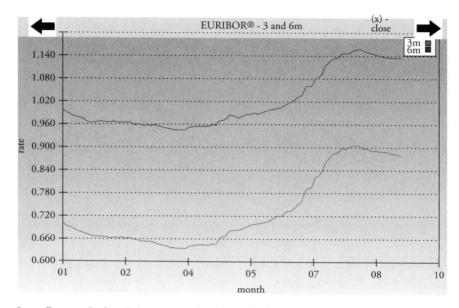

Source: European Banking Federation, permission by attribution.

Australia Bank Bills

After Australia Bank Accepted Bills are settled for the price of the Australian dollar, the Australian Financial Markets Association (AFMA) calculates and releases the Bank Bill Swap (BBSW) reference rate. AFMA manages this rate through bids and offers to swap Australian dollars by 14 banks that comprise the committee of bankers. Bids and offers are submitted to two decimal places with a bid/offer of a five-basis-point spread in each maturity on either side. AFMA institutes established spreads for BBSW in each maturity that are reviewed annually. Currently, the one-to-two-year swap rate attaches to it a six-basis- point spread, the three-to-five-year spread's rate is eight basis points, the 7- to 10-year is 10 basis points, and the 15 -year rate is 14 basis points. This comprises the entire Australian Yield Curve and the bounds of fixed-spread swap rates.

After bids and offers are submitted, AFMA discards the highest and lowest bids and offers, averages the remainder, and releases BBSW rates to four decimal places promptly at 10:00 a.m. Sydney time on their web site for one-to-six-month maturities. This time coincides with the 10:00 a.m.

Sydney Australian dollar/U.S. dollar fix, an important time in Australia trading due to bids and offers for Australia dollar/U.S. dollar. Remaining rates can be viewed by subscription to AFMA or through Thomson Reuters or Bloomberg. This process is again repeated as swap rates are released at end of day at 4:45 p.m. Sydney time in order to further price Australian dollar interest-rate swaps as trading moves to Europe.

The method to factor swap rates and spreads is calculated against Australia Bonds. The three-year bond futures contract's last traded price is employed to factor the two-to-six-year swap, while the 10-year bond futures contract is used to calculate the 7-to-15-year swap. A yield rate is given for one-year maturities.

So what is the price of Australia dollar/U.S. dollar in Australia trading? Swap spreads like the EONIA example are the greatest determinant beside yield-curve changes that would allow Australia dollar/U.S. dollar its best movements. Because the Australia dollar yield curve is stable in terms of bond issuance and the economic situation is currently resilient, swap spreads will determine the answer. There are a number of factors for consideration.

The Australia Securities Exchange (ASX) trades a three- and 10-year swap futures contract. The difference between the three- and 10-year swap contract and the three- and 10-year bond futures contract is the coupon. Interest rate swaps have a 6.5 percent coupon while the Treasury bond has a 6 percent coupon.

Swap curves will always be higher than government-bond curves because swap borrowings occur above bond rates and have a higher cost due to their risk and higher yields. Government yield curves are considered the risk-free rate while the swap curve is the risk because it is above what is considered safe risk. As swaps spreads widened, government bond yields go up and bond prices go down, while a narrowing sends bond prices up and yields down. The question is which side of the Australia dollar/U.S. dollar equation to trade. The perfect scenario is the narrowing of spreads, because bond prices will rise along with Australia dollar/U.S. dollar while Australia dollar/New Zealand dollar will drop and vice versa. Swap spreads in Australia can only be viewed by subscription to AFMA.

New Zealand Swap Rate

For the New Zealand wholesale markets and the swap market in particular, the swap rate is produced by the New Zealand Financial Markets Association (NZFMA). The NZFMA produces reference rates and overseas market rate auctions, and collects, calculates, and reports reference rates for the New Zealand wholesale markets through NZ Data, a growing subscription data feed that allows users to view reference rates in real time. Current subscriptions have been trending up as more banks and institutions around the world become familiar with New Zealand's stable and growing markets. Yet for $100 NZ, anyone can view New Zealand's wholesale rates in real time.

Swap rates are auctioned at end of day between 4:30 and 4:45 p.m. NZ time and reported through SwapClose at 4:46 p.m., a section of NZ Data. Exhibit 7.4 is an example of swap close. Swap rates are factored for New Zealand's government bonds that range from 1- to 15-year maturities. In addition, swap-to-spread pricing is factored for corporate fixed coupon bonds, local authority fixed-coupon bonds, floating-rate notes, and Kauri bonds.

The swap-to-spread basis is created from end-of-day bond fixings released by NZFMA for the New Zealand government and the bonds at 4:45 p.m. New Zealand time. Spreads are added to interpolated yields against various maturities. This is known as the outright yield. This prices the New Zealand dollar as well as interest-rate swaps, both important components of Royal Bank of New Zealand (RBNZ) funding operations. Consider the 2010 report from the Executives Meeting of East Asia Central Banks, an organization comprised of 11 regional central banks.

From January to September 2009, 48 percent of RBNZ funding operations were conducted in FX Swaps. Yet the RBNZ has a "high reliance on FX Swaps, particularly Overnight and Tom/Next trades to meet daily liquidity."(Executive meeting report 2010). One reason why may be the present economic crisis and possibly because NZ exports in another currency. What makes New Zealand attractive is the dominance of yield differentials due to New Zealand's positive and high Official Cash Rate (OCR). The RBNZ

EXHIBIT 7.4   SwapClose, Market Timing

Description	Swap Close Times (NZT)
Market Clear Down	16:00
Contributor Input Times	16:35–16:45
Calculator	16:46
Override Times	16:46–17:30
Market Reset Times	18:00

Source: NZ Financial Markets Association.

swaps New Zealand dollars into another currency and converts back into New Zealand dollars later. New Zealand's institutions conduct business in the interest of the New Zealand dollar but particularly as it relates to appreciation of New Zealand dollar/U.S. dollar, their foremost pair of interest.

The true swap rate for New Zealand's markets is the Bank Bill Reference Rate (BKBM) released about 10:45 New Zealand time and used to settle and adopt new trades such as interest-rate swaps and other various fixed or floating deals during market hours.

End-of-day fixes coincide perfectly with the August 2008 Williams/ Reuters 14:00, 2:00 p.m. New Zealand time fix of the New Zealand dollar/ U.S. dollar. End-of-day swap and bond fixes allow pricing and trading to occur all night throughout other markets until the next New Zealand fix. But the 10:00 a.m. New Zealand fix allows the New Zealand dollar/U.S. dollar to be priced in New Zealand markets in terms of swap and bond pricing. This is another sample of the brilliance of New Zealand's institutions, because not only is the yield curve factored against swap rates but as trading occurs throughout the night in other markets, the price of New Zealand dollar /U.S. dollar represents a true price and a method to gain appreciation of New Zealand's benchmark currency pair. New Zealand's dilemma is time differentials and the ability to connect financial instruments to other markets around the world. Consider a New York morning is a New Zealand night and that summer in New York is winter in New Zealand. New Zealand must constantly be creative to allow the connections to world markets.

Trade Swaps against New Zealand Dollar/U.S. Dollar

The equation of narrowing swap spreads leading to a fall in New Zealand dollar/U.S. dollar is written explicitly and often in news releases at the New Zealand's Stock Exchange (NZX), as well as throughout New Zealand's newspapers such as the *Dominion Post* and the *NZ Herald.*

Spreads narrow and bond prices fall along with the New Zealand dollar, called the Kiwi, is a commonly reported story as newspapers educate the investing public. The spreads of reference are always reported as the shorter-dated two-to-five-year maturities. This accuracy is without question. Possibly the reason for the five-year spread reference is so much bond issuance is brought to market by funding a fixed rate against the five-year swap rate (NZDX). Yet notice Exhibits 7.5 and 7.6 and notice how important and how many rates exist at the short end of the swap and Government-bond yield curves. This is where traders will find answers to New Zealand

EXHIBIT 7.5 ANZ Government Bond Indices

Daily	8-Nov Monday	5 -Nov Friday	4-Nov Thursday	3-Nov Wednesday	2-Nov Tuesday	Duration	Modified Duration
Gross Returns Index							
ANZ NZ Government Stock	1162.55	1163.47	1162.13	1163.54	1164.73	4.01	3.91
ANZ NZ Trading Bonds	1198.52	1199.47	1198.09	1199.54	1200.77	4.01	3.91
ANZ 0- to 3-year maturities	304.79	304.83	304.72	304.90	304.99	1.61	1.58
ANZ 0- to 5 -year maturities	284.48	284.57	284.44	284.68	284.83	2.36	2.31
ANZ 3- to 7-year maturities	341.51	341.78	341.54	342.03	342.38	3.96	3.87
ANZ 1 year & longer maturities	338.63	338.90	338.51	338.92	339.27	4.01	3.91
ANZ 5 year & longer maturities	323.89	324.39	323.65	324.23	324.83	6.72	6.55
ANZ 7 year & longer maturities	359.99	360.55	359.73	360.38	361.04	6.72	6.55
ANZ Call Deposits	547.55	547.42	547.37	547.33	547.28		
ANZ 30D Bank Bills	574.92	574.78	574.73	547.68	574.63		
ANZ 90D Bank Bills	577.52	577.37	577.31	577.26	577.22		
ANZ NZ Inflation-Indexed	314.50	314.56	314.38	314.36	314.47		4.68

Source: NZ Bond Market, permission by attribution.

EXHIBIT 7.6 New Zealand Indices, Swap Indices Nov 8, 2010

Index ID	Index Name	Index Level	Index Move	Yield	Duration	Mod Duration
NZXSW1_10	ANZ All Swaps Index (1Y to 10Y incl.)	141.664707	0.048999	4.698070	3.975543	3.884300
NZXSW1_3	ANZ Short End Swap Index (1Y, 2Y, & 3Y)	137.386797	0.062451	4.062700	1.914446	1.876331
NZXSW1_5	ANZ Short-Mid Curve Swap Index (1Y to 5Y incl)	139.887675	0.060258	4.343085	2.790165	2.730864
NZXSW3_7	ANZ Mid Curve Swap Index (3Y to 7Y incl)	143.554558	0.055459	4.617459	4.262591	4.166400
NZXSW5_10	ANZ Mid-Long End Swap Indices (5Y, 7Y, & 10Y incl)	145.286650	0.028313	4.945654	6.131490	5.983527
NZXSW7_10	ANZ Long End Swap Index (7Y & 10Y)	145.837085	0.019479	5.055051	6.940673	6.769570
NZXSW1Y	ANZ 1-Year Swap Index	132.527171	0.046715	3.559755	0.974971	0.957910
NZXSW2Y	ANZ 2-Year Swap Index	138.178410	0.080336	4.000694	1.929358	1.891499
NZXSW3Y	ANZ 3-Year Swap Index	141.522855	0.060840	4.273105	2.841746	2.782276
NZXSW4Y	ANZ 4-Year Swap Index	143.116399	0.067605	4.452701	3.700959	3.620332
NZXSW5Y	ANZ 5 -Year Swap Index	144.086523	0.04 5760	4.607936	4.512089	4.410448
NZXSW7Y	ANZ 7-Year Swap Index	145.345148	0.047307	4.886049	5.995412	5.852409
NZXSW10Y	ANZ 10-Year Swap Index	146.283374	0.008 528	5.182145	7.885669	7.686480

Source: NZX, Permission by attribution.

dollar/U.S. dollar direction in New Zealand markets. Further notice how duration and modified duration is employed as a tool to track the index. Moreover, New Zealand's benchmark indices can be tracked against the New Zealand dollar/U.S. dollar.

The ANZ swap indices include the one-year swap index, 2 year, 3 year, 4 year, 5 year, 7 year, and 10 year. Aggregate indices include the All Swaps Index that covers the 1- to 10- year maturities. The ANZ Short End Swap Index for one-, two-, and three-year maturities, the ANZ Short Mid Curve Index that covers one to five years, the Mid Curve are three-, five-, and seven-year maturities, the Mid Long End covers 5-, 7-, and 10-year maturities, and the Long End covers 7- and 10-year maturities. Additionally, a Kauri Bond Index, two Bank Bill indices, and a host of government bond indices are perfect measures of New Zealand dollar/U.S. dollar. Due to the importance of the short end of both the government and swap curve, New Zealand Bank Bill-futures traded on the ASX should be viewed as the most important barometer of New Zealand markets and the New Zealand dollar/U.S. dollar. For swaps, narrowing of the two- and five-year spreads sends New Zealand dollar/U.S. dollar down and widening spreads sends it up.

Japan

A 2006 phenomenon inside Japan and among domestic Japanese banks is the swap market. Many reasons exist for this.

The Bank of Japan (BOJ) restructured their operating target in 2006 from outstanding balance of accounts to present connection to Japanese Call rates (Baba). This led to a slow growth into interest rate swaps, but those swaps were initially employed primarily by overseas institutions (Baba).

Not mentioned is the Japanese Bank for International Cooperation, which through the Japanese Finance Corporation developed relationships outside Japan, financed imports and exports, invested in overseas enterprises, and developed relationships to ensure that oil, natural gas, and iron ore would continue to flow into Japan's manufacturing sector. Yet many enterprises were established within the respective nations that trade with Japan to ensure access to natural resources and were financed by foreign currency bonds (Japanese Bank for International Cooperation). Swap trades were vital to these endeavors and the continued health of the Japanese economy because yen had to flow between various nations.

Interest rate swaps were employed using the OIS rate against or included six-month LIBOR against Japanese Government Bond (JGB) futures. As the call rate became a more familiar phenomenon, trades in the OIS rate were used for hedging and/or gain advantage in interest rates since the call rate is a floating daily rate (Baba). Prior to the use of swaps, Euroyen futures were employed for hedging. The second aspect of slow swap market growth is due to the structure of Japanese Banks.

The Japanese banking sector is organized into public and private institutions with each bank serving a distinct function. Public and private banks include six city banks, 64 regional banks that serve only the prefecture in which they reside, 61 foreign banks that account for 0.8 percent of the overall banking market, 19 trust banks, 162 credit cooperatives, and 740 Agricultural Cooperatives. Life insurance companies are deeply intertwined within this structure (Japan Bank Association). There are a number of factors for consideration.

Despite the change to call rates as the BOJ target, the Japanese since 2004 had swap trades completely figured. By 2005, practice trades from fixed to floating and floating to fixed were in the implementation stages by the Ministry of Finance. Not only was a JGB curve established but a swap curve was implemented based on a Quadratic Gaussian model and chosen due to its linearity because of low call rates (Ministry of Finance). This is known more formally as the Hull and White method.

The JGB is the heart of the Japanese economy so swap trades had to be factored to the nth degree before an official trade was implemented. Yet this is normal Japanese analytics. Another problem included the hesitation to publish JGB yield-curve data because a new 40-year JGB was in the planning stages and scheduled for a 2007 release (Ministry of Finance). The proposal at the time was to release JGB interest rates only, and that would equal swap interest minus the spread to satisfy the curve.

Original trades factored as a measure to manage interest rate risk especially large bond redemptions. So a long-term swap included fixed versus floating receipt while the medium term included a floating payment against a fixed receipt. The JGB curve equaled an estimation of the swap curve plus the swap spread. Despite a lengthy study, swaps still represent a small portion of Japanese trading within their banks and institutions for a number of reasons.

The first factor is the call rate is 0.10 percent, and that rate has slight volatility. TIBOR would suffice, but would this rate factor as a fixed or floating leg of a swap and what would be the domestic instrument that could be used against it? For U.S. dollar/Japanese yen, which side of the equation would be employed in a currency swap? To solve this dilemma, the Japanese employ basis swaps where yen LIBOR is exchanged for U.S. dollar LIBOR or vice versa. This leaves the OIS rate.

The OIS rate began in 2007 as a trading vehicle with 31 mostly foreign institutions and nine domestic banks involved in trades (Ministry of Finance). OIS swaps were paired with JGBs, interest-rate swaps, and Euroyen futures. Despite the initial introduction to Japanese society, OIS is still not a huge portion of overall trading and not employed as a funding vehicle by the BOJ.

Overseas swaps represent huge transactions but those deals are tied to currency bonds of the respective nation of business. In European markets, a number of vehicles exist to measure the yen that will be addressed later. The answer for the Japanese market to profit with respect to U.S. dollar/Japanese yen is the JGB or Euroyen futures. The only other alternative to measure risk is watch the credit default swaps that trade on the Tokyo Stock Exchange (TSE).

The Tokyo Stock Exchange in conjunction with Markit iTraxx now trades a series of credit default swap indices. For the Japanese market, the benchmark Japan series 12 is the five-year credit default swap index most watched and reported by market professionals to gauge market risk. It is referred to as the hedge index due to the ability to buy and sell protection against other market positions. The Series 12 index encompasses 50 investment-grade Japanese entities (TSE). As spreads increase, credit deteriorates. This is a sell U.S. dollar/Japanese yen as the cost of finance increases.

Trade Web, LCH Clearnet, and ICAP

All three organizations support swap trades. Trade Web trades yen interest-rate swaps and JGBs against six-month LIBOR from 9:00 a.m. Tokyo time to 4:00 p.m. London time. (Trade Web). ICAP through i-Swap trades interest rate swaps, OIS, cross currency basis swaps, and EONIA. LCH Clearnet clears more than 40 percent of the interest-rate swap market (LCH Clearnet). All are worldwide organizations and all can be employed to track the swap market.

United Kingdom and British Pounds

Interest-rate swaps or better-termed British pound-swap rates are factored based on sterling overnight rates. Sterling overnight rates encompass two aspects, SONIA and British pound six-month LIBOR. Both represent the floating rate side while Overnight Indexed Swaps or OIS are fixed legs.

The OIS side are swap rates that are market-driven rates rather than a rate set by a market association.

SONIA-OIS represents the shortest maturities because of its function as an overnight rate. Contracts rarely exceed six-month terms and most banks trade SONIA-OIS due to interest rate speculation or to meet funding needs (Joyce, 2008).

LIBOR swaps settle against six-month British pound LIBOR with maturities ranging from 2 to 30 years. LIBOR swaps are employed to reduce funding costs and hedge longs in cash markets. (Joyce).

Spreads equal the difference between gilt yields and swap rates. If the spread between British pound LIBOR and OIS widens, interbank lending falls. This is a sell British pound/U.S. dollar. Three methods exist to measure swap rates: government liability curves, bank liability curves, and implied probabilities.

Government liability curves for the BOE is a measure of zero-coupon yields for gilts and GC repo rates with maturities out to two years. This is a daily release by the BOE. Bank liability curves measure shorter maturities such as LIBOR, short sterling futures, and forward-rate agreements for the short forward curve. Interest-rate swaps are included for a longer bank liability forward curve. But the measure here is more to gauge the BOE's Bank Rate rather than a swap rate measured against gilt yields. A final method exists to factor both.

Suppose an instrument was chosen to measure an underlying distribution for the OIS rate and the LIBOR-OIS spread. A distribution should be bounded below zero. Assume a log normal distribution with means equal to the forward OIS rate and forward LIBOR-OIS spread. Aggregate the OIS rate and LIBOR-OIS spread distribution to give the sum of OIS minus the (LIBOR minus the OIS). Compare option-implied LIBOR distributions and search combinations of distributions for OIS rates and LIBOR-OIS spreads to find the best replication of option-implied LIBOR distribution. This is the indicative distribution, a probable distribution for OIS rates and LIBOR-OIS spreads.

The problem associated with the BOE's bank liability curve and implied probabilities is the measure of the BOE's bank rate measured forward over a short period of time, usually three months. Neither method is perfect to measure swap rates, but a better measure of the current 0. 5 percent bank rate. Yet all three can indirectly measure swap rates and the swap curve, as the bank rate will provide direction to the swap rate. The original purpose of swap rates was to supply funding slightly above gilt yields due to the premium involved in the swap transaction. So indirectly swap rates should equal gilt yields of various maturities.

OIS rates were once very stable rates and rarely moved in terms of basis points so OIS represented a perfect fixed-leg option to the SONIA and LIBOR floating leg. Economic crisis caused OIS rates to skyrocket and move far out of market norms. This further caused OIS and the floating interest-rate swap legs to become floating as market uncertainty grew. As OIS became the norm and stable fixed rate, SONIA and LIBOR represented the unsecured portion of the floating leg. Now both are treated as unsecured.

So a better measure was needed to gauge swap rates and gilts against interest rate swaps.

The BOE factors swap spreads as the sum of two-year interest rate swap settles on six-month LIBOR minus two-year OIS plus the sum of two-year OIS rate minus two-year generic gilt spread.

Canada

Canada employs CDOR-OIS as a means to finance interest-rate swaps, yet overnight transactions account for 10 to 20 percent of daily trading volume in U.S. dollar/Canadian dollar (Canadian FX Committee 2010). FX swaps account for 64.3 percent of daily trading volume, 23.8 percent in spot transactions. This says the majority of Canadian official business is financed by a currency other than the Canadian dollar. The vast majority of all U.S. dollar/Canadian dollar transactions were done for seven days or less with the U.S. dollar as the primary foreign currency. Between 2005 and 2010, FX swaps volume remained stable. The last fact is spot U.S. dollar/Canadian dollar spreads on $50 million or more was 8 to 10 points before the economic crisis but widened to 20 to 25 points during the peak of the crisis (Canadian FX Committee 2010). Another aspect to finance is the fixed OIS against a floating CORRA rate. Swap rates here are based on CORRA, Canada's overnight repo rate. As swap spreads widen, sell U.S. dollar/Canadian dollar or long Canadian dollar/U.S. dollar.

Swiss Swaps

SARON is the official overnight rate for the Swiss and is employed in interest-rate swaps. For research, the SNB is by far the worst. If the answer is not found at the SIX Swiss Exchange, a search for Swiss information throughout the Swiss government is futile.

On the SIX Swiss Exchange along with the interactive yield-curve function is the ability to interactively employ Swiss and other nation's swap rates against any nation's yield curves. It is a fabulous tool and worthwhile for traders of all investment instruments due to its high reliability. One can perform bond-nation comparisons with any maturities or individually, compare individually, or compare interest-rate swaps and deposit rates.

United States

Two methods exist to measure the U.S. market. The 30-day Fed funds futures contract tracks the overnight Fed funds rate for a month. But the three-month OIS more closely tracks effective rates and it provides a guide to expectation and probabilities of those rates. The key word is probability as U.S. markets track Fed funds-rate increases or decreases based on probabilities. Other nations use different methodologies.

To calculate, Futures price minus 100, 1.00 minus 0.98 with an expected 25-basis-point change.

$$(\text{Target fed funds}) - (\text{implied rate}) = \text{rate spread}$$

$$\frac{1.00 - 0.98 = 0.02. \ (\text{rate spread})}{(25 \text{ basis point change})} = \text{percent chance of 25 basis point change}$$

$$0.02 \ / \ 0.25 = 0.08$$

No confidence in a rate hike at this point.

What is tracked is U.S. interbank deposit rates that settle based on actual/360. An inverse relationship exists between interest rates and the OIS contract. If interest rates head higher, the contract price falls and vice versa. It's a longer-term gauge inside deposit rates and a great method to trade FOMC meetings and rate expectations.

The purpose for a swap transaction is varied. Some may wish to hedge an interest-rate risk using OIS contracts while others may employ OIS as a forward contract that exchanges fixed for floating streams. Currency swaps are varied as well. Some may borrow in one currency and lend in another currency. Some employ these methods for conversion purposes, while others will for example sell U.S. dollar debt in exchange for another currency. Canada for example employs interest-rate cross currency swaps to fund foreign-currency reserves by issuing fixed-rate domestic bonds then swap into fixed- or floating-rate debt. Many facets of the swap market exist as well as many variations of a swap curve from nation to nation due to the difference in focus to employ monetary policy that meets three-month target rates. Yet since the Lehman Brothers' collapse, the major focus for central banks and traders is the focus on the short term due to market uncertainties and because so many financial instruments now exist that focus on the short end.

Central banks have a three-month horizon with a daily monitoring of overnight rates with the opportunity to hedge any market risk. Money must constantly move in order to keep it working within an economy. For this reason, the swap market can provide vital information in terms of a spot transaction.

The further reason for the increased focus on the swap market is the recent development that central banks employ eight monetary policy meetings a year. These meetings determine policy rates and gauge economic development in the future. This further enhanced the short-term economic focus.

The gauge is the spread. As spreads widen, it's always a sell position as the cost of business is too high. To understand this varied market is to understand the forward market.

Outright Forwards

The method to connect interest rate swap conditions is to employ forward-implied rates. The forward price of a currency must relate to an interest-rate differential between two currencies. The classic definition says it assumes an arbitrage condition is possible if parity doesn't exist.

A formula to look at this relationship is:

$$t_i^* - i_t = se_{t+1} - s_t + p_t$$

where

t_i^* = foreign period nominal interest rate,
i_t = domestic period interest rate,
s_t = spot rate (foreign to domestic in logs),
se_{t+1} = market one step ahead forecast for the spot rate at t, and
p_t = risk premium.

This formula captures bond-yield differentials that reflect expected exchange-rate movements over the life of the bond, plus risk. This methodology is termed covered-interest parity and is designed to determine where the spot price is trading in relation to the forward rate. The correct term is uncovered Interest Parity but if a position is covered by an interest rate, it's no longer uncovered. The purpose of both serves as a method to determine interest rates and conditions of parity. Much has been written on this topic in the 30 years since its early inception. Forward points actually found its beginnings since World War II, but its importance as a trading vehicle began when the gold standard was set aside in exchange for floating exchange rates.

The formula

$$F = S\,(1 + r/1 + rf\,)t$$

where

F = the current forward rate,
S = current spot rate,
r = domestic interest rate for term t,
rf = foreign interest rate for term t, and
t = time to delivery.

The formula can also be viewed as

$$F = S(1 + \text{rate cc1 } t)/(1 + \text{rate cc2 } t)$$

where

F = Forward rate,
S = spot,
cc1 = interest rate of currency 1,
cc2 = interest rate of currency 2, and
t = time.

The key term is foreign to domestic interest rate. This category is where overnight rates are factored, LIBOR, effective interest rates, repo rates, yield curves and market rates such as a T-Bill. A spot price and forward point can be found within the calculation.

A forward points is the most important and vital link to understanding currency spot prices as well as their relationship to other pairs and financial instruments.

The key to forward points is points per day, which is the link to determine the cost of maintaining a position overnight through either a Tom/Next, overnight, or spot/Next trade. These are rollover rates and are debited or credited to accounts at the 5:00 p.m. EST closing.

Outright forward points trade at a discount or premium depending on which side of the currency pair is the lesser or greater interest-rate currency. Forward points are quoted against spot. A long or short position is debited or credited based on interest rates that translate to forward points and factored into a spot price. The determination to roll over daily is how many forward points are debited or credited based on the 5:00 closing.

If a trader is long the greater interest-rate currency pair, that account will be credited and debited for the lesser interest-rate currency to reflect the premium or discount in each pair. The greater interest-rate side of a pair is the premium, while the lesser pair is the discount. Its market is determined based on any day's trading.

More important to forward points is the prediction to determine possible future spot prices. Outright forwards and forward curves are good factors, a future prediction based on present market conditions based on interest rates. Today's forward points drive future forward predictions.

Forward points are bounded by the interest rate differentials within each currency pair. Those interest-rate differentials are reflected in the market by traders that anticipate changes to monetary policy made by central banks. Both sides are bounded by interest rates, but short interest rates change daily so forward points will change daily. Central banks maintain rates 25 to 50 basis points from current rates yet markets and traders anticipate future rates reflected in bonds, yields, and forward points. Sometimes the market over-shoots the target, sometimes not. So forward points are bounded within the context of a spot price by the bond/yield interplay on one side and monetary policy on the other. Monetary policy means rates rise, fall, or stay the same and it's the overall driver of spot prices.

The twist is that each central bank meets eight times yearly but not at the same time. So currency pairs maintain monetary policy within its price based on two monetary policies. The interest rate is the measure and is found in the markets because it streamlines the tedious process to factor every economic announcement, every bond issuance, every cash flow, and every basis point yield.

So a forward point represents an interest rate, an expected rise, fall, or stasis condition and is reflected in the bond/yield interplay on a daily basis. Because currency pairs are two-sided equations between two nations, yield-curve spreads could be measured by forward points to arrive at a daily spot price. Yet as markets, bond prices and yields change, so do forward points and spot prices. Forward points can rise and fall within a trading day. Fixing times are most important for pairs and forward points because they establish a spot reference price for central banks, importers and exporters, banks, and major companies to lock in a price. Fixing times are best points for profit because they distill confidence in a price and the market will follow its price, so volatility may occur if the market price is far from the fix.

The idea of interest-rate differentials is the method how and where money must seek its yield, yet it is the cost of capital. Forward points represent interest income or the cost of capital.

For example, forward points are quoted as 0.0094, which means multiply by either 100 or 1000 and the price of interest is established for one side of a currency pair. If the other side is, for example, 74, multiply by 100 or 1000 and the other side is established. Interest payments are factored. To receive the 94 in interest from the bid side, a buy forward/sell spot is transacted or a sell spot/buy forward. To gain the 94 interest, buy spot and sell the other side of the pair forward, the 74. Forward means from one day to 10 years. Positions can always be rolled over if a trade was entered for a short duration. A rolled position means rolling over the same trade for a longer time frame. The offer side works the same, sell forward/buy spot. The methodology is to buy/sell, sell/ buy. Look at bids and offers as lend/borrow. And look at forward points as the guide to interest income. Refer to the currency swap examples above. All take the form sell/buy, buy sell. A nation like Japan with a deflationary environment and low interest rates must seek higher yield in other markets. Monetary policy in Japan has been stifled by current and past conditions, so traders and investors sought yield in higher interest-rate paying nations. This was the basis for the methodology for carry trades that later became accepted practice and the basis for the yen to become the funding currency. Lastly, it became the basis for the Japanese to transfer operations to offshore markets.

Market anticipation in terms of forward curves alludes to construction of the curves. Banks may employ OIS strips, zero-coupon strips, or forward/forward FRA strips to discount two different yield curves.

As time progressed and the use of swaps became an increasing phenomenon, forwards were factored for implementation in various currency-swap arrangements.

Forward traders are actually spot traders. The difference is forward traders trade based on forward points, interest-rate differentials. Those interest-rate differentials are found between two nations' yield curves and depend on which of two maturities is the focus.

Calculate Forward Points, Yield Curves, and Spot Prices

The formula is:

Interest rate differential × number of days × outright/interest rate base
(Day Count) × Spot × 100

Suppose Australian dollar/U.S. dollar yield spread is 418.9 bp or 4.189 percent/U.S. yields 2.625 percent.

FX points midday = 790 = 0.8786/0.8706 2 year outright/Spot = 0.9581/84. From above formula-4.188 percent × 730 (2Year) × 0.8796/365 × 0.95825 (Mid spot price) × 100 = 2689.148/38090.27 = 7.059935/100 = .0705 points market forward.

Or suppose $1 is invested in Australia at 6.813 percent and $1 is invested in the United States at 2.625 percent for one year. The difference would be the dollar's discount reflected in spot points 0.95825 × 0.04188 = .0401 or 401 pts, twice that is 802. Mid forward = 790.

As financial instruments constantly trade, interest rates will change along with fast market movements. So a calculation must be made constantly to find a mismatch of rates. Calculations are provided for forward points.

There are two factors for consideration within the formula. Day counts must be specific and interest payment schedules must be factored in monthly, quarterly, semi-annual, or as bullet pay. *Bullet pay* is defined as no interest payments. Principal and interest is paid upon maturity.

Forward points in terms of a currency price can be factored against many financial instruments. The key to other calculations is to divide the cash rates by the futures rates. A stock market index can be factored against a spot price by fair value calculations. The key is to determine index points and factor those points against spot forward points.

In bond terms, a U.S. 30-year Treasury is priced in thirty-seconds is $312.50 each thirty-second or $3,000 per point. One basis point on a 10-year bond is $1,000 plus interest flows quarterly, semi-annually, or annually. A foreign bond is equal to one basis point British pound 1,000 and British pound 3,000. Foreign bonds trade 0.01 percent. The key to understand foreign bonds in relation to spot prices and forward points is to understand and measure cash flows.

In the United States, average treasury yields on any given day trade about 1.48 for the two-year, 2.18 for the five-year, and 3.21 for the 10-year. Each nation's yield curve must be measured against these rates for U.S. dollar traded pairs.

Conclusion

This chapter focused on the various types of swaps. It began with currency swaps, cross currency swaps, and basis swaps and examples were provided, as well as types of traders that would employ each type. Swaps comprise many types, such as OIS swaps, and connect to other revenue sources. All types were provided by explanation and example, as well as types of markets that employed these instruments. Forward points and outright forwards were highlighted and explained and examples provided for each instrument.

CHAPTER 8

Stock and Bond Markets

The focus of this chapter is nation-to-nation stock and bond markets and the dynamics of the two markets in relation to currency prices. Bond markets are indicators to stock market direction because of their early opening from formal stock market opens. This interplay as an indicator prices yields and yields price currency pairs. An in-depth look into each nation and the dynamics of each structure will be highlighted, as well as the characteristics of each currency pair within the respective market.

Stock markets in the respective nations that are attached to one side of a currency-pair trade can provide vital answers to direction of that pair for many reasons. The first point is stock markets determine direction of the interplay between bonds and yields. In this instance, it answers the question whether to go long or short a pair in a particular market. This represents profits or losses.

Secondly, stock markets must be looked upon as a risk indicator. In the United States, Germany, and Canada, rising stock markets are measures of risk because government bond yields rise with the currency. Stock markets ebb and flow, so currency pairs will ebb and flow as pairs follow the bond yield interplay.

Rising stock markets represent the fact that LIBOR, repurchase agreements, effective, and swap rates all fell into a perfect pattern that allowed the rise. Currency pairs move based on interest rates, so sometimes the proper alignment of the most important of rates allows stock markets to rise, yet an improper alignment allows stock markets to fall. This equation is not necessarily written in stone as outside developments can disrupt the balance, but it's always better to follow the equation as a high probability for stock-market moves. Economic performance is the sole reason for stock-market movements, up during good times and down during bad.

Stock markets provide either early warning down signs or positive up signs that ensure currency pair direction. Yet they provide answers as to which pair to trade and in what direction to take that particular pair. Because the Australian Stock market opened doesn't mean only the Australian dollar/U.S. dollar should be traded. Almost any pair can be traded in any market. The question must be which pair and what direction, long or short? If a stock market chooses not to rise or fall and instead ranges, that can be a vital source of profits as range tops and bottoms can be bought and sold. For this reason, stock markets should be evaluated as closely as any currency pair and measured against ranges.

To hold currency pairs through many markets means a further evaluation and proper knowledge of other nations' stock markets. Stock markets have definite opening and closing times within nations, but in many instances stock market openings and closings overlap around the world. This could have dramatic effects on a trade held throughout many markets. An up market in Australia doesn't automatically presuppose an up market in Japan, so an exit may be necessary from the Australian market before the Japanese opening. But continuity may exist, so a trade can possibly run throughout other markets. London, Frankfurt, and the SIX Swiss Exchange all trade at some point together on any trading day, while Canada and the United States open later in the day—that leaves these five markets trading at the same time. This situation could represent enormous profits, but without proper knowledge, huge losses.

Stock markets around the world sometimes correlate, sometimes not. Correlations occur provided an economic situation doesn't force a change of direction. Wars, natural disasters, and even political personnel changes can force dramatic and immediate directional changes.

Correlations normally occur within regions such as Australia and New Zealand, or the United States and Canada. Yet each nation is completely a separate entity with various monetary policies, various interest rates, and various objectives to achieve its goals. For this reason, stock markets will react very differently. A 100-point rise in Japan doesn't correlate to the United States market rising 100 points. Correlations indicate ups or downs rather than exact point movements. The key to correlations is to follow the leaders as they provide direction, yet leaders doesn't necessarily correlate as the United States or Europe, because anything can occur throughout the markets within a trading cycle. A leader could be Australia as easily as Japan.

For currency pairs in U.S. markets, always look at yen crosses as the measure of stock-market risk. Australian dollar/Japanese yen should move in conjunction with Australian dollar/U.S. dollar if confidence exists. Canadian dollar/Japanese yen is the premier measure of risk in Canada trade simply because of its correlation to oil. Confidence in Canada and the U.S. economic system means Canadian dollar/Japanese yen should move in conjunction with Canadian dollar/U.S. dollar. British pound/Japanese yen should move in conjunction with British pound/U.S. dollar. euro/Japanese yen should move in lockstep with euro/U.S. dollar. A rising stock market may see for example euro/U.S. dollar rise, but if euro/Japanese yen doesn't follow, the stock market bond/yield interplay is not a sign of confidence. Without confidence in stock-market moves, any rise in, say, euro/U.S. dollar without euro/Japanese yen as a follower, means euro/U.S. dollar can't hold any gains. Euro/Swiss franc, however, will always maintain its dominance as the premier measure of risk. U.S. dollar/Swiss franc and Swiss franc/U.S. dollar confidence must be measured with euro/Swiss franc, especially during European trade. Yet euro/Swiss franc serves well as a risk measure in U.S. markets.

Stock markets, just like currency pairs, tend to function in wave patterns during normal economic periods. Each nation or region experiences tops or bottoms throughout any given year. To know tops and bottoms helps to understand how to profit with various currency pairs.

All markets and all financial instruments experience this wave pattern and the patterns are as definite as the seasons of change. It's as if each nation receives a turn in the wave-pattern structure. Through this structure, stock markets find tops and bottoms, currency pairs experience tops and bottoms, bonds and yields experience tops and bottoms, and LIBOR experiences tops and bottoms. One must wonder if wave-pattern structures were a manmade design as a consequence to ensure that every nation prospers or the Invisible Hand of self-regulating markets first outlined by Adam Smith in 1759 in *The Theory of Moral Sentiments* and later in 1776 in *An Inquiry into the Nature and Causes of the Wealth of Nations.*

With the introduction of the euro in 1999, the newly formed G-20 Finance Ministers began regular meetings to discuss world economic events. At the time of the 1997 Asian crisis, when Asian currencies crashed, the introduction of the euro was foremost on their minds. The statement in 1999 from the first meeting in Berlin began with a policy to "make globalization work." Further, "evaluation by nations' compliance with international codes and standards in transparency and financial sector policy" and "examination of differing exchange-rate regimes and role to cushion impact of international financial crisis." They sought reform and globalization, an integration of the world and markets.

The 2000 Montreal meeting sought to "reduce countries' vulnerabilities to financial crisis including exchange-rate arrangements." From 1999 onward, governments began the policy of management in terms of capital flows, trade policy, movement of goods, taxes, debt, and strengthening of international institutions to carry out these policies evidenced by further communications.

Further, the G-10 nations, the forerunner to the G-20, voted in 1999 to change the name and mandate of the Bank of International Settlements (BIS) euro Currency Standing Committee from a mandate that monitored off-shore deposits and lending-market issues to the Committee on the Global Financial System to recognize, analyze, report, and monitor threats to financial stability (BIS). Whether manmade or the Invisible Hand, one may never know. The import is to understand market ebbs and flows, but be aware of policies that may disrupt the present global-market order.

All financial instruments ebb and flow in waves, so each can be employed as an indicator as a check on the other. Fall is the premier time for the euro/U.S. dollar to top in its wave pattern, but then it changes as the wave-pattern falls and a new leader reigns. To be successful at trading means only to know and find these patterns and understand the structural changes. Unusual economic times may temporarily disrupt a pattern, but eventually all markets normalize and revert back to the mean of seasonal wave patterns.

The caveat to stock price rises and falls is the measurement of equity prices. For example, how can a 50-point rise in the New Zealand stock market be measured? In New Zealand dollar terms, the rise is high, but compared to U.S. dollar terms the rise is minimal. The same scenario holds with New Zealand bond and yields. Some wonder why New Zealand dollar/U.S. dollar doesn't move much in Wellington trading, and the answer is sometimes it can't because rises and falls in stock market, bond, and yields don't move enough for change to occur in U.S. dollar terms, but they are sufficient for New Zealand dollar terms.

Bonds and yields move currency prices rather than equity markets. Equity markets are the indication of the overall structure that is measured in local nation dollars and an insight to bond/yield direction.

The other caveat to New Zealand movement is this market begins a new trading day and trades by itself for the first few hours of trade.

Many methods exist to measure stock market indices. Some employ Price to Earnings (P/E) Ratios as measured by Index level/Earnings per share are equal to Index P/E or dividend yields where yields are equal to Dividends per share per index level. Others employ a volatility gauge, an indicator such as a moving average, or mathematical formula such as a Sharpe Ratio.

Fair Value

The Chicago Mercantile Exchange (CME) employs an Index Fair Value formula:

$$\text{Index Futures} = \text{Cash} \ (1 + r \ (x/360)) - \text{dividends}$$

The formula encompasses current index level, index dividends, futures days to expiration, and present interest rates. Fair value is defined as futures priced to cash. A vast majority of index pricing occurs around a fair-value price (CME).

To calculate:

S&P 500 Futures price = 1157.00 pts,
S&P Cash index = 1146.00 pts,
interest rates = 5.7 percent,
dividends to expiration of futures = 3.47 pts converted to S&P Index pts and factored by addition of dividends in index divided by index divisor, and
days to expiration of futures = 78 days.

$$\text{Fair Value} = 1146 \ (1 + .057 \ (78/360)) - 3.47 = 1156.68$$
$$1157.00 - 1156.68 = .32 \text{ futures overpriced (CME web site example)}.$$

S&P 500 Dividend Yield = 1.40, convert to
S&P points = 1146.00 × .0140
= 16 pts yearly, 78/360 (CME website example).

Notice the term futures priced to cash. This says in the market or on the sidelines to hold cash.

Theoretical Fair Value is the relationship between a stock or the index that comprises that stock, in this instance the Canadian S&P/TSX 60. Theoretical Fair Value allows a short in one market and long in another. The formula is:

$$F = S \ (1 + (i - d) \ t/365)$$

where
F = Theoretical fair value of futures contract,
S = Spot index value,
i = interest rate reflecting cost of funds,
d = dividend rate, and
t = number of days remaining until expiration of the futures contract.

Bonds

Bond markets open before stock markets in many nations. This dynamic can presage the performance of stock markets. It's the premier indicator to determine if a stock market will open up or down, if a trade can run long or short.

Stock-market openings ensure that currency-pair direction is established, whether the trade can run, and how far. The method to check this dynamic is to monitor the interplay of government bonds and yields. U.S. stock markets that continually rise means bond yields continue to ascend. Stock markets that range indicate bond prices and yields ebb and flow throughout any trading session or through given periods. And down U.S. stock markets indicate bond prices are rising. Any one of the three dynamics may mean a trend or range. And any of the three dynamics represent profits.

Anyone can track stock markets around the world from any computer, from any news service, day and night. Stock prices and market information may be delayed by as much as 20 minutes when viewed from an open computer, real time from a news service. Yet the SIX Swiss Exchange allows real-time prices to be viewed. The time to really watch is at the time of an important news announcement in the United States, because all prices rebalance between the two markets.

Bond prices and yields work the opposite way in the world from the U.S. examples. In the United States, stock markets rise along with yields as bond prices fall. The opposite scenario holds in other nations. Bond prices are connected to stock market rises and falls and yields move counter. For example, as the Financial Times and the London Stock Exchange (FTSE) stock index falls in London trading, so does the government gilt Bond price, while yields rise. The government gilt bond is then tied to economic performance of the overall British economy. The British pound/U.S. dollar then falls as the euro/British pound rises.

The reason for the British pound/U.S. dollar fall is not necessarily the bond price, although that is important in itself, but the yield may be too high to borrow in British pound terms along the yield curve. Euro/British pound is employed then to temper the exorbitant borrowing cost for the premier currency pair of Great Britain.

Understand the importance of the yield curve in terms of spreads and the widening, narrowing, and flattening of curves. All have profound importance for a currency-pair trade in terms of direction, and it answers the question how far will a pair travel.

Yields are factored as 0.01 is equal to 1/100th of a point. The proper term is basis point. Bonds are quoted almost the same for most nations, except for the United States, where it is measured as thirty-seconds of a U.S. dollar.

British gilts are traded on a price basis in 1/100ths with a t + 1 settlement based on actual/actual semi-annual coupons. Prices are clean as opposed to index gilts, which are dirty priced due to their index link, whose price floats.

Japanese Government Bonds (JGBs) are traded and quoted based on a yield basis, while Canada bonds are traded on a price basis in decimals quoted in hundredths of a point.

Central banks compare, contrast, and calculate each other's stock markets, bonds, and yields. The purpose is to measure economic performance in other nations in terms of inflation, targets, and gross domestic product (GDP). Most important is to understand other countries' economic performance in terms of their own borrowing costs, and highlight possible future scenarios. Central banks are normally far ahead of any yield curve in their models, calculations, and possible future scenarios. A few examples follow.

Swiss franc, British pound, Australian dollar, and New Zealand dollar move in their own markets based on sovereign bonds. If, for example, the British pound/U.S. dollar rises in price during London trade and gilt purchases aren't matched by the British pound/U.S. dollar buying, the British pound/U.S. dollar move was false. It lacks trend and confidence and could be due to market speculators or possibly from a one-time major purchase in the spot market by a central bank. Many scenarios exist as to why. The important takeaway is that trends must have confidence and conviction backed by interbank instruments to support the spot price. Without support, price moves are false and can be sold at their peak. This example holds for Swiss franc, Australian dollar, and New Zealand dollar. Yet it holds for any pair.

Reserve versus Funding Currency Pairs

Before we look into the bond-price yield scenario, it's important to understand the currency-pair arrangement as it relates to a bond. Currency pairs are arranged as financing mechanisms to fund cross-border trade, to finance government bonds in whatever nation's currency, and used as a means for carry trades.

Carry trades fund one side of a currency pair by selling one interest rate currency for another. The Japanese yen was the most popular funding currency over the years, due not only to its low interest rate but continuous drop in interest rates. The yen was then paired with Australian dollar, British pound, euro, Swiss franc, U.S. dollar, New Zealand dollar, and Canadian dollar in this general manner, Australian dollar/Japanese yen. Notice Japanese yen was always the second part of the equation. In this instance, the Japanese yen was the funding currency while the first pair in the equation is known as the reserve.

A low interest-rate currency will always exist to be matched against a higher interest-rate currency. It's the nature of the markets in economic terms. This strategy worked to earn interest for traders and investors, and allowed cross-border funding to be completed by importers, exporters, major companies, and governments.

In bond terms, the strategy in the respective market aligned with the Japanese yen will always be to sell the funding currency and buy the reserve. A low-yielding currency will always be attached to a higher-yielding currency, it's the difference between a successful and nonsuccessful economy. So the British pound/Japanese yen would always be a buy in London trading, as stocks in London rise along with gilt prices, and sold as stocks drop along with gilt prices so the yen will seek its yield. A higher interest-rate currency will always outperform a low interest-rate currency when matched. But what if the arrangement was not this simple?

Suppose British pound/Australian dollar was matched against each other as a misalignment of a funder against a reserve. In this case, Australian dollar has a 4.50 percent interest rate that rose over the years against 0.50 for the British pound that dove over the years.

In gilt bond terms, the British pound would always be sold against the Australian dollar as the U.K. economy deteriorated and the gilt price followed. In Australian bond terms and in Australian markets, no reason exists to buy this pair. It doesn't serve any of the above purposes. The result has led to a continuous downtrend for British pound/Australian dollar since 2002. Yet this represents overall directional trend. It doesn't mean that quick short-term gains can't be earned in up British pound markets as the gilt rises. Gains will be very short term and they will come quickly, but the possibility exists to profit. This strategy goes against trend and it's never recommended, but for quick profits, it's always possible because currency-pair prices are always mobile.

The same scenario applies for euro/Australian dollar. Australian dollar rates rose as euro rates decreased, so nobody saw a need to ever buy this pair, so in turn it, too, dropped. But this scenario represents overall direction and it doesn't mean possibilities do not exist for example to profit quickly in the euro market. In down Australian markets, quick profit opportunity may exist, but take profits quickly. What if interest rates are closely aligned and what if much cross-border trade occurs within one pair? British pound/Swiss franc fits this category.

British pound/Swiss franc has a 0.50 percent rate for British pound and 0.25 percent interest rate for Swiss franc, so this represents an excellent trade in terms of a funding and reserve currency pair to represent a balance. Both sides of this pair need each other to satisfy cross-border trade rather than an advantage in interest rates. These pairs represent range trades over a period of time, as Swiss franc will be bought in up markets on the Swiss Market Index (SMI) and sold in down markets as Swiss bonds decline. Likewise the British pound will be bought in up London markets, as British pound will follow the gilt price up, and sold as the gilt price falls.

What occurs is a range trade until one side or the other changes interest rates one way or another. If one side changes its rates and the other side doesn't, a trend situation will occur and disrupt the present balance. The reserve versus funding structure will then align itself in another manner, depending on which side changes its rates and in what direction those rates change. The possibility exists to even drop this pair from funding and reserve arrangements in favor of another pair more conducive to funding arrangements in interest-rate terms. Currency pairs fall in and out of favor over years as interest rates rise and fall between nations.

For example, when the Federal Reserve signals that interest rates will be low for a considerable period in the future, it's the green light to markets that the U.S. dollar can be employed as a funding currency against a reserve. In this instance, sell the U.S. dollar against all other currency pairs just as the Japanese yen was sold against all its currency pair alignments. With present low interest-rate environments as exist today, more than a few pairs can be chosen as a reserve. Until the economic situation changes and interest again rises, this arrangement will be the market order.

Globex and the Currency Bond/Yield Interplay

Currency pairs once shared the bond price/yield connection between each other, but the historic connection changed with the introduction of Globex in 1992 by the CME. It's a matter of semantics.

For example, when it's said the U.S. dollar follows a yield or bond price in another nation, the meaning is actually tied to the Dow or Standard & Poor's (S&P) futures price. The semantics changed with the introduction of Globex.

Globex is an electronic trading system that allows CME products to be traded after normal U.S. market hours close. Globex allowed world traders to be connected, trade other markets, and monitor trades from market to market around the world. More importantly, it allowed the U.S. dollar to be a free-floated instrument when futures and options were introduced along with the S&P 500 futures contract in 1993 (CME).

The Japanese connected to other world markets when futures began trading on the Nikkei 225 in 2004. Now Tokyo and U.S. markets had a solid connection around the clock. The U.S. dollar/Japanese yen relationship then had a more profound meaning.

No longer was the bond yield connection monitored based on one market. It was now monitored between two markets so the meaning and purpose of yield curves became more pronounced as a gauge to monitor and evaluate currency pairs. Yet the bond connection became more crystallized as well when trading of currencies ventured into the retail market.

Retail traders can now connect with other currency markets around the world with the help of the Globex connection through use of the home computer. The Globex web site now allows interactive charts to be managed by anyone, as well as an insight into volumes based on futures contracts on the S&P 500.

New Zealand

The majority of the world watches and reports on New Zealand's top companies that comprise the NZX 50 index that trades on the New Zealand Stock Exchange. Yet the NZX Mid-Cap Index that comprises 35 medium-sized companies plus the NZX 50 is the better barometer to gauge the health of New Zealand's stock market and overall economy. It's a broader index of companies, therefore a broader index to measure New Zealand's stock market.

The NZX Group at the NZX issues an operational report every month that highlights, among other points, trading volumes. September 2010 saw $2.2 billion of stocks bought compared to $104, 355, 670 in fixed-interest instruments better known as debt instruments. June 2010 saw $1,716 million stocks bought and $133 million in bonds. What is missing in this equation is the delineation between government and corporate bonds.

The New Zealand Debt Exchange (NZDX) is New Zealand's bond market. The bond market opens for a pre-opening from 8:45 a.m. to 9:00 a.m. New Zealand time, while the formal market opens at 9:00 a.m. and closes at 4:45 p.m. This is the opportunity to evaluate trades before the formal market opens. The New Zealand dollar 11:00 a.m. fix occurs while the market is open. This should be viewed with more importance than stock-market performance because it establishes the New Zealand price for the New Zealand market. This aligns the New Zealand dollar to the bond price. New Zealand government bonds are tied to economic performance of the New Zealand economy, so in turn is the stock market. A rising bond price means a rising stock market.

New Zealand's NZX pre-open is from 9:00 a.m. to 10:00 a.m. The NZX begins at 10:00 a.m. and closes at 4:45 p.m. New Zealand time.

The New Zealand markets do not trade futures, but that will change in 2011 as index futures and options will begin trade. Whole Milk Powder futures began trade October 2010 while Skim Milk, Cheese, Milk Fat and Butter Anhydrous remain in the planning stages. For New Zealand this represents a huge opportunity, as these products are of profound importance to the health of New Zealand's economy. Whole milk powder, Skim Milk Powder and Anhydrous Milk fat futures and options began trade in New Zealand while the remaining products are in planning stages.

To calculate the NZX 50:

$$\text{(Gross Index t)} = \Sigma \text{ (Indexed Shares)} \times \text{(Last Price)}$$
$$+ \Sigma \text{ (Indexed Shares)} \times \text{(Distribution per Share)}$$
$$\times \text{(Gross Index t} - 1)/\Sigma \text{ (Indexed Shares)}$$
$$\times \text{(Adjusted opening price)}$$

The NZX is a free-float market capitalization. NZX 50 companies include 18 services, 6 properties, 5 energy companies, 7 goods companies, and 14 primary companies.

Trade Strategy

New Zealand government bonds are tied to economic performance of the New Zealand economy. This means that during good economic times bond prices, along with stock markets, will always rise simultaneously. Currently, economic performance is fine in New Zealand, so evaluate New Zealand dollar/U.S. dollar in this context. As stock markets rise, the bond price rises and in turn New Zealand dollar/U.S. dollar will rise. This is a long position and short when stock markets dive with bond prices

New Zealand stock markets top somewhere in the April to May period. Historically, April to August see down markets. Up and down markets for

New Zealand generally means two-to-three hundred, even 400 points a month, on rare occasions.

Measured in New Zealand dollars, when stock markets dive during summer months in the United States, which is actually winter in New Zealand, Australian dollar/New Zealand dollar rises. View Exhibit 8.1, a historic chart of Australian dollar/New Zealand dollar along with Exhibit 8.2, a historic chart of the NZ 50 stock market.

May is the premier uptrend month for Australian dollar/New Zealand dollar. A note of caution as this pair is very volatile and the payout is small in U.S. dollar terms and for U.S. traders. A 100-point gain equates to about $50 in exchange-rate terms.

Trade the New Zealand markets like this. Down stock markets will see New Zealand dollar/U.S. dollar down and Australian dollar/New Zealand dollar up as the government bond price falls along with stock markets. Australian dollar/New Zealand dollar rises along with New Zealand bond yields and falling stock markets. This serves for trends and general daily ebbs and flows. Both pairs can be bought and sold continuously as bonds and yields ebb and flow throughout any trading day.

EXHIBIT 8.1   Historic Chart of Australian Dollar/New Zealand Dollar

Source: Market Scope 2.0. Note: granted permission by FXCM with Attribution.

EXHIBIT 8.2   Historic Chart of NZ 50 Stock Market

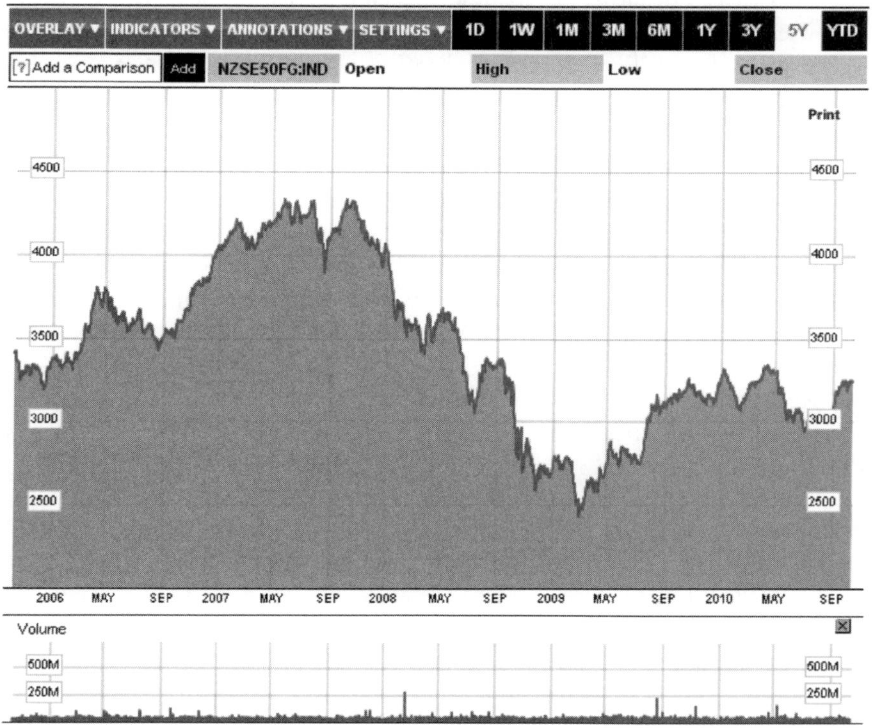

Source: Bloomberg Finance, L.P.

Yet the real measure for direction of New Zealand markets is the S&P 500. When U.S. markets close, New Zealand opens, so New Zealand serves as a direct connection to the U.S. markets. If U.S. markets close down, chances are good New Zealand markets will trade down and probably close down because the S&P 500 futures contract will still reflect the down U.S. day. Directional changes occur only if a market event changes the direction.

New Zealand dollar/Japanese yen is another important pair to consider. Generally, Japanese yen likes bond yields. But like its counterpart Australia, the New Zealand economy is generally performing well. What does this say to bonds measured by economic performance and a rising stock market? It says yields won't perform quite as well for the Japanese. So look not to sell New Zealand dollar/Japanese yen, look to buy New Zealand dollar/Japanese yen for Japanese purposes.

The Japanese would love the yen to be tied to the economic performance of New Zealand in terms of Japanese yen/New Zealand dollar. It then earns New Zealand dollars against the yen as the economy continues to perform well. Both sides of New Zealand dollar/Japanese yen should be considered before a strategy is implemented. One side will always top as the other pair bottoms.

Measure New Zealand dollar/Japanese yen against yields between both nations. As spreads widen, it's a sell New Zealand dollar/Japanese yen and buy when spreads narrow. This is a measure of trade and borrowing costs, higher spreads are more costly. New Zealand dollar spreads narrow when the NZX is down and the Nikkei 225 is up as Japanese yields will fall and compression will occur between the two yields. Spreads widen when NZX is up and the Nikkei is down.

Again the interest-rate disparity with New Zealand and the remaining nations of the industrialized world must be considered, because capital flows into New Zealand both as investments and as flows into New Zealand markets, which are quite good. The official cash rate (OCR) in New Zealand is 2.75 percent, far above any nation we discuss in this tome except Australia. So any pair against New Zealand dollar should be sold in New Zealand trading hours. Pairs such as New Zealand dollar/euro, New Zealand dollar/Swiss franc, New Zealand dollar/British pound, and New Zealand dollar/Canadian dollar are all sells, provided the bond-yield scenario holds. In other markets, present arrangements may or may not work. A reconfiguration of pairs may be necessary. New Zealand dollar/U.S. dollar should always be a buy-on-dip strategy, provided economic conditions hold.

What about the British pound/Swiss franc in New Zealand markets? The answer is why trade it since it doesn't have a connection to New Zealand or its markets, nor does the British pound side have a connection because their markets are not yet opened for trading nor is the Swiss. There is never an intersection between the two markets.

When New Zealand opens for trading, it trades by itself for about two hours while the world awaits the ASX opening in Australia. At this time, the U.S. market closed about two hours prior. U.S. markets will set direction for New Zealand markets.

Think about the New Zealand dollar 4:00 p.m. fix and its relation to other markets. Once New Zealand markets close, the New Zealand dollar must be priced for other markets, but New Zealand time zones are quite different. At 4:00 p.m. New Zealand time, New Zealand is ahead of euro trading in Frankfurt and Swiss franc trading in Zurich by 11 hours, ahead 12 hours for London trading and the British pound. At 4:00 p.m. New Zealand time, it's 4:00 a.m. in London. The New Zealand dollar hardly touches the major European markets. Instead, the Canadian and U.S. markets in terms of New Zealand dollar/Canadian dollar and New Zealand dollar/U.S. dollar are prime trading times for the New Zealand dollar. Plus British Bankers Association (BBA) LIBOR is released at 11:00 a.m. London, 11:00 p.m. New Zealand, after the New Zealand market closes. The LIBOR release at 5:00 a.m. New York time is important to watch for New Zealand dollar direction.

As New Zealand markets close, the New Zealand dollar is no longer tied to its bond market, so it will seek yields in other markets. The New Zealand dollar/U.S. dollar will follow S&P direction on Globex until the formal opening of the New York Stock Exchange. Once New York opens, New Zealand dollar will seek yields in rising New York markets as Treasury Bonds fall. New Zealand dollar/U.S. dollar is a long in rising New York markets and a short when the market falls.

Canadian markets open at the same time as New York, so New Zealand dollar/Canadian dollar could be a viable trade option. As the Toronto Stock Exchange (TMX) in Canada rises, go long New Zealand dollar/Canadian dollar as Canadian bonds fall and yields rise, and go short when the Canadian markets fall. Once New York closes, trade will again come back to New Zealand and New Zealand dollar will again attach to its bond price.

Australia ASX

Australia's ASX Stock Market, known formally as ASX Limited, is currently in merger talks with Singapore's Stock and Derivatives Exchanges (SGX), subject to approval by Australia's Foreign Investment Review Board. The intent is to create the largest exchange in Asia by volume.

Trading begins at pre-market open at 7:00 a.m. Sydney time and a formal opening at 10:00 a.m. Stock orders are entered into the system during premarket opens with best-priced orders to trade first. The 10:09 a.m. full opening occurs about the same time as the 10:00 a.m. Australian dollar fix. This dual-purpose opening can forecast valuable information as to direction of Australian dollar/U.S. dollar as well as Australian dollar/New Zealand dollar.

The equity index to view for trading purposes is the S&P/ASX 200 because it includes only the highest capitalized Australian companies. Approximately 65 percent of the index comprises financial and material companies in the ASX total listing of 2,192 companies. Yet 78 percent of the index accounts for total market capitalization. The ASX closes at 4:00 p.m. Sydney time, midnight in New York. The S&P/ASX 200 index is a market-capitalization weighted index. The formula: total market capitalization of index stocks divided by the divisor.

Futures markets that include interest rates, Bank Bills, cash rate, bonds, swaps, and options begin trade from the second Sunday in March to the first Sunday in November at 5:14 p.m. to 7:00 a.m. and 8:34 a.m. to 4:30 p.m. From the first Sunday in November to the second Sunday in March, markets open between 5:08 and 5:14 p.m. to 7:30 a.m. and between 8:30 and 8:34 a.m. to 4:30 p.m. The purpose for the varying times is to coordinate daylight savings time, especially in the United States, since U.S. Sunday-night market openings are actually Monday mornings in Sydney. At the Australian opening, Wellington, New Zealand, trading on the NZX has been open for three hours.

New Zealand Futures that trade on the ASX open from 5:40 p.m. to 7:00 a.m. and 8:30 a.m. to 4:30 p.m. Bank Bills, cash rate, and 3- and 10-year bond futures trade. Yet the bond futures contract is not widely traded and should be excluded from consideration as an indicator of reference and instead replaced with the Bank Bills contract as an indicator.

From Exhibit 8.3, the five-year chart of the S&P/ASX200, one would notice no definable pattern exists as to highs and lows from year to year. This is what it means to tie bonds to economic performance. They're tied directly to stock market movements and all movements have pointed straight up over five years.

Australia is an economy currently performing quite well. As long as Australia's economy performs well, no shorts will exist in Australia's stock market nor will they exist in Australian dollar/U.S. dollar. Yet this represents overall trend rather than short-term performance.

If lows for the year will materialize, they will occur somewhere in the April to August period as new budgets are passed and funded. Any drastic lows experienced were due to shocks to the world economic system from 2007 to the present day. Australia's economy absorbed the shocks and rebounded. This would explain the volatile movements in Australian dollar/ New Zealand dollar to some degree, yet this pair has always traded quite sporadically.

The ASX never experienced large point swings. Like its counterpart in New Zealand, 100- or 200-point trading days are rare. Instead 30- or 40-point days are more representative of the ASX. But it's a market that trends, so Australian dollar/U.S. dollar will trend.

One measure of risk for the ASX is the new S&P Volatility Index that began trade September 2010. This volatility index is a VIX index measured by a weighted average of implied volatility of put and call options on the

EXHIBIT 8.3 S&P/ASX 200 5-Year Chart

Source: Bloomberg Finance, LP.

ASX 200. No options are listed on the index, it's a measure of XJO overall put and call options against the S&P/ASX 200. XJO options are cash settled, exercised in the European style and are index options over the S&P 200 that are measured in points rather than Australian dollars. The term XJO is the formal name of these options.

Generally a high reading implies market uncertainty; some would imply, probably correctly, an overbought situation, while a low reading implies certainty. Others would argue it means an oversold market ready to go up. The volatility index is an end-of-day calculation and is basically the same VIX Index in purpose, calculation, and measurement that trades on the Chicago Board of Trade. One difference is 30-day volatility is measured by settlement prices of puts and calls on the ASX 200 using the RBA overnight rate and one-, two-, and three-month Bank Bill Reference Rates (BBSW) to interpolate the risk-free rate for each maturity.

Trade Strategy

As Australia's bonds are tied to economic performance, stocks and Australian dollar/U.S. dollar will continue to rise. Further, as long as interest rates in Australia continue to rise and continue to be the highest of the industrialized world, economic performance and money flow into Australia and Australia's markets will be good. Any dips in Australian dollar/U.S. dollar during Australia trading hours should always be bought.

Australian dollar/Japanese yen, like its counterpart New Zealand dollar/Japanese yen, is a sell Japanese yen against Australian dollar during good economic conditions in Australia. Yet the Japanese would prefer a buy Japanese yen/Australian dollar so Australian dollars can be earned against yen. A disparity of interest rates won't allow this under present economic conditions. Measure Japanese yen/Australian dollar against Australian dollar/Japanese yen, as one side will experience a top as the other side bottoms. With interest disparities, Australian dollar/Japanese yen is the preferred trade.

Yet look for compression of both yield curves as a buy and widening curves as a sell. This is measured against the Nikkei 225. A narrowing occurs when Australian markets are down and the Nikkei is up. This is a buy Australian dollar/Japanese yen and sell when Australia is up and the Nikkei is down.

The rising Australian stock market and healthy economic conditions with a wide disparity of interest rates says sell any pair against Australian dollar during Australian trading hours. Pairs such as Australian dollar/British pound, Australian dollar/euro, Australian dollar/Swiss franc, and Australian dollar/Canadian dollar are all buy positions, as Australia's bonds and the ASX rises and yields fall. Stated differently, these pairs are all long trades as the ASX rises along with the bond price. In other markets, these arrangements may or may not have to be reconfigured.

Once the ASX closes, Australian dollar is not tied to its bond market. Instead, it will seek its yields in other markets. The S&P 500 should be monitored in terms of Australian dollar/U.S. dollar direction until the formal opening of New York trading. Once New York opens, Australian dollar/U.S. dollar is a long, as a rising stock market will send yields up and bond prices down, and a sell when the stock market falls, as yields fall when the bond price rises.

Australian dollar/Canadian dollar is a long in rising Canadian markets as yields will rise when the bond price falls. The monitor for this trade is the New York markets. If New York markets are up, it lends further confirmation, as the TMX has good chances of following rising New York markets. If both markets are down, sell Australian dollar/Canadian dollar. Be aware of an interest rate factor in this trade, 4.75 percent against Canada's 1.00 percent. A sell trade in down New York and Toronto markets is never long term due to interest rate differentials. This pair at times is not a major mover, which can only say not much interest lies in this pair. One reason may be limited trade between Canada and Australia, or maybe it doesn't serve as a funding pair. The last reason may be this pair is a pure commodity pair and its fortunes may be tied to other factors for its movement such as the CRB Commodity index.

Australian dollar/British pound is a long in London trading only if the FTSE is down along with the gilt price as yields rise. The disparity of interest rates in this configuration allows this pair to be bought for the long term and sold as British pound/Australian dollar.

In the Australian dollar/Swiss franc arrangement, both are tied to their respective bonds in their respective markets. Neither market connects simultaneously. After Australia closes, Zurich will eventually open. Either configuration for this pair poses a problem due to an interest-rate disparity, but it's also not a viable trade in terms of risk/reward. For example, the only method to go long this pair occurs when the SMI is down along with Swiss Confederate bonds. Australian dollar will rise based on yields. But the Swiss economy is tied to performance based on a rising bond price. What if the arrangement was Swiss franc/Australian dollar? This pair loses based on interest-rate disparity, 0.25 for Swiss franc and 4.50 for Australian dollar. A long trade in U.S. or Canadian markets would be an option if this Australian dollar/Swiss franc configuration was arranged.

FTSE and British Pound

The majority of the world reports and focuses on the FTSE 100 Index that trades on the London Stock Exchange. This index comprises the best-capitalized companies that trade on the London Stock Exchange. But it's the FTSE 250 Index that serves as the better barometer and measure of health of the economic situation in England and direction of the British pound because those 250 companies are more U.K. represented. Point movements will always be more broad in the FTSE 250 than the FTSE 100.

See Exhibit 8.4, a five-year chart of FTSE 100. The *Financial Times* of London always credits this index as its benchmark and this view can be accepted.

EXHIBIT 8.4   FTSE 100 Five-Year Chart

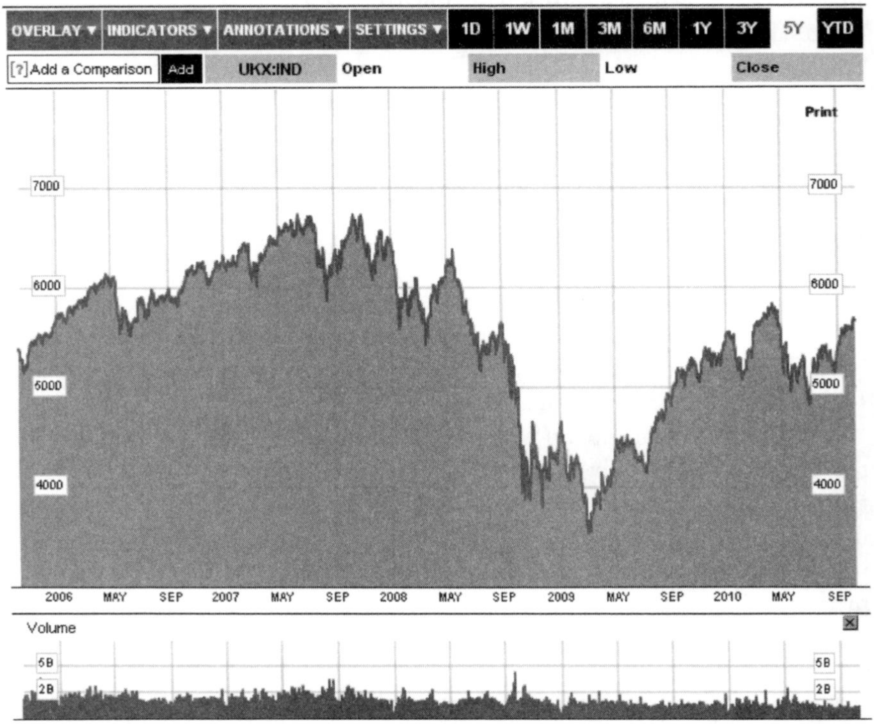

Source: Bloomberg Finance, LP.

Further, the FTSE 250 allows for a better view of possible tops and bottoms measured year to year where the FTSE 100 is not clear in that delineation. Yet it must be understood that at times that measure can be quite difficult because the gilt bond /stock market measure is strictly based on economic performance. Years of great economic performance can undermine the search for a clear top and bottom. Likewise, years of economic turmoil cannot necessarily presage a rise.

If any period exists to measure a top and bottom year to year, it occurs with an April/May top that trails off in the summer and builds again in the October/ December period as new budgets are debated and passed. See Exhibit 8.5, the five-year chart of the FTSE 250. This was measured against a five-year chart of the FTSE 250 from 2005 to the present. But this measure is not consistent year over year, as economic performance completely drives this system.

EXHIBIT 8.5 FTSE 250 Five-Year Chart

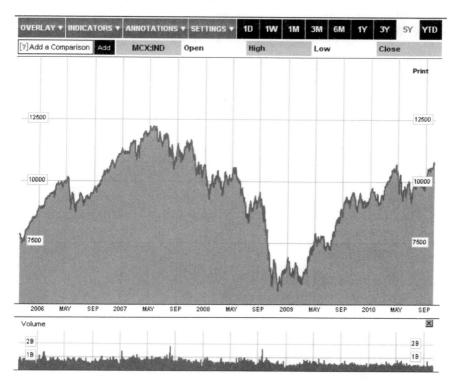

Source: Bloomberg Finance, LP.

Approximately 2,696 companies trade on the London Exchange as of August 2010 with an average daily value of approximately $4,127,251,785 (London Stock Exchange). Compare that figure to an average daily value in 1997 of 819,319,487 and one will notice tremendous growth. Part of that growth is explained by the 2007 merger of Borsa Italiana, Italy's stock exchange, new company listings that rose over the years, and a host of new products introduced. Ironically, stock P/E ratios are not published from company to company nor is it assumed that P/E ratios are published for the FTSE 100 or 250, so an overbought or oversold market can't be determined by P/E ratios. So this market must be measured in terms of gilt bond prices and yields.

However, following the FTSE calculation will not only determine an index value, but P/E Ratios can be determined. For FTSE 100 and all FTSE indices in the United Kingdom:

$$\sum_{n+1} ((P_i \times e_i) \times s_i \times f_i)/D$$

where

   $n = 1, 2, 3 \ldots, n,$
   n = number of securities in the index,
   p = price last trade of component security or previous day index close,
   e = exchange rate - exchange rate required to convert security's home currency into index base currency,
   s = number of shares in index,
   f = free-float factor applied to each security to allow weighting, expressed between 0 and 1 where 1 is equal to 100 percent free float, and
   d = divisor-total issued share capital of index at base date, adjusted.

The base value has been 1000 since its 1984 launch. The index is chain linked using the Paasche method and is calculated every 15 seconds. Index divisors can be factored by dividing the market value by the index value. Yet a market value is equal to the change in index points multiplied by the index divisor.

PE Ratios are factored as:

$$\frac{\sum_{i-1}^{n} p_i \times s_i \times t_i}{\sum_{i=1}^{n} e_i \times f_i}$$

   n = number of shares,
   s_i = share in issue for ith component,
   p_i = price of ith component security,
   e_i = aggregate earnings of ith component, and
   f_i = free float factor for 1th component.

The London Stock Exchange is a market that can move. In May 2007, the FTSE 100 traded at about 12,203, saw a low of 5,543 during the November 2008 economic crisis, and rose to present-day values of approximately 10,725 (all quoted in British pounds). Plenty of opportunity exists to profit with deployment of currency pairs during London trade.

Monthly gilt summaries are released by the London Stock Exchange Group. Summaries include gilt sales, redemptions, index-linked, and non-index-linked gilts. Gilts trade on either the Professional Securities or Main Market.

The London Stock Exchange advertises itself as the largest debt market in Europe because of the large number of corporate- and government-debt issues offered to the trading public. Currently 89 different companies offer various debt maturities traded on the London Exchange. This lends credence to the Bank of England's (BOE) focus in the *Quarterly Bulletin* on corporate debt as a measure of future economic health across Europe. More debt issuance usually denotes corporate expansion.

In September 2010, gilts were offered to the retail public for the first time. gilt purchases and sales flow through to the Electronic Order Book for Retail Bonds on the London Exchange. This allows the public to see two-way continuous pricing in 49 different gilt maturities. Previously, gilt sales and purchases had high minimum purchase sizes and were for institutional investors among others.

The London Stock Exchange opens for trading at 8:00 a.m. London time, 3:00 a.m. New York time and closes at 4:30 p.m. London time, 11:30 a.m. New York time.

The last two hours of London trade rolls into the first two hours of New York trading. Further, the last two hours of London trade coincides with the first two hours of trade on the Toronto Stock Exchange, so British pound/ Canadian dollar becomes an important trade during this time. A 10-minute auction process begins every trading day in London at 8:00 a.m. and ends at 8:10. The auction process provides vital information as to the direction of the formal opening.

At the London open, New Zealand and Australia are closed while Tokyo is closing. Yet Tokyo's JGB Futures markets remain open for the first three hours of London trade, and it is vitally important to gauge a British pound/ Japanese yen trade in terms of a yield curve and bond strategy. Be aware that the close of the three-hour window is the 11:00 a.m. London, 5:00 a.m. New York time BBA LIBOR announcement. But the 8:00 a.m. London opening is 4:00 p.m. Tokyo. So the close of JGB futures trading rolls into BBA LIBOR and is an important time to measure the Japanese yen. This time brings volatility due to repricing of assets after the release. Plus U.K. and European economic announcements are released about this time. This period is one of the most volatile episodes within a 24-hour trading cycle. It's a time to profit, or to lose if one is not careful.

One hour after the London opening, Frankfurt and Zurich open for trading, so the euro and Swiss franc become important at this time.

Trade Strategy

The equation to trade the British pound/U.S. dollar is quite simple. As the FTSE stock market rises, gilt bonds will rise. So in turn will the British pound/U.S. dollar. How far up depends on bond movements. The short end is rich with possibilities to measure how far, so this represents the start to monitor any trade.

Conversely, as the stock market and bond price decline so will the British pound/U.S. dollar. These equations assume trends. Yet markets may range trade up and down during a trading session or through periods. This means bond prices, yields, and the FTSE will ebb and flow throughout a trading day or period of time. It allows for continuous buys and sells throughout the trading session

Ranging markets simply say bonds, yields, and stock prices fall within the parameters of their respective prices and are not ready to break new highs or lows. The British pound/U.S. dollar price will be contained within these same parameters. A breakout will occur only when the bond/yield equation breaks its range. If the British pound/U.S. dollar breaks its range without a bond/yield breakout, British pound/U.S. dollar overshot the range targets and will fall back inside the range. So if the British pound/U.S. dollar range was broken on the upside, it's a sell British pound/U.S. dollar and it's a buy if it broke the downside target, provided bonds and yields didn't break their range.

Yet the FTSE, bond prices, and yields move well enough on any given day to easily profit. Reaction to market movements occurs quickly in London and Europe, so caution is advised to stay abreast of market action if one trades short term.

To gauge future movements, compare bond prices to yields. The FTSE is more than an ancillary indicator due to its focus on exchange rates, so it should be employed as a measure between bonds and yields.

The overall direction for the British pound/U.S. dollar is always up toward weakness as good economic conditions are the goal for policymakers and the BOE. What they seek is a rising bond price with a rising stock market. That means a British pound/U.S. dollar headed higher toward weakness. London trading is quite different from New Zealand and Australia because movements occur—and sometimes rather quickly.

Remember British pound/U.S. dollar is the premier pair for the BOE, policymakers, and the general U.K. public due to its connection to the U.S. economy and as a measure of its own economic health. It's the pair widely known, widely viewed, widely understood, and widely reported in the U.K.

for its importance as the vital link. All stock markets report this pair, and investors watch the U.S. markets with concern to gauge direction of their own currency pairs, investments, and economic direction. Many world stock markets stream U.S. news and the New York Stock Exchange averages are reported directly on respective sites. The world truly watches the U.S. dollar.

Another measure of the British pound/U.S. dollar is the German bund due to the importance of the German economy as a benchmark indicator of economic conditions throughout Europe. The approach is to measure yield spreads between the German bund and the gilt. The question for consideration should always be how much and who benefits; which side receives the better side of the deal in British pound or U.S. dollar terms.

Notice how the British pound/U.S. dollar is configured. Both are opposite to each other. Only one side can win on bond terms while the other side will win in yield terms, but never at the same time. Imagine borrowing in British pound yields at one price, then paying back the borrowed money in bunds at a higher bund yield. It's a losing situation. The bund yield is the U.S. dollar side of the equation. A few examples follow.

As spreads widen in favor of the German bund, this is a sell British pound/U.S. dollar because the cost of borrowing in British pound terms is greater than U.S. dollar terms. The cost is prohibitive in British pound terms because replication of British pounds can't be earned, and that must be the overall goal. If spreads narrow, buy British pound/U.S. dollar as the cost to borrow decreases. In this instance, it's the cost of conducting business across borders that increases or decreases and yields define the terms. As spreads widen, it says the gilt/bund price widened.

This scenario on a larger scale transpires as spreads widen in favor of bunds, the British pound/U.S. dollar falls, gilt prices rise, and the FTSE rises while the opposite scenario holds. As spreads narrow, buy British pound/U.S. dollar as the FTSE and gilt prices rise. Stated differently, if the German Stock Index (DAX) in Frankfurt is down and the FTSE is down, buy the British pound/U.S. dollar, and sell when the DAX is up and the FTSE is up. How about euro/British pound?

Euro/British Pound

As those same spreads widen, now euros are borrowed and paid back in British pounds. This is a buy euro/British pound situation. As spreads narrow, sell euro/British pound because business will be conducted instead in British pound/U.S. dollar, the premier currency pair that will earn more

British pounds for the UK. euro/British pound in this instance is the funding pair, and performed as expected when these pairs were introduced in the latter part of the 1990s. It was meant to facilitate finance across borders when cost became too high in the premier currency pairs.

In terms of U.K. trading, euro/British pound will always move counter to British pound/U.S. dollar. If gilt prices and the stock market rise, euro/British pound will always fall. Conversely, if gilt prices fall along with the stock market, euro/British pound will always rise. Euro/British pound as configured is a yield seeker, so it looks for its yields opposite a British pound/U.S. dollar gilt follower. Euro/British pound is not connected to the bond price nor is it measured in terms of economic performance, but it can be viewed in its price term as a measure of economic performance.

A high euro/British pound price in London trading warns that economic performance is not healthy so one can note its price in terms of British pound/U.S. dollar as an overall indicator. Since both move counter to each other, one pair is always a short while the other pair is always a long. If for whatever reason both move together, this represents market uncertainty and a market gift, because one pair will be sold or bought to normalize the market. The profit potential can be enormous when market gifts are offered in this manner. In U.S. dollar terms, euro/British pound pays almost $2 per pip, better than British pound/U.S. dollar at $1 per pip.

Yet British pound/euro will react quite differently because it becomes tied to gilts and the FTSE while the euro side attaches perfectly to bund Yields and the DAX. If the DAX is up in Frankfurt and the FTSE is up in London, British pound/euro is a clear long, and a clear short if both are down.

The recommendation is to trade pairs during London trading that are euro, British pound, Japanese yen, or U.S. dollar related and arrange the pairs based on gilt and yield movements. It is not recommended to trade for example Australian dollar/Canadian dollar or any unrelated pair attached to the gilt yield configuration.

In U.S. trading, British pound of euro/British pound follows the Treasury bond price up and down while the euro seeks Treasury Yields and follows yields up and down.

Japanese Yen

As the three-hour time frame ends to trade JGB futures in London trading, the connection for Japanese yen will switch to Nikkei 225 futures and Globex will be the measure of direction. Japanese yen in the second part of the currency-pair equation will connect to the Nikkei for the remainder of London trading.

The British pound/Japanese yen will then connect as the British pound to the gilt price and Japanese yen to the Nikkei 225. As yield spreads narrow, buy British pound/Japanese yen and sell when spreads widen. Spreads narrow when the FTSE is down and the Nikkei is up. Spreads widen when the FTSE is up and the Nikkei falls.

U.S. Dollar

The U.S. dollar as the second side of the currency-pair equation can be measured by the S&P 500, and again Globex is the measure. British pound/U.S. dollar will be tied to gilts and the U.S. dollar to the S&P 500.

British Pound/Canadian Dollar

Canadian interest rates are currently1.00 percent and Great Britain is 0.50 percent. This present equation is slightly misaligned if this was a trade to go long. Since the Canadian market is a yield seeker and the British pound is tied to gilt performance, the only method to go long this pair in the last two hours of London trading is if the FTSE is down and the Canadian stock market is down. Spreads would then compress and allow profits on the long, but this trade must be held only for the last two hours of London trade because the British pound configuration will change once London trading closes. The opposite effect also holds. If spreads widen, it's a clear short, particularly when the gilt is tied to performance that sends gilt yields down and the Canadian market seeks yields as the TMX rises. Stated differently, why would anyone borrow British pounds at 0.50 percent and pay it back at 1.00 percent? The overall trend is down in this configuration and up as Canadian dollar/British pound.

British Pound/Swiss Franc

This is an unusual pair, because both are tied to respective bond economic performance. The British pound present interest rate is 0.50 percent and Swiss franc is 0.25 percent. Swiss franc in Swiss markets rise when the Domestic Bond Index, the SBI, rises. If the SBI is up and the gilt price is up along with the FTSE, go long the British pound/Swiss franc and go short when both fall. In U.S. markets, the Swiss franc will rise and fall with Treasury bond prices, while the British pound will rise and fall with bond yields. All three markets will eventually trade together during a trading day. New York markets will dominate direction. Due to present interest-rate configurations, the overall trend is buy British pound/Swiss franc and sell Swiss franc/British pound.

British Pound

As London trading closes, British pound will no longer tie to the gilt price. British pound will then seek yields in Frankfurt, New York, and Canadian trade. Frankfurt has one hour of trade remaining, so the Canadian and New York markets become the best trade opportunities for British pound.

In Canadian markets, British pound/Canadian dollar would work well. As the TMX rises on the Toronto Exchange and Canadian bonds fall, yields will rise. This is a long British pound/Canadian dollar, provided London is closed and the gilt connection is broken. If London is open and the FTSE and TMX are up, British pound/Canadian dollar is an easy long trade.

For U.S. markets, as the New York market is up, yields will rise and bond prices will fall. This sends British pound/U.S. dollar up, and down when New York markets are down with yields as the bond price rises.

Japanese Nikkei 225 and TOPIX Indices

As can be expected, the Japanese are quite different in their methodology and calculation of their stock indices, the TOPIX and Nikkei 225, because both are light years apart and have various meanings.

The world reports and focuses on the Nikkei 225 because it is calculated in yen while the Tokyo Stock Price Index (TOPIX indices), are factored in point terms. TOPIX indices are calculated by the Tokyo Stock Exchange while the Nikkei is calculated by Nihon-Keizai Shimbun, a popularly read newspaper in Japan distributed by Nikkei Digital Media. TOPIX indices are free-float adjusted with a market capitalization weight while the Nikkei is an average-price weight where higher-priced stocks impact the index.

The Nikkei is comprised of 225 top Japanese companies while TOPIX indices are multi-faceted indices that comprise the TOPIX, 30, 70, 100, 500, and 1000 and include economic sectors such as the TOPIX Transportation index, Bank index, Energy, and Electric appliances to name a few of the many that exist. The Nikkei comprises 225 companies, while total TOPIX companies include 1700 traded on the TSE. The BOJ and Japanese Government focus on TOPIX to gauge economic conditions, while the Nikkei is never considered. This means the Nikkei 225 is a market measure while the TOPIX is an economic measure for policymakers. The Nikkei 225 in yen traded outside Japan for about 20 years while Nikkei 225-U.S. dollar terms was introduced in 2004. Both trade on the CME.

The TSE opens at 9:00 a.m. and closes at 3:00 p.m. Tokyo time. Futures trading on the TSE holds the same hours, except evening trading in JGBs from 3:30 p.m. to 6:00 p.m. From 11:00 a.m. to 12:30 p.m., the exchange is closed for lunch, but consideration is under way to extend lunch for one hour.

Tokyo openings represent a one-hour trade difference between Sydney and Tokyo so pairs such as Australian dollar/Japanese yen should be evaluated. Wellington, New Zealand, represents a four-hour difference, so New Zealand dollar/Japanese yen should also be evaluated before or during Tokyo trade. The three-hour JGB extended opening allows JGBs to be carried over and traded for the first three hours of London trade. This allows Japanese yen to be priced in London and Frankfurt markets.

The overall trend for the Nikkei has been down since 2005 due to horrid economic circumstances. Consider a few examples from the TSE 2010 Fact Book.

Currently, stock dividends are taxed at 10 percent with a scheduled 10 percent increase in 2012. Capital gains are currently taxed at 10 percent with a 10 percent increase scheduled in 2012. Three percent of the 10 percent tax is an inhabitant tax that is standard across all prefectures. JGBs have a separate and equally abusive tax. That explains why the majority of Japanese trading occurs from offshore accounts outside of Japan. Overall the Japanese economy has been in an economic slump since the Asian crisis in the late 1990s and has not experienced good times since.

If any seasonal trend exists year to year, April is always a down month while May experiences ups. It's not unusual to see 80, 100, even 150 point days for the Nikkei 225.

The JGB Futures 5- and 10-year contract and the 5- and 10-year options contract is the only instrument to gauge the U.S. dollar/Japanese yen relationship because the Japanese lack an actively traded bond market.

The Nikkei Index was first calculated in 1950. All stocks represent the full spectrum of the Japanese economy and are equally weighted in the index. Today's criteria is a 50-yen par value. To calculate: divide the sum of stock prices of Nikkei 225 stocks by a divisor. Round two digits after the decimal point to calculate the average. The divisor in September 2010 was currently 24.869 and is regularly published by Nikkei. The divisor is the trigger, the guide that holds the index steady in light of stock splits, additions, or subtractions of stocks.

Trade Strategy

In the U.S. dollar/Japanese yen arrangement, the Japanese yen is a yield seeker while Japanese yen/U.S. dollar sees Japanese yen as a bond follower. This is a tricky arrangement for the Japanese. With U.S. dollar/Japanese yen, as the Nikkei rises, bond futures will fall, and bond yields will rise along with the U.S. dollar/Japanese yen. Japanese yen/U.S. dollar works opposite. As the Nikkei falls, bonds rise, yields fall, and the Japanese yen/U.S. dollar rises. The preferred arrangement for the Japanese is Japanese yen/U.S. dollar in Japanese trading, yet that means stock market falls hinder their companies as well as overall economic conditions. It's a precarious situation for the Japanese and made more precarious by a call rate of 0.10 and a falling U.S. dollar. One can understand the move for the Japanese to establish overseas for their fortunes. Fundamentally, both pairs should be evaluated in terms of bonds and yields. Yet a tracker is the Nikkei 225 in yen and Nikkei 225 in US dollar terms. One should rise as the other falls. Both trade on the CME.

The British pound/Japanese yen will perform best as a buy when Japanese bond future prices rise and gilt prices fall as the spread narrows, and sold when the spread widens.

This scenario holds for Australian dollar/Japanese yen and New Zealand dollar/Japanese yen. If New Zealand markets are down and the Nikkei 225 rises, yield spreads will narrow, so buy New Zealand dollar/Japanese yen and sell when the reverse occurs because spreads will widen. The same scenario holds for Australian dollar/Japanese yen. Yet refrain from pairs such as Canadian dollar/Japanese yen, Australian dollar/Canadian dollar, and Australian dollar/Swiss franc during Japanese trading as no need exists to trade these pairs due to limited cross-border trade. These pairs should be traded during their respective markets or in New York trading hours.

Deutsche Boerse DAX, STOXX, Bunds, and the Euro

What is known as the Xetra Dax 30 that trades on the Deutsche Boerse, formerly known as the Frankfurt Stock Exchange, is comprised of DAX as an index to measure stock prices and Xetra is the electronic trading system employed by market professionals to report DAX movements. DAX is actually a family of indices such as the MDAX—comprised of 50 medium sized German and foreign companies, TEC DAX—comprised of 30 of Germany's largest tech companies, and SDAX—comprised of 50 German small-cap companies, to name a few.

The Deutsche Boerse actually calculates approximately 2700 indices daily, the vast majority comprise DAX indices for other global markets such as volatility indices, strategy indices, short stock indices, and real estate indices. Domestically, DAX indices comprise 18 economic sectors and nine subsectors that include financials, utilities, and consumer goods to name a few. This methodology is the same as the Japanese format. The format allows an economic assessment to be rendered sector by sector by government officials and market professionals.

Yet the world reports and focuses on the DAX 30 because it was the first to form in the index family in 1988. It's the index closely aligned to the German bund price and yield, and approximately 50,000 financial products are tied to the index (Boerse Reports). But the HDAX can be viewed as a more informative indicator to measure economic performance, a benchmark, because it comprises 110 companies contained in DAX, MDAX, and TEC DAX. Ninety-five percent of total market capitalization comprises HDAX (Boerse).

The Dax 30 is a free-float index calculated every second using a Laspeyres formula with a 1987 base value of 1000. Prices are quoted in euros and reported on the Deutsche Boerse web site in close to real time, so a trading decision can be evaluated quickly. Approximately 134,154 domestic and 54,055 foreign equities trade on the Boerse. The 2009 annual report states approximately 10,000 to 15,000 equity trades occur per month, for a 167,270,994 yearly total with a total turnover of 2,222,071 and 90 percent handled through Xetra.

Xetra is the premier electronic trading platform for the Deutsche Boerse, where a vast majority of trades are handled from many European exchanges such as derivatives, futures, and options traded on Eurex, Scoach Schweiz derivatives and floor transactions on the Boerse. Consider the 2009 annual report that states 341,000 certificates and warrants, 3,000 retail funds, 547 index funds, 10,000 securities, 26,000 fixed income, and 380,000 trade-able instruments trade through Xetra. Total 2009 trading volume equaled euro 1,163.3 billion, with 167.3 million transactions conducted without failure. All trades are conducted with precision and efficiency. This exchange is well managed in all aspects of its operations.

A 2010 study was under way to improve the speed of Xetra. Currently, Xetra handles a million quotes a second in under one millisecond per quote. It is a fast-moving and sophisticated market.

The Deutsche Boerse opens for trading at 9:03 a.m. and closes at 5:45 p.m. Frankfurt time, 3:00 a.m. to noon New York time with a one-hour difference during U.S. daylight savings. This time is referenced to the close of Xetra. Floor trading continues until 8:00 p.m. Frankfurt, 2:00 p.m. New York. This time would coincide with the close of futures trading on the CME.

London has been trading for one hour when the DAX opens, and closes one hour before Frankfurt while Australia, New Zealand, and Tokyo are closed. The caveat is this methodology follows New York EST. The last two-and-a-half hours of Frankfurt trading coincide with the first two-and-a-half hours of New York and Toronto Stock Exchange trading. Euro/Canadian dollar is an important consideration during this period. All will follow U.S. dollar up or down in London and Frankfurt trading, so the S&P 500 will be the measure for U.S. dollar.

See Exhibit 8.6, the five-year DAX 30 chart and notice April down months with a trend that develops in August and trends to the end of the year. This period begins the yearly euro/U.S. dollar top during the November-December period.

The DAX index is a market capitalization, free-float index calculated every second using a Laspeyres chain-linked methodology. To calculate:

$$\text{Index}_t = K_T \times \frac{\sum p_{i,t} \times ff_{i,T} \times q_{i,T} \times C_{i,t}}{\sum p_{i,o} \times q_{i,o}} \times \text{Base}$$

where

$c_{i,t}$ = adjustment factor of company I at time t,

$ff_{i,T}$ = free-float factor of share class I at time T,

n = number of shares in the index,

$p_{i,o}$ = closing price of share I on the trading day before first inclusion in the index,

$p_{i,t}$ = price of share I at time t,

$q_{i,o}$ = number of shares of company I on trading day before index inclusion,

$q_{i,T}$ = number of shares of company I at time T,

t = calculation time of index, and

K_T = index-specific chaining factor valid as of chaining date T where

T = day of last chaining.

EXHIBIT 8.6   Five-Year Dax 30 Chart

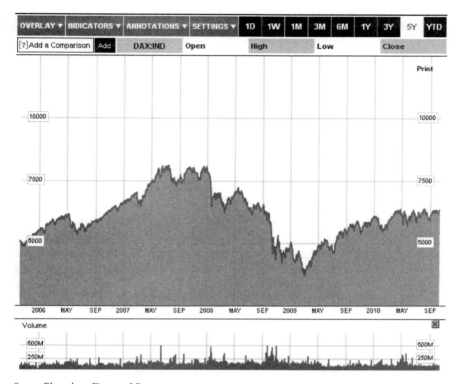

Source: Bloomberg Finance, LP.

Weightings:

$$\text{Index}_t = \frac{\displaystyle\sum_{i=1}^{n} p_{i,t} \times \left(K_T \times \dfrac{ff_{i,T} \times q_{i,T}}{\displaystyle\sum_{i=1}^{n} q_{i,o}} \times 100 \times c_{i,t} \right)}{\displaystyle\sum_{i=1}^{n} p_{i,o} \times \dfrac{q_{i,o}}{\displaystyle\sum_{i=1}^{n} q_{i,o}} \times 100} \times \text{Base} = \frac{\displaystyle\sum_{i=1}^{n} p_{i,t} \times F_i}{A} \times \text{Base}$$

whereby: $A = \dfrac{\displaystyle\sum_{i=1}^{n} p_{i,o} \times q_{i,o} \times 100}{\displaystyle\sum_{i=1}^{n} q_{i,o}}$

and

$$F_i = \frac{K_T \times ff_{i,T} \times q_{i,T} \times 100 \times c_{i,t}}{\sum_{i=1}^{n} q_{i,o}}$$

In simple terms, using F_i, multiply the current price by F_i weighting factor, take the sum of these products and divide by base value A, which remains constant until a modification of the index.

German Bunds

There are two methods to track German bunds. Eurex links spot and futures markets through electronic trading of bunds and iBoxx indices. iBoxx indices comprise two benchmarks for the euro and British pound bond markets, iBoxx and iBoxx consolidated. Both were the first indices developed to track the European bond market. iBoxx trades gilts and bunds while iBoxx consolidated determines spreads to measure yield curves. Yield-curves data are based on actual and updated market bid/ask spreads.

The benchmark German bund is the 10-year, and is employed as a comparison to other nations' yield curves to determine direction for the euro and other financial instruments. Yet it's not an imperative for the 10-year to be employed for trading decisions. German and other bonds can be viewed on Eurex, accessible directly from the Deutsche Boerse web site. Here bund prices, turnover, and volume can be viewed almost in real time.

Euro Trade Strategy

German bund yields follow the DAX in up markets and down in falling markets while the bund price moves in opposite directions. To trade the euro/U.S. dollar, follow German bund yields.

As the DAX is up along with bund yields, the euro/U.S. dollar will go up, a buy the euro/U.S. dollar. Sell the euro/U.S. dollar when the DAX is down along with bund yields. The U.S. dollar side follows the German bund price up and down.

While this statement may be correct and can be employed as an evaluative tool, the S&P 500 is the better measure because it can determine overall DAX and U.S. dollar movements until the New York Stock Exchange opens. The euro will always outpace the U.S. dollar side due to buying and selling of the euro either in the spot market or through other financial instruments connected to the euro such as futures and options. A number of measures exist to ensure euro direction.

The STOXX 50 is an index comprised of 50 of the biggest Blue Chip European companies. The DAX will move in the same direction as the STOXX 50. The SDAX is a measure of short DAX positions in the DAX 30. It's correlated 99.89 percent with the DAX 30 (Deutsche Boerse). All indices can be viewed directly on the Deutsche Boerse web site.

The Germans measure the DAX and other equity indices based on further DAX indices termed DAX Plus that are known as strategy indices. As free-float indices such as the DAX 30, it doesn't measure risk. The current Deutsche Boerse newsletter outlines one such risk strategy.

The DAX Plus Maximum Sharpe Ratio is a measure of excess return to risk calculated using standard deviation. Sharpe Ratios are defined as

$$S(X) = (R_b - R_t)/ \text{Standard deviation of } X$$

where

    X = investment,
    R_b = average rate of return of X,
    R_t = best rate of return of a risk-free asset, and
    standard deviation X = standard deviation of Rb.

Since standard deviation is the square root of the variance that measures risk, measure the variance of DAX 30 using the DAX Plus minimum variance. A high variance means volatility will increase which is measured against the DAX Plus Risk Trigger index. This methodology says as volatility rises, equity prices will fall and vice versa. This is a sell euro/U.S. dollar as volatility rises.

In simple terms, Sharpe Ratios using standard deviation, say, as a stock's return varies from the average return, the more volatile is the stock or the financial instrument as the measure. Sharpe Ratios were used to measure two portfolios against each other.

During Frankfurt trading, British pound/U.S. dollar is locked into the gilt price while Australian dollar/U.S. dollar and New Zealand dollar/U.S. dollar will follow bund yields up and down along with the DAX 30 and the euro/U.S. dollar.

Euro/Japanese yen, Australian dollar/Japanese yen, and New Zealand dollar/Japanese yen will always be questionable due to the Japanese side of the equation. Measure Japanese yen based on the Nikkei 225.

For euro/Japanese yen, sell when spreads widen between the Nikkei 225 and the DAX 30 and buy when spreads narrow. If the DAX is down and the Nikkei rises, buy euro/Japanese yen because yield spreads narrowed. If the DAX is up and the Nikkei falls, sell euro/Japanese yen because yield spreads widened and the cost to borrow is too high.

It appears Australian dollar and New Zealand dollar lack a connection to European markets, yet this is not the case and will be addressed in the next chapter. For now, the Nikkei 225 is the measure against Australian dollar/ Japanese yen and New Zealand dollar/Japanese yen, and know that Australian dollar and New Zealand dollar trade in London and Frankfurt to seek yields. The purpose of Australian dollar and New Zealand dollar is to earn reserves for their economy when trading outside their own markets.

So again measure the euro/U.S. dollar to the DAX and S&P. Both markets move in the same fashion, rising stock markets means rising yields and falling bond prices. A rising DAX is euro/U.S. dollar -supported in Frankfurt markets and may mark trends. Both stock markets can be measured against the euro/U.S. dollar to determine a support or resistance level.

If both markets are up, go long the euro/U.S. dollar and go short if both markets are down. If the DAX is up and the S&P is down, it is still euro/U.S. dollar-supported because the euro is the home nation. If the DAX is down and the S&P is up, watch the euro/U.S. dollar for direction heading into New York markets. Normally the S&P provides overall direction. The same scenario would work for the British pound/U.S. dollar as it closely follows the euro/U.S. dollar.

As the DAX formally closes, the euro will find direction in U.S. markets by following yields in rising U.S. stock markets as the Treasury bond falls. So euro/U.S. dollar is a buy in rising markets and a sell in falling markets.

Euro/Canadian Dollar

This pair has equal interest rates at 1.00 percent and Frankfurt trades its last two-and-a-half hours into the first hours of trade in Toronto that opens at 9:30 a.m. New York time. If the DAX and the TMX in Toronto are both up, euro/Canadian dollar is a clear long, and a sell when both markets are down. If U.S. markets are up, it's a further indication for this pair to go long. Yet if the U.S. market is up, Frankfurt is closed, and the Canadian market is up, it's still a clear long, and a sell when both are down.

Euro/Canadian dollar should never be reconfigured under present interest rate-conditions and under the present perfect two-market arrangements. Both sides of this pair seek yields in their respective markets and both sides will find them easily when both markets are up. If economic circumstances change for the better among both pairs and interest rates remain the same, euro/Canadian dollar will fly up. Only a change of interest rates that favors one side or another can change the present balance.

In terms of U.S. dollar/Canadian dollar, euro/Canadian dollar goes long and rises as U.S. dollar/Canadian dollar goes short. Combine the pairs, and the equation becomes Canadian dollar/Canadian dollar and euro/U.S. dollar. Canadian dollar becomes either short with euro/Canadian dollar or long with U.S. dollar/Canadian dollar or vice versa.

Euro/Swiss Franc

This is a tricky pair for many reasons. Both the Swiss National Bank (SNB) and european Central Bank (ECB) have huge interests in this pair, but both have interests in opposing configurations. The Swiss want Swiss franc/euro to rise while the ECB want euro/Swiss franc to rise. Both markets pull against each other and that continues in U.S. markets.

One reason is the DAX rises on yields while the SMI stock index that trades on the SIX Swiss Exchange is tied to Confederate bonds and both are tied to economic performance. This equation seems quite simple but it will not work in every instance with this pair.

It's not the euro side that's complicated but rather the Swiss franc side. So it's important to view Confederate and Bund futures on the SIX Swiss Exchange web site. bund and Confederate futures are the key indicator, more so than the SMI. The web site actually provides all the necessary information to trade this pair in real time and all is provided as market indicators. Interesting about this pair is it can be a big mover because the payout is big in U.S. dollar terms. Yet if the matrix is understood between the two markets, it's an easy pair to trade.

So to trade this arrangement as the DAX rises, bund prices fall, and yields rise along with the euro. The SMI needs to rise along with the SBI in order for the Swiss franc to rise. If the DAX falls and the SMI falls, spreads compress so this might be the long trade opportunity. If Confederate and bund futures rise, euro/Swiss franc is a short.

The Swiss SMI is not an essential element in this equation because the SMI can rise while the SBI Index is down. SBI and Confederate futures is the essential element for the Swiss franc side. Both or either must rise in order for Swiss franc to rise. This can be tricky on some days, so caution is advised. If problems arise while in a trade and it doesn't work as expected, bail out and wait for a better day. Those problems lie in the push and pull of both central banks' interests and the exchange rate element in the SMI calculation.

In U.S. markets, euro will follow Treasury yields up and down and Swiss franc will follow Treasury bond prices up and down. Rising U.S.

stock markets sends Treasury yields up and Treasury bond prices down. U.S. markets will dictate direction in all three markets once New York trading formally opens.

The methodology for U.S. trade is view euro/Swiss franc the same as euro/U.S. dollar. Because U.S. dollar/Swiss franc is an opposite pair to euro/ Swiss franc, they will move in opposite directions. Swiss franc/U.S. dollar is another configuration that moves in opposite directions as euro/Swiss franc. In Swiss franc/euro terms, U.S. dollar/Swiss franc and Swiss franc/U.S. dollar would both run counter to Swiss franc/euro. The overall strategy should be watch euro/Swiss franc because it's a forward indicator to euro/U.S. dollar due to interest for both central banks to employ it for cross-border trade rather than a speculative investment.

SIX Swiss Exchange

The SMI is the widely reported and popularly known index that marks direction for all stocks traded on the SIX Swiss Exchange. The SMI comprises 20 of Switzerland's biggest companies. Yet the SMIM is a broader index that includes 30 of Switzerland's largest mid-cap companies. A total of 256 shares trade on the SIX Swiss Exchange, represented by the All Share Index.

All stock indices operate based on a Laspeyres index, a free float that is calculated every second by dedicated market professionals at the SIX Swiss Exchange. The formula is:

$$Is = \frac{\sum_{i=1}^{M} p_{i,s} \times x_{i,t} \times f_{i,t} \times r_s}{D_t}$$

where

t = current day,
s = current time on day t,
I_s = current index level at time s,
D_t = divisor on day t,
M = number of shares in index,
$p_{i,s}$ = last paid price security I,
$x_{i,t}$ = number of shares of security I on day t,
$f_{i,t}$ = free float for security I on day t, and
r_s = current Swiss franc exchange rate at time s.

The Domestic Government Bond Index is not only the most important index to monitor and evaluate trades, but it's by far the most widely traded. The index is termed the SBI Domestic. Only Swiss Government fixed interest-rate bonds with maturities 12 months or longer with Swiss franc $100 million comprise the index. The SBI is calculated based on a Laspeyres capital-weighted index.

The SBI 52-week high and low ranged from 110.82 to 119.96 with a daily high and low that ranged from a low of 117.96 and high of 118.11 (SIX Swiss). Daily movements in this range do not speak volumes about stock market ranges.

To monitor the SMI, a volatility index was introduced in 2005 called the VSMI. Volatility is based on SMI 30-day options traded on Eurex. The index is calculated based on a Sharpe Ratio as trades enter the Eurex system. The calculation is:

$$\text{SMI index level}, X \times \sqrt{(30:365)} \times \text{VSMI in percent per year}$$

High volatility says the SMI price is high and low volatility implies the index is low.

Bond trading begins at 8:30 a.m. Zurich time, 2:30 a.m. New York time and closes at 5:30 p.m. Zurich, 11:30 a.m. New York. The 8:30 a.m. opening includes a two-minute randomized opening. If bond prices with maturities less than 15 years deviate 1 percent in price at the opening, trade is stopped for 15 minutes. If bond prices with more than 15-year maturities deviate 3 percent in price, trade is halted for 15 minutes. The SIX Swiss Exchange opens at 9:00 a.m. and closes at 5:30 p.m., which is 3:00 a.m. to 11:30 a.m. New York time.

At the Swiss opening, Australia, New Zealand, and Tokyo are closed. The SIX Swiss Exchange closes 30 minutes before the close at the Frankfurt Exchange. The London close occurs simultaneously with the SIX Swiss Exchange. The last two hours of Swiss trading coincide with the first two hours of the New York Stock Exchange trading as well as the Toronto Stock Exchange.

SIX Swiss Exchange Trading Services

On the SIX Swiss web site are a number of useful trading services that deserve mention. The bond calculator offers an option to determine yields based on price and price based on yields to include accrued interest. A bond can be factored based on maturity, coupons, settlement, price, and day counts.

Charts allow charting of the Swiss markets in terms of equities, bonds, and indices. A charting comparison between markets is offered as well.

A sophisticated colored heat map allows individual stocks, sectors, industries, and stock indices to be viewed in terms of different periods, volume, and turnover not just for present trading periods but historical markets as well. It's valuable as a measure of the Swiss markets.

An updated exchange rate table along with the ability to measure U.S. dollar and cross pairs in terms of an interactive conversion table is offered. This may appear simplistic on the surface, but exchange rates must be measured in terms of the larger picture of worldwide traders and market professionals.

Resident U.S. traders may find no value in an Australian dollar/New Zealand dollar trade because the number of Australian dollar/New Zealand dollar converted into U.S. dollars is quite small. Yet the exchange rate may be sufficient in Australian dollar and New Zealand dollar terms and for Australian dollar and New Zealand dollar resident traders who may find profit. Japanese traders may find profit in, say, British pound pairs. All currency pairs have a different payout depending on exchange rates and the conversion factors in whatever currency, according to the particular world market.

Switzerland Confederate Bonds

Confederate Bonds are tied to economic performance of the Swiss economy and serve as the benchmark for trade of Swiss franc.

Trade Strategy

U.S. dollar/Swiss franc and Swiss franc/U.S. dollar can be tricky trades. The SBI Domestic Bond Index provides the most important indicator in terms of direction for both pairs. Typically, when the SBI and SMI are up Swiss franc/U.S. dollar is up and U.S. dollar/Swiss franc is down, a long and a short. The SMI is an ancillary indicator in this equation, and doesn't necessarily correlate directly with the SBI. Yet both are by far the most widely traded instruments on any given Swiss trading day. The tricky aspect occurs when the SMI is up, say, 10 points and the SBI can actually trade in negative territory. This can send U.S. dollar/Swiss franc and Swiss franc/U.S. dollar in quite different directions. For this reason, the SBI is the key guide. Confederate Bond futures play a role of almost equal importance.

Typically, the SBI and Confederate Futures follow each other, sometimes not. Confederate Bond futures sometimes follow German bund futures, sometimes not. To navigate, employ SBI as the overall guide because SMI again fails as an overall correlational tool. When the SBI is up, Swiss franc/ U.S. dollar is up and U.S. dollar/Swiss franc falls. Better to trade the Swiss franc/U.S. dollar configuration in Swiss markets. Euro/Swiss franc will typically follow the direction of U.S. dollar/Swiss franc, while Swiss franc/euro will not. Caution is advised in Swiss markets because sometimes trades are easy and other days they are not. The SMI web site allows a full view of the SMI, SBI, Confederate, and bund Futures to be viewed on one screen.

In U.S. markets, Swiss franc in U.S. dollar/Swiss franc will follow Treasury bond prices up and down while U.S. dollar will follow yields. As the U.S. stock market rises, yields will rise and the bond price will fall. When both markets trade together, U.S. markets provides direction to U.S. dollar/ Swiss franc and Swiss franc/U.S. dollar and also provide direction to Swiss markets in terms of the SBI.

Go long U.S. dollar/Swiss franc when U.S. markets are down and short when markets rise. Go long Swiss franc/U.S. dollar when U.S. markets rise and short when U.S. markets fall.

Euro in euro/Swiss franc follows Treasury bond yields while Swiss franc follows Treasury bond prices, so some continuity exists from market to market to some degree for this pair. It's another reason euro/Swiss franc can be employed as the premier risk indicator. The question for euro is risk to follow yields or safety of bond prices by Swiss franc. It's a gauge of a market that seeks risk or safety, caution against risk.

British pound/Swiss franc in U.S. markets trades as British pound is the Treasury yield seeker while Swiss franc follows the bond price. Negative U.S. stock markets will see British pound fall as Swiss franc rises and vice versa. The best opportunity for British pound/Swiss franc is go long in rising U.S. markets, short when markets drop because of the British pound dominance in interest rates and movements over Swiss franc.

Australian dollar/Swiss franc and New Zealand dollar/Swiss franc have possibilities in U.S. markets only as a long trade and only if U.S. stock markets rise because of the wide disparity in interest rates between these two pairs. Both pairs are long trends due to the disparity of interest rates.

In terms of DAX comparisons, one must triangulate the pairs. Euro/ U.S. dollar and U.S. dollar/Swiss franc is actually euro/Swiss franc if U.S. dollar is cancelled. U.S. dollar works as a cancellation because Swiss franc becomes the U.S. dollar measure in terms of market risk for both pairs. A long euro/U.S. dollar is a short U.S. dollar/Swiss franc and vice versa. Euro seeks yields in terms of bunds and yields in terms of U.S. Treasuries. It's a pure risk indicator as opposed to Swiss franc as a pure measure of safety as it follows Confederate bonds, U.S. bonds, and German bonds. What if euro/ Swiss franc was measured as euro/U.S. dollar and Swiss franc/U.S. dollar? This is actually a proper arrangement of the pairs because equal positions are held in terms of the bond-yield configuration. The final analysis is still euro/ Swiss franc as a measure, because the SMI sometimes fails as an indicator.

Toronto Stock Exchange

The TMX Group operates the Toronto Stock Exchange to trade stocks, the Montreal Exchange to trade Canadian derivatives, the Boston Options Exchange to trade equity options electronically, and the Natural Gas Exchange to trade and clear natural gas contracts.

The S&P/TSX 60 is the primary equity index that covers 73 percent of total equity capitalization. The S&P/TSX Composite is a broader market measure that includes common stock and income trust units. Income trust units are defined as an equity type investment structured to distribute cash flows in a tax efficient manner. Currently 155 are traded, that includes 92 business trusts, 13 energy trusts, 38 real estate investments trusts, and 12 power and pipeline trusts. Income unit trusts are employed as a corporate formation in Canada to allow the development of Canada's natural resource-rich commodities such as gold, minerals, oil sands, mining, oil, and gas and natural gas. Dividend yields have been known to be quite high over the years, especially as underlying trusts became full-fledged companies.

The S&P/TSX Composite is a comprehensive measure of equities in terms of the S&P/TSX 60, S&P/TSX equity, and S&P/TSX Completion Indices.

In October 2010, the S&P/TSX VIX index was launched to measure 30-day volatility of the S&P/TSX 60 equity index. The index is derived from near- and next-term options on S&P/TSX 60. The Canadians employ CORRA and CDOR one-, two-, and three-month rates to interpolate risk-free rates for each maturity.

The Montreal Exchange is a sophisticated and well-managed trading forum for options, futures, interest rate, equity indices, yield curve spreads, and swap hedges. The guides and strategies section is a fabulous tool as a learning guide into Canadian financial traded instruments.

Can Deal reports Canadian Treasury and bond prices in terms of a bid and ask price, a bid and ask yield, and price changes throughout any trading day directly on the Toronto Stock Exchange web site. This is most important to trade the Canadian dollar. The Canadian bond market opens at 8:00 a.m.

New York time or EST, while stock trading begins at 9:30 a.m. and closes at 4:00 p.m. Canadian economic announcements are released about 8:30, the same as the United States.

Standard and Poor's, a company formed in 1941 by the merger of Standard Statistics Corporation and Poor's Publishing, calculates all Canadian stock indices. The TSX is factored by dividing the total float-adjusted market capitalization of index stocks by a divisor. Float adjusted are publicly traded shares. An investable weight factor (IWF) is employed. For each stock IWF is equal to available float shares divided by total shares outstanding.

$$\text{The float-adjusted index} = \Sigma_j (P_j \, S_j \, IWF_j)/\text{divisor}$$

where

P_j = price of stock j,

S_j = total shares outstanding of stock j,

IWF_j = investable weight factor, and

divisor = index divisor.

The divisor is not released for public consumption.

Trade Strategy

The Canadian market trades as the TSX rises, and bond prices fall while bond yields rise. This combination sends Canadian dollar up toward weakness, a long position. So Canadian dollar/U.S. dollar would work in rising Canadian markets while U.S. dollar/Canadian dollar is a short because Canadian dollar's configuration was changed to reflect the bond price rather than the yield.

The Canadian arrangement will always be tricky because both the U.S. and Canadian markets reflect yields as both stock markets rise and bond prices fall. One side must reflect a bond price while another must reflect the yield. The question on any trading day is which combination works. The determination can be tricky.

U.S. dollar/Canadian dollar won't work as a long if Canadian markets rise and U.S. markets fall. A short is a questionable arrangement. If both markets fall, short U.S. dollar/Canadian dollar. If both market rise, long Canadian dollar/U.S. dollar, so trade the Canadian dollar/U.S. dollar arrangement. This is the proper order, not necessarily perfect, but U.S. dollar attaches to a bond price while Canadian dollar attaches to its yield. The Canadian market must be thought about first before a trade strategy is implemented, yet U.S. markets may provide overall direction.

In interest-rate terms, Canadian dollar rates are 1.00 percent while U.S. dollar is 0.25 percent. The longer term says Canadian dollar/U.S. dollar is the preferred combination as a longer-term long trade. Yet interest-rate dispari-ties should always arrange as the dominant rate in the first position of any currency-pair arrangement.

Due to the unique Canadian dollar yield arrangement and pres-ent interest-rate disparities against other pairs, normal Canadian dollar configurations will be strange. For example, see the euro/Canadian dollar. Canadian dollar rates are 1.00 percent as opposed to euro 1.00 percent. But both are yield seekers. When the DAX and TSX both rise, how should pair arrangement work? To some degree, it's long without looking back unless either side changes its rates and provided economic condi-tions hold steady or improve. Australian dollar/Canadian dollar and New Zealand dollar/Canadian dollar have the same arrangement in U.S. and Canadian trading. Both pairs seek yields, so it's again long under present configurations.

Canadian dollar/Swiss franc in present form works fine. Go long Canadian dollar/Swiss franc in rising Canadian markets, especially because Canadian rates are 1.00 percent and Swiss rates are 0.25 percent.

The Canadian dollar is a yield seeking currency, which classifies it as a risk asset. Risk assets can only be traded against measures of risk such as the new Volatility Index. High volatility is normally a sign of high risk or overbought conditions, while low volatility represents oversold conditions with low risk. The Canadian dollar should be traded based on rises and falls of the TSX with volatility as the overall guide to determine direction. Based on its yield nature, the Canadian dollar will always be a funny-moving pair even loony at times. Add the vast amounts of corporate oil interest in this pair who wish to lock in a particular price, and prices can at times become really loony.

New York Stock Exchange

The New York Stock Exchange and Euronext combined in 2007 to form New York Stock Exchange, Euronext which claims 8000 varying financial instruments traded, including derivatives, futures, options, stocks, and stock indices. Two most important instruments to trade currency pairs are the Dow Jones and S&P indices. Both are important, yet very different in calculation, methodology, size, and age.

Charles Dow calculated the Dow 12 stocks in 1896 while Standard Statistics Corporation first introduced the S&P 90 in 1926, S&P 500 in the 1950s (DJ Indexes, S&P). Dow indices are price weighted while S&P are market-capitalization weighted (DJ Indexes, S&P). Dow indices represent only blue chips while S&P are the largest capitalization companies, at least $3.5 billion by Standard & Poor terms. Dow 30 captures about 25 to 30 percent of the market while the S&P 500 covers about 75 percent (DJ Indexes, S&P). Dow Jones offers the Dow 30 and Composite 65 while the S&P offers S&P 100, Mid Cap 400, Small Cap 600, and S&P 1500 that comprises S&P 500, 400, and 600 (DJ Indexes, S&P). All indices are represented by U.S. companies and calculated in U.S. dollars. Dow Jones indices update every two minutes on the NYSE web site, S&P are time delayed by 20 minutes. Both indices are calculated within seconds.

Both companies offer Treasury bond indexes to track Treasury bond prices. Dow Jones offers the CBOT Treasury Index that comprise a 30-year bond, a 10-year note, and a 5-year note futures contract that measures the default-free U.S. dollar capital market returns (DJ Indexes). It's calculated every 15 seconds and prices are reported in real time.

The S&P/BG Cantor U.S. Treasury Series includes subindices such as the U.S. Treasury Bill Index, one- to three-year index, three- to five- year, five- to seven-year, 7- to 10-year, 10- to 20-year, and 20-plus-year indices (S&P).

The S&P 500 comprises info technology—18.8 percent, financials—15.7 percent, healthcare—11.6 percent, consumer staples—11.3 percent, industrials—10.8 percent, energy—10.9 percent, consumer discretionary—10.4 percent, utilities—3.6 percent, materials—.5 percent, and telecommunication services—.2 percent. The Dow 30 comprises industrials—22.07 percent, technology—17.37 percent, consumer services—13.54 percent, consumer goods—10.70 percent, oil and gas—0.15 percent, financials—9.92 percent, healthcare—7.99 percent, telecommunications—4.15 percent, and basic materials—4.11 percent (S&P).

The S&P 500 index value is a "quotient of total float-adjusted market cap of constituents and its divisor and is calculated as each stock weight is proportional to float adjusted market value". To calculate:

$$\text{Index level} = \frac{\Sigma_i P_i \times Q_i}{\text{Divisor}}$$

The numerator is calculated as "the price of each stock × the number of shares in index calculation." The divisor is by S&P's example. "If the numerator is equal to $11.8 trillion and the divisor is equal to $9.4 billion, the index is equal to 1250" (S&P). The S&P Index is a modification of a Laspeyres Index.

$$\text{Laspeyres Index} = \frac{\Sigma_i P_{i,1} \times Q_{i,o}}{\Sigma I_{p_{i,o}} \times Q_{i,o}}$$

"If Qo is replaced by Q1, the numerator equals market value and the denominator is replaced by a divisor represents initial market value and sets the base value." Recognize the similarities of the SMI and the German DAX indices.

Dow Jones indices are float adjusted and price weighted. Price weight means the weight is commensurate with price (DJ Indexes). Charles Dow calculated his index by adding stock prices and dividing by the number of stocks (DJ Indexes). Today, add prices of components and divide by the current divisor. The divisor is published daily in the *Wall Street Journal* and is employed to hold the index steady in terms of stock splits, mergers, and acquisitions (DJ Indexes). The base value 40.94 of the Dow 30 Industrial Average is derived from 1896 (DJ Indexes). Dow Indices that include the Dow 65 Composite, Utility and transportation averages are calculated every two seconds, every 15 seconds during German DAX trading.

The Dow Transportation index comprises 20 of the top transportation companies and predates the Dow 30 average by almost two years (DJ Indexes).

Transportation Index, New Zealand Dollar/U.S. Dollar and Australian Dollar/U.S. Dollar

Consider the Dow 30 year to date increased 9.74 percent, the Dow Transportation Average increased 17.51 percent, Australian dollar/U.S. dollar price increased year to date from 8800 to 1.0110, and New Zealand dollar/U.S. dollar increased from 7041 to 7970.

Some Things to Consider

Traditional Dow Theory aligns with the supposition that the Dow Industrial averages is the measure of manufacturing health while the transportation index is the measure of transporting manufactured goods. Each index moves traditionally in conjunction with each other as a measure of an economy in proper order. Australian dollar and New Zealand dollar can be measured in terms of the transportation index due to the vital importance transportation plays in the shipment of Australian dollar and New Zealand dollar goods to and across the United States. The idea is a healthy economy will see shipment rates in terms of rail, air, and land decrease and benefit both currencies. This is not the only Australian dollar and New Zealand dollar measure but both pairs strongly correlate to transportation indices. Rare mention is rendered due to many new instruments with a short-term focus.

The Dow Utility average was first calculated in January 1929 with a base of 86.64 and 15 present stocks in the index (DJ Indexes). The index comprises electric and natural gas companies (DJ Indexes). Traditionally, rising utility prices was a sign of falling interest rates, and rising interest rates saw averages decline as interest cost to electric companies rose and fell. Some argue this phenomenon doesn't hold any longer due to deregulation (DJ Indexes).

U.S. Dollar/Swiss Franc and Dow Jones Utility Average

Consider 2010 year to date total returns of 6.42 percent, 4.06 percent total for five years, with a 2010 dividend yield in 2010 of 4.30 percent (DJ Indexes). Now consider U.S. dollar/Swiss franc began 2010 at 1.0265 and sits at 0.9598 presently. The inverse correlation is fairly consistent year to year, which could say that the Utility Index tops during year end as the currency price drops under a normal wave pattern.

Treasury bond, S&P, and Dow Jones futures trade almost around the clock on Globex and are quite easy to track.

Interest Rates

Most important in terms of currency pairs is the purpose of trade and movements in interest rates, and interest rates are determined first by the most interest-rate sensitive instruments. In the United States, Fed funds is what prices bonds and bonds are what determine direction for stock markets. OCR determines New Zealand and Australia movements in terms of bonds and stock markets.

Consider Fed funds contracts begin at $5 million, $5 million for Australia OCR contracts. The course is to follow the smart money. But during the course of any trading day, rates can change up or down depending on market circumstances, so the focus switches to bonds, yields, and stock markets. Stock markets are always ancillary indicators, while bonds, yields, and interest rates are primary indicators because the cost of money is determined, so therefore can a cost be valued for currency pairs. Currency pairs are money-market instruments, so prices are reflected in interbank trading as bonds and rates are factored. The methodology should be to focus on those short-term instruments first before the bond, yield, and stock market.

Conclusion

The bond/yield interplay is reflected and priced into stock markets. Stock markets as an indicator are then a factor that can be used to gauge spot prices. Each currency pair has a characteristic in its movement and purpose from market to market. Each market is quite different depending on the pair. The euro is one pair where movements are the same throughout all markets.

CHAPTER 9

Currency Cycles, Currency Futures, Options, and Volatility

The purpose of this chapter is first to understand currency cycles and how those cycles were first applied to market instruments. To know inverted pairs is to know how to apply the right indicator. Gann and Elliot are the premier indicators and offered with detailed explanations. A pure cycle indicator, how it is applied, methodology, and formula are explained in depth. E-Quivalents are discussed at length due to its insight as not only a market tool but its many functions as an insightful market guide.

A detailed and insightful discussion of options is offered, including how to factor option premiums, how to know and detect barrier options, and implied volatility and its calculation.

Volatility and volatility indicators in terms of various formulas, calculations, strategies, purposes, and uses are discussed with a step-by-step detailed approach. Popular risk models and their purposes and uses are addressed.

All essential information, calculations, formulas, purposes, methodologies, and historic frameworks are discussed in depth and detail in order for those methods to easily be applied in any trade plan.

In order to properly measure such currency pairs as euro/U.S. dollar and U.S. dollar/euro, it's imperative to understand these pairs in relation to currency cycles and cycle measurements, a topic with firm adherents or diametrically opposite views. The concept of cycles particularly as it relates to currency trading is certainly not new and is quite popular among researchers and found in many different research reports. All reports vary however in lengths of cycles in relation to time. If historic currency-pair tops

269

and bottoms can be the measure since the euro introduction, currency cycles last anywhere from 12 to 16 weeks, although 16 is on the high side as that occurred only once since the euro inception in 1999. Notice the correlation with cycle tops and bottoms and seasonality. The variation of reports may be because only one side of the inversion is measured. Another may be related to the historic understanding of cycles.

Cycles in the modern day were measured in terms of business peaks and troughs to predict recession and expansion and many can be credited historically. Nokolai Kondratieff identified 54-year cycles, Simon Kuznets found 18-year cycles, Clement Juglar is noted for the long nine-year cycle, and Joseph Kitchens identified the four-year cycle. Joseph Schumpeter in 1939 published a definitive two-volume set called *Business Cycles*. It was only a matter of time before market professionals employed various cycle methods to predict stock prices.

In simple terms, William Gann's great contribution to technical analysis was to divide time and price by geometric angles, while Ralph Elliott's five-wave pattern employed Fibonacci numbers to measure each wave. Both are wave-pattern forms, but both can be measured in relation to time and price with accuracy.

The basics of Gann say a price over time is equal to a one-by-one angle drawn at 45 degrees. The idea is that prices rise and fall based on time. Angles provide support or resistance and highlight where the market is trading at any given moment. Gann devised nine lines, nine angles, each with various degrees relative to price and time.

Elliott's waves comprise five: A, B, C, D, and E. The basics of Elliott in up trends says A waves rise, B waves correct, C waves rise, D waves are down, and E waves rise. Then the down waves begin with E waves falling to an A, B becomes an upward correction, and C continues the downtrend. Smaller waves may exist within the patterns, called impulse waves, so Fibonacci numbers are employed to measure time and price in relation to dominant waves.

The exact timing of the study of pure-cycle analysis in markets is anyone's guess. One possible source is JM Hurst's 1970 classic *Profit Magic of Stock Transaction Timing*. With degrees in mathematics and physics, Hurst built on the work of nineteenth century mathematician Joseph Fourier and the Fourier Transform and applied it to stock transactions.

Hurst invented a cyclic system that claimed "8.9 percent yield per transaction every 9.7 days" (Profit Magic). The book is a highly recommended read, but it is not for the mathematically challenged.

The basic components of Hurst are summarized in *Technical Analysis, the Complete Resource for Financial Market Technicians* by Charles Kirkpatrick and Julie Dahlquist. Three basic aspects are measured by cycles: amplitude, period, and phase.

"Amplitude is measured as the distance of the horizontal axis from peak to trough, period is the distance between consecutive lows or consecutive highs and phase is how far from the y-axis cycles begin. The location along the cycle of each point is measured by this formula: $f(x) = a \times \cos(bx + c) + d$, where a = amplitude, bx = period (constant b times $\times$ time in radians), c = phase in radians and d = error factor." (Kirkpatrick and Kahlquist) Lastly, "Hurst measured period lengths in multiples of two or three longer or shorter than next larger or smaller cycles. A 20-day cycle says another longer cycle of 40- or 60-day length exists. Cosine waves, multiple waves are each calculated and added to form a summation." The question of does this method work, can be answered with just as well as Elliott and Gann, but much more exists to the methodologies presented here. For example, Hurst factored frequencies, parameters of prices, and measured corrections. Hurst stated in *Profit Magic* that his methodologies took 10 years to perfect. The study of cycles in this modern day can possibly be credited to Hurst and incorporated by others.

For example, Doug Schaff invented an indicator for currency traders called the Schaff Trend Cycle that was based on a variation of Hurst. This is the first of its type, and is based on Schaff's years of cycle research. Schaff's idea was to find an indicator that traded into the dominant cycle trend. This was accomplished by blending an Exponential Moving Average and Fast Stochastics with a cycle component.

For currency pairs, the best measure is by far the ABC pattern, where A and B are up candles and C corrects down, or A and B are down candles and C corrects up. Compare this pattern to Elliot's five waves and one can understand critical arguments to cycles.

Currency pairs cycle from peaks to troughs, as one inverted pair tops, then the other bottoms, or relatively close. The question is the measure of inversions.

CME Group Equivalents

An extraordinarily useful tool to traders is Equivalents, offered by the Chicago Mercantile Exchange (CME). Equivalents operates 23 hours a day from Sunday to Friday and can be viewed by anyone around the world from any computer at cmegroup.com/equivalents. Equivalents allows traders to view currency-pair futures prices live in any contract month, and view live volume and notional amounts. More useful is the ability to determine spot prices, cash positions, and a four-time daily update of forward points.

First, view high, lows, and last trades to determine the parameters of the market. Then determine market bids and offer prices, important because these prices can represent major support and resistance; more important is the ability to view market liquidity.

Liquidity is the key to determine if a pair will break a support or resistance point or if a pair will bounce and maintain a range. Nearest-term contracts are always represented first. Futures contracts settle quarterly based on International Money Market standards, M = June, U = September, Z = December, and H = March.

Bids are buy prices and offers are sell prices. What is shown is how many contracts are bid and offered at various bid and offer prices. This will determine market direction in terms of longs and shorts. If 200 contracts are bid at a certain price and 50 contracts are offered at another price, this says the market is long, so spot prices can go long. Bids and offers can be seen in longer-dated contracts.

Another tool is to convert futures prices to spot equivalents. Euro is the most widely traded of all currency pairs and trades at $12.50 per tick, which converts to $125,000 euros per contract. The formula is number of contracts multiplied by contract size is equal to currency denomination. For example, 50 contracts multiplied by $125,000 is equal to $6,250,000. This represents how many euros are offered. For bid prices, 200 contracts multiplied by $125,000 is equal to $25,000,000 euros bid. The market can now be viewed in euro liquidity terms.

Japanese yen/U.S. dollar trades yen at 12,500,000, British pounds/U.S. dollar at 62,500, Canadian dollar/U.S. dollar at Canadian100,000, Swiss francs/U.S. dollar trade at Swiss francs 125,000, 100,000 for Australian dollar/U.S. dollar. Ticks are equal to 0.0001, except for the yen quoted at 0.000001 (CME).

The point here is the quote conventions. The question is how many U.S. dollars will it take to buy one euro? U.S. dollar pairs are quoted directly as how many dollars to buy X amount of another currency.

In this situation, euro was well bid at a certain price. This says the market sees a long euro/U.S. dollar. In inverted cycle terms, the market also sees a short U.S. dollar/euro. This example serves for the British pounds/U.S. dollar, Australian dollar/U.S. dollar, and New Zealand dollar/U.S. dollar, all traded pairs at the CME and offered through Equivalents.

The opposite holds for non-dollar pairs such as Japanese yen/U.S. dollar. This is the standard arrangement of trade for the yen. It's called an indirect quote. It asks how many yen to buy one U.S. dollar? This example could be any pair arranged in this manner. For Japanese yen/U.S. dollar, determine direction in terms of contracts, and evaluate in U.S. dollar/Japanese yen terms which pair to trade. How far each will trade in cycle terms can be found in cash equivalents.

Forward points are shown at bid and offer prices. Forward points represent interest-rate differentials between currency pairs, important because they establish cash equivalents for each currency pair. All pairs will have different forward points due to different interest rate differentials. An interest-rate change in a nation can change forward points dramatically. The CME updates forward points four times daily to reflect interest-rate changes in the short term. Interest-rate changes are reflected in cash prices. The formula is futures rate minus forward points is equal to spot cash equivalents.

The methodology now is to evaluate spot-cash prices to futures prices. Cash prices are almost always above futures prices, it's the cost of capital now instead of the future. More important is what is the relationship between spot and futures prices. Forward prices are established in this manner by forward price is equal to spot price plus forward points.

Spreads are factored as:

$$\text{Spot} \times (\text{European foreign currency} - \text{Eurodollar deposit rate}) \times (t/360) \times 100 \text{ or } S \times (\text{Eurodollar rate European foreign currency}) \times (t/365) \times 100 \text{ (CME)}$$

This equation answers the question is futures trading at a discount or premium to the cash spot price? Both formulas establish either the direct or indirect quote convention. This methodology allows a view in terms of central bank meetings, rate determinations, and direction to pairs when interest rates are raised or lowered. A caveat, Eurodeposits are established daily for not only U.S. dollar but the euro, British pounds, and Swiss francs are also priced and reported shortly after the British Bankers Association (BBA) LIBOR release.

Forward points are calculated as:

$$\text{Spot quote/Bid} \times (\text{I quote} - \text{I base}) \times \text{time}/360 \times 100$$

Add forward points to the spot quote and it's a forward quote. A forward quote is what the market is willing to pay for future spot. This is the measure to factor inversions. Yet it is not necessarily the method to factor forward-exchange rates. Forward exchange rates are found in forward interest rate formulas.

Approximately 30 years ago, the International Standardization Organization (ISO) located in Switzerland determined quoting conventions for currency pairs. Today it's called the International Standards Organization. Pairs quoted as the foreign currency first such as euro/U.S. dollar or British pounds/U.S. dollar is termed the American-quote convention, a direct quote in market parlance, while U.S. dollar/Japanese yen or U.S. dollar/Swiss francs are known as European quotes and quoted as an indirect quote. The establishment, methodologies, and factors of those decisions derived from the ISO 4217:2008 country-codes sectors of the ISO.

The proper name is Codes for the Representation of Currencies and Funds is and maintained by SIX Interbank Clearing, located in Zurich, Switzerland, but they fall under responsibility of the British Standards Institution, an ISO member from the United Kingdom(ISO).

The purpose of 4217 is to enhance trade, commerce, and banking across borders with identifying features (ISO). Nations are identified by a three-letter alpha and three- number numeric code. Alpha U.S. dollar is identified by numeric 840 and includes nations that use U.S. dollars in exchange. The Alpha euro is identified by numeric 978 and includes all nations that use the euro in currency exchanges. ISO also establishes decimal points for *minor currencies*. The last ISO list was published in 2008, while the prior list was published in 2001 (ISO).

Currently, 41 pairs trade at the CME and a vast majority are offered on Equivalents. Pairs such as British pounds/Japanese yen, Australian dollar/Japanese yen, Canadian dollar/U.S. dollar, and U.S. dollar/Swiss francs can all be evaluated for direction and inversion terms. A further method is the March 2009 introduction of the E-micro contracts.

E-Micro

E-Micro currency futures contracts are one-tenth the size of standard contracts so euro is attendant as .001 = 1 point and Japanese yen at .01 = 1 point. Currently six pairs trade on Globex around the clock on the trading floor, and all can be viewed on Equivalents with the same features as standard contracts. The six pairs are: euro/U.S. dollar, Australian dollar/U.S. dollar, British pounds/U.S. dollar, U.S. dollar/Japanese yen, U.S. dollar/Canadian dollar, and U.S. dollar/Swiss francs. The point of note is pair arrangements.

Standard futures contracts trade Japanese yen/U.S. dollar, Canadian dollar/U.S. dollar, and Swiss francs/U.S. dollar, while E-Micro contracts trade U.S. dollar/Japanese yen, U.S. dollar/Canadian dollar, and U.S.

dollar/Swiss francs. This is termed spot market, interbank market, or cash markets to align market parlance properly. Since both contracts trade opposite arrangements, no better instrument is available to measure inversions. As one pair cycles up, the inverted pair cycles down. But inversions, like cycles, never match perfectly at times so what is important is directional determination of each paired inversion.

Options and Volatility

The latest preferred method to trade currency pairs is by option premiums and volatility. Such a new and sophisticated strategy can only say old methodologies are no longer useful as a strategy nor even as a guide.

For example, Put/Call ratios were once the measure to determine if the market was long or short. If call buyers exceeded put sellers across all strike prices, the market is considered long, while put sellers exceeding call buyers is considered a short market. Traders would then pick and choose strike prices that aligned to their preferred time frames and determined ratios of longs to short. While put/call ratios still may work for stock options or other markets, it appears to be outmoded as a currency-trading plan. The next method was risk reversals.

Popular market-risk-reversal definition says it's the difference in implied volatility between a currency option same strike, same expiration of an out-of-the-money delta 25 put and delta 25 call. The purpose is to measure future volatility in relation to deltas, but more importantly to gauge market direction. As future volatility increases, deltas will increase as the value of options increase due to higher premiums expected by the market. The Chicago Board Options Exchange (CBOE) definition of delta is "the amount an option's theoretical value will change for a one unit change in price of the underlying instrument." Out-of-the-money options are employed as a strategy to follow the underlying currency pair. Delta is a 30-day time frame and the shortest of the Greek options: Gamma, Vega, Theta, and Rho. From an opposing view, as an option moves toward expiration, deltas decrease and end at zero at expiration. Some then graph and plot strategy based on a skew, yet it accompanies successes and failures. This is because enormous fallacies are associated with this strategy.

The first question must be what type of options were measured: over the counter, exchange-traded options, or both. The second question: were European and/or American options considered? This is vitally important because European options are exercised at expiration while American options can be exercised anytime. This point changes the entire equation, because both accompany different formulas and methodologies and neither can be employed together. For example, some track the S&P 500 against VIX Options that settle European exercise. Secondly, American options trade five hours longer than European options and that must be held account in any trading plan (CME Options Rulebook). The methodology is European options are employed to hedge and American options are widely traded.

The Black Scholes formula originated in 1973 in the *Journal of Political Economy* and is employed to measure European options both over the counter and exchange traded. The vast majority of over-the-counter options are European exercised.

The Barone, Adesi, and Whaley formula originated in 1987 in the *Journal of Finance* to factor American exchange-traded options (CME). The question for both was how to price and value options, but both formulas must be employed against its respected type. Consider traded options.

Formulas must factor call and put options, time to expiration, price, strike price, and interest rates. Interest rates must be factored as a risk-free rate. The T-Bill is widely employed, but that rate is twice removed from an actual BBA or internal LIBOR.

John Cox, Stephen Ross, and Mark Rubenstein published a binomial pricing model in the *Journal of Financial Economics* in 1979 that valued trades based on arbitrage that factored a currency pair and currency option. In one way, Cox-Ross, as it's known in market parlance, can be viewed as the risk measure to the two main option pricing models currently in existence. The Canadians at the Montreal options and derivatives exchange widely employ Cox-Ross. All three models set standards that haven't been surpassed since inception.

In 1983, Mark Garmen and Steven Kohlhagen advanced the Black Scholes formula with introduction of an interest-rate factor measured against each side of a currency pair. The purpose was to factor the risk-free rate between a currency pair that accounts for exchange rates. Finally, is the question of implied volatility.

Implied volatility is defined by the market as the expected return. The CME defines implied volatility as "implied by a market price of an option based on option pricing models. Volatility through models yields a theoretical option value." Despite a definition that said nothing, the key word is implied. Implied volatility is expected, not guaranteed, but expected if the market reacts as anticipated. Some say a formula doesn't exist to calculate implied volatility hence the purpose to follow a delta strategy. Implied correlation is the preferred method due to its statistical component.

Volatility is an estimate based on American or European formulas using option-market prices as an input. By using past and present prices, implied volatility is found by running the models backward. These are what-if scenarios that incorporate a futures price, strike, option price, days to expiration, and interest rates. Formulas are factored as F(S, O, D, R).

Market events in a delta strategy can disrupt an expected forecast and destroy a risk-reversal strategy especially when the return is expected within a 30-day period. The assumption is volatility within a currency pair will increase the price of deltas. Yet it's not a guaranteed strategy simply because currency markets can trade sideways, and move in infinitesimal ranges with price congestion for long periods. Time will surpass the strategy. Implied volatility may work well in other markets, but spot prices and its fast rate of change or no change can impinge the overall measure of volatility unless the strategy was perfected. Today's strategy is trade at the money options. A risk measure is employed by taking the one month interest rate differential and divide by the implied volatility from the one month at the money call or put option. It's a measure of currency options but can be employed to trade equitiy indices.

Volatility and Volatility Indicators

To measure risk is to measure volatility. The question is how far will prices vary in relation to expected returns? Two instruments can realize different returns based on variations because we are squaring the difference from the mean as a measure of variability. So volatility must be measured by squaring the variance to obtain a standard deviation to obtain an accurate view of volatility.

Volatility is measured by standard deviation calculated by standard deviation of daily returns over X trading days to annualize the figure. This measures the spread of prices around the mean—the average. When prices are close to the mean, standard deviation is low, and high when prices are far away. The general strategy should be buy the low and sell the high.

Standard deviation asks the question how far apart is the distribution. Normal distribution says prices should be 68 percent within one standard deviation of the average, 95 percent within 2 standard deviations, and about 96 percent within three standard deviations. This outline is known as realized, actual, or market volatility that's generally measured in one- to three-month time frames, one year to measure historic volatility. Looked at another way, suppose as suggested by prior research that a 252-day simple moving average was plotted, a mean based on past year price closes that considers U.S. foreign exchange

(FX) trading days and holidays. Much dispersion occurs around the mean over a yearly period. How to capture those short-term variations in volatility terms has been the subject of intense research over many years, more so in the present day as option trading increased with new financial instruments. Consider that in Whaley's historic 1987 paper, 30 American options traded on the CME.

The main point associated with volatility and volatility indicators is it tends toward mean reversion where prices oscillate around a long-term average. Whether low or high volatility, it mean reverts. A rate of return of volatility as an annualized standard deviation percentage index or indicator can be converted to shorter time frames. For example, a 20 percent index value converts to a monthly value by multiplying 20 percent by square root of one-twelfth, for a 5.77 forecast that predicts movement of one standard deviation over one month of $+/-$ 5.77 (ASX example). This formula addresses the question of stressed rates.

Stress rates ask the question what is the probability z scores change based on whatever standard deviations are measured in relation to the square root of time? The formula is:

$$S_e^{z\sigma\sqrt{t}}$$

where

s = spot in logs,
e = the natural logarithm,
z = a z score, sigma (SD) at the square root of t.

It's a strategy not only to determine spot prices but other market instruments such as options. Market professionals view this methodology as a measurement of a time series employed for the short term. The purpose is to capture only volatility that deviated from normal trend.

Another strategy widely employed by central banks is to measure volatility between two pair's exchange rates and correlate.

The formula

$$\sigma\frac{2}{12} = \sigma\frac{2}{1} + \sigma\frac{2}{2} - 2_p\sigma_1\sigma_2$$

where

volatility 12 $=$ cross rate volatility,
volatility 1 $=$ volatility of exchange rate 1,
volatility 2 $=$ volatility of exchange rate 2, and
p $=$ correlation between currency 1 and 2.

Prior research measured volatility in terms of options, and measured volatility by Garch models, Arch models, time-series models, long-term volatility, and short-term volatility. Papers measured single-market instruments, combined markets, and instruments. The study of pure volatility began in the summer of 2000 in the *Journal of Alternative Investments* by Robert Krause and intensified over the years.

Krause proposed then a pure volatility contract, later finalized and outlined in the 2010 issue of the Swiss Derivatives Review. Many questions were settled with formulation of the CME's 2011 introduction of Krause's volatility contracts on six currency pairs, euro/U.S. dollar, British pounds/U.S. dollar, Canadian dollar/U.S. dollar, Australian dollar/U.S. dollar, Swiss francs/U.S. dollar and Japanese yen/U.S. dollar. Vol (Trademark) contracts are cash settled and settle to either the 1 or 3 month realized volatility.

The formula is:

$$RV = 100 \times \sqrt{252/n \left(L_n \frac{P_t}{P_{t-1}} \right)^2 \sum_{t=1}^{n} R_t^2}$$

where
  n = number of trading days,
  r_t = continuous compounded daily returns calculated by
  $r_t = L_n \dfrac{P_t}{P_{t-1}}$ and,

where
  L_n = natural logarithm,
  P_t = underlying reference price at time t, and
  P_{t-1} = underlying reference price at time t period preceding time t.

The formula is calculated as an annualized standard deviation of log returns of daily settlement. Any volatility contract should begin with zero as the foundation point. To define a mean, it begins at a zero point and deviations occur from that point.

At the Volatility Institute at New York University, many time-series charts for various financial instruments are available for daily review at the vlab, as well as many published papers and lists of courses. Robert Krauss updated volx.us with an abundance of information, papers, and trade strategies.

Option Premiums

On any screen shot of American currency options is a view of volume, futures price, option price, and strike price for each option offered. American currency options trade at premiums in half-point strike price increments and represent 85 percent of total CME volume (CME Options Rulebook). Premiums are quoted in U.S. dollar points per foreign currency. The notional values equal the same underlying price convention, $12.50 euro, $62,500 British pounds.

The formula to determine premium is:

$$\text{Points} \times \text{Contracts} \times \text{Tick value}$$

For example, a 1.4430 euro/U.S. dollar call option bid at 75 × 150 contracts is equal to 0.0075 multiplied by $125,000 equals $937.50. To sell the option 150 multiplied by $937.50 equals $140,625. A premium quote is reported as the equivalent of a live price in the OTC market (2010 Option Rulebook). To know currency options is to know liquidity in the market related to any currency pair combined with the futures and cash prices. The overall question is where is the market in terms of liquidity and at what strike price, a determination of a long or short market.

Barrier Options

The importance of this section is not to understand barrier options, how to trade those options, and price methodologies. Rather it's important to know where barriers are located within spot currency prices to determine if a break or bounce will occur at a particular price once a barrier is reached.

Importers, exporters, and major companies routinely employ barrier options to facilitate trade across borders. For example, Canadians employ barrier options to facilitate oil flows and other trade to U.S. markets, its largest export partner. Japanese exporters routinely employ barrier options to facilitate a multitude of trade in various products to various world destinations.

A multitude of barrier options can routinely be found within yen prices in various currency-pair arrangements. Since the United States is the second-largest export market, Japanese yen/U.S. dollar and U.S. dollar/Japanese yen must be evaluated to determine where barriers are located since barriers may restrict a price break at certain levels.

Barrier levels at certain prices are either defended successfully, in which a bounce will occur in the opposite direction, or an unsuccessful defense occurs and prices will continue a forward path. Barrier options are employed to lock in a particular price.

Other currency pairs may contain barrier options to hedge other financial instruments. Other types of barrier options exist such as a Binary or Plain Vanilla, but they don't have the market power as a full barrier option simply because of a higher-priced barrier. The question for deployment of barrier options is how important is the price and cost to defend it. European-style options are by far the most popular deployed, yet American- and Bermuda-style are also employed (US FX Committee 2005 Report). Bermuda options allow expiration relative to time, but specific dates relative to exercise must be stated in prior arranged agreements. For traders, it's the nondiscrete barrier options to monitor because they are determined by the spot rate (FX Committee 2005).

Barrier options began trade with formal outlines implemented by the U.S. FX Committee and other organizations such as the International Swaps and Derivatives Association in 1998 with an additional update in 2005 and 2006. Highlights from the updated report follow.

A barrier event was further defined. The committee question was how does one know a barrier was reached? A barrier-determination agent was introduced as a third-party confirmation a barrier event occurred. Determination dates and rate calculations were further defined. Barrier and other options are backed by extensive agreements that outline the terms between two parties. The real purpose to this supplementary report was to further define barrier options and single- and double-No-Touch and One-Touch binary options. It was a forward report, as most of these reports are facilitated by market professionals.

Two types of barrier options exist for our purposes, Knock in/Knock out and Double Knock in/Double Knock out. Knock-out options terminate if spot trades at or beyond a defined barrier before expiration. The closer the knock out to the spot rate, the less expensive it is because the probability that the barrier is reached will increase.

A knock-in option is inactive but becomes live if spot trades at or beyond a barrier before expiration. The closer Knock in trades to spot, the more the option will increase because the probability exists that the barrier will be hit (FX Committee). Double Knock-in and Double-Knock out options include another barrier. News organizations that specialize in currency markets routinely report locations of barrier options.

The problem with movements at times of an export currency such as the U.S. dollar/Japanese yen is barrier options are routinely located within various price points of U.S. dollar/Japanese yen that at times restrict movements. It's not unusual to see a $5 or $10 million barrier located at a certain price.

Volatility and Value-at-Risk Models

Volatility affects market prices as a function primarily from outside forces. Inflation, interest rates, political changes, economic disasters, military escapades, and wars all affect markets in terms of volatility levels and levels can change dramatically.

Dollars at Risk seeks to determine such factors as yield-curve movements in relation to currency prices and employed as a measure of risk. Dollars at Risk ask questions as to how many basis points does a 10-year Treasury bond move in relation to a target price or stop loss order, and what about two-year-bond basis points? The preferred method is to factor fixed-income returns against a constructed yield curve using various risk measures that account for volatility.

Value-at-risk (VAR) models assess risk using "statistical techniques on worst-case scenarios that can't exceed a particular confidence level. It measures risk in relation to leverage. New components include volatility, correlations, and exponentially weighted moving averages to assess risk" (Jorion 2007).

Conclusion

After a historic walk through past economists such as Schumpeter and methodologies of economic business cycles, an introduction of currency cycles was offered in terms of inversions. The methodology of currency cycles is in the measurement. Since currency-pairs invert, past inventors of indicators widely employed today such as Gann and Elliot were offered as a methodology to help in understanding how and why cycles occur, with a further idea that methodologies can be applied easily to a chart.

Volatility was discussed in all its minute details of historic importance as well as offered formulas to calculate and measure market instruments and currency pairs, volatility in relation to options and premiums, and barrier options. Risk models in terms of VAR and dollars at Risk were addressed.

CHAPTER 10

Technical Analysis

This chapter highlights in depth and detail many market tools and various indicators. Volume and open interest is discussed due to its wide use and effectiveness. Formulas, trade strategies, trading methodologies, and past history to understand its modern-day context are all highlighted. Commitment of traders' reports, where to find them at the Commodity Futures Trading Commission (CFTC) and Chicago Mercantile Exchange (CME), how to read the reports, and which ones to read, as well as their points of reference in order to evaluate a trade plan is explained step by step. The Baltic Exchange, its derivation, products, purpose, functions, and evaluative tools are addressed in order to track commodity currencies. Correlations, then regression lines and other trend lines, are shown and methodologies highlighted to understand how to plot lines on a chart to measure currency and other market prices. Special Drawing Rights (SDRs) and the International Monetary Fund (IMF) may be a future indicator due to wide use of the SDR financial instrument. Pivot points, Bollinger Bands, and Ichimoku, and their purpose, derivations, calculations, and formulas along with full explanations of how to measure currency and other market prices is fully explained.

Currency-pair prices trend, range, or cluster in a zone for periods of time, while other periods of time account for volatility. How to measure various phenomena can be gauged by market tools and/or indicators.

It's imperative to know a range of indicators to account for various market periods, yet it's also imperative to be able to shift indicators as market periods meld from one type to another, such as range to trend. Indicators are never perfect, but they provide reasonable estimates of various market periods. Reasonable estimates are derived from indicator calculations.

For example, Bollinger Bands are widely deployed to account for both volatility and moving-average components. Moving averages measure mean time series over time, pivot points measure support and resistance, and Ichimoku measures moving averages for present and future market conditions. All work equally well to capture profits, but none have the perfection of a pure mathematical model. Yet markets are never perfect so it's imperative to allow confirmation in every market scenario.

The import of any indicator is to know its minute details as well as any currency pair for its various characteristics, because all have variations. Some indicators work well in trends, others work better in short-term market moves.

Volume and Open Interest

Volume and open interest studies trace their roots to commodity trading with passage of the Commodity Exchange Act on September 21, 1922. It was formerly titled the Grain Futures Act, but was amended in June 1936 to include other traded commodities such as wheat, rice, corn, oats, and other agricultural products (Bear, 1948).

The Chicago Board of Trade (CBOT), established in 1848, was mandated by the Agricultural Department to maintain volume and other extensive records for open inspection for at least three years. Commitment of Traders (COT) Reports today still maintain a three-year history for public view. The main purpose for the records was to maintain integrity of the markets due to the importance of agricultural products to the American public in staple and export terms.

Open interest is assumed to be a byproduct of future market developments. Yet the Chicago *Daily Tribune* reported open interest for wheat contracts as early as 1926.

The New York Stock Exchange traces its roots to the 1792 Buttonwood Agreement where 24 brokers signed an agreement to trade securities by commission (NYSE). Possibly volume and open-interest studies trace their roots to these early days and became a natural byproduct with establishment of organized commodity exchanges.

As two of the oldest indicators, volume and open interest hasn't been a focus in the modern day due to more popular, ready-made indicators. Yet volume and open interest have been a constant staple for market professionals since inception.

Ken Shaleen of Chartwatch can be credited with writing the definitive book in 1992, called *Volume and Open Interest*. Outside Ken Shaleen's work, volume and open interest has been contained within the confines of market professionals because not much has been written since Shaleen. Ironically, market professionals know nothing about popular indicators, nor do non-market professionals know anything about professional tools. Market professionals employ pure mathematical models while nonprofessionals employ indicators, and neither interest intersects.

Open interest is defined by the CME as total futures contracts long or short in a delivery month entered into but not offset by delivery. Only one side of the transaction is calculated. Volume is simply the number of contracts bought or sold for a given time period. Volume in days past was an essential ingredient as a hedge, called price insurance (Baer 1948). Open interest was the trading method. Today, volume and open interest together are employed to determine trends, market sentiment, and direction by monitoring contract flows.

Under daily settlements on the CME web site is where volume and open interest information is found. Anyone can view foreign exchange (FX) futures, FX options, or both for open interest and volume reports. The new addition is FX Micro contracts and the key is to study open interest and volume because Micro contracts are arranged as spot transactions, so a full view of standard and FX Micros can be determined.

Three different reports may be employed: futures only, options and put/call totals, and Micro contracts. For options, volume and open interest is now available for each strike price. Long-term traders would be interested in near- and next-term contracts while short-term traders would be served by nearest contracts. Floor trading and Globex are the two reports of interest. An initial report is issued after market closes that includes floor trading, and final reports are issued before market openings the next day that include floor trading and Globex trading from overnight. There are a number of scenarios to monitor.

A trending market occurs when volume and open interest is up. Prices rise on increased volume and open interest. Low volume may be a correction, but it depends if open interest rises (Shaleen). A rise is a correction, a fall could be a reversal. Average volume is a range trade. When volume and open interest is up and prices decline, chances are good it's a downtrend (Shaleen). Average volume and flat open interest represent congestion, an unsure market, or a wait-and-see approach to outside events (Shaleen).

The key is to compare Japanese yen/U.S. dollar futures and options against U.S. dollar/Japanese yen Micros to determine direction. Same for Canadian dollar/U.S. dollar and Swiss franc/U.S. dollar futures and options against Micro U.S. dollar/Canadian dollar and U.S. dollar/Swiss franc. Traders should look at option-strike prices with the understanding that American options are the vast majority of trade.

COT Reports

The weekly COT report is still a valuable tool studied by market professionals to determine market direction, sentiment, and trend. Two types of reports are released weekly for financial futures and options. Legacy reports for currency pairs highlight commercial and noncommercial positions, longs and shorts for each currency pair, open interest, open interest as a percentage by trader type, and weekly changes. Commercials could be hedgers or wish to manage risk, while non-commercials are everybody else. Futures only and futures and options combined reports are available weekly free of charge from the CFTC.

The recommendation is to view each report separately to determine open interest for futures and options because futures and micro contracts are reported together. U.S. dollar/Japanese yen must be viewed critically due to the Japanese yen/U.S. dollar futures arrangement. This is why options must be viewed separately to determine sentiment. COT reports are without question a vital tool and worth every trader's time and effort. The report to view should always be reportable positions.

August 2010 marked the first publication of *Traders in Financial Futures* (TFF). The reports contain the same information but classification of traders are identified and their market activity.

The first of four categories of large traders are Dealers/Intermediaries who represent the sell side of the market. Asset Managers/Institutional are pension funds, portfolio managers, and mutual funds to name a few. This category represents the buy side of the market. Third are Leverage Funds, who are money managers and hedge funds who represent the buy side of the market. Finally Other Reportables represent hedgers.

A category of spreading was introduced to both the legacy and TFF reports. The CFTC "computes spreading amount equal to offsetting longs and shorts held by a trader. It's calculated as the amount of offsetting in different calendar months or offsetting futures and options in the same or different calendar months" (CFTC).

Since COT reports all futures and options for all traded instruments, confirmation of proposed or ongoing currency pair trades can be validated by its respective instrument. For example, euro/U.S. dollar can be validated by oil.

Both are risk assets that move together. Agricultural commodities are risk assets and confirmed by Australian dollar/U.S. dollar and New Zealand dollar/U.S. dollar since both move together.

Australian dollar/U.S. dollar prices are moved more by coal and metal prices for exports more so than any other commodities. New Zealand dollar/U.S. dollar prices respond to logs, dairy, wool, and meat. U.S. dollar/Canadian dollar is a commodity currency that must be measured critically against oil and specific commodities inherent to Canada's trade flows. Corporations, importers, exporters, and central bankers with oil interests can swing Canadian dollar prices as they seek to lock a respective oil price. Metals are risk assets and can be measured against all risk currencies. For example, industrial gold exported from Australia is another measure for Australian dollar/U.S. dollar risk.

Bollinger Bands

John Bollinger recently celebrated the twenty-fifth anniversary of his Bollinger Band introduction. Its wide use in all markets attests to its success, and forex is no different because it has survived the test of time. The purpose of Bollinger Bands is to capture highs and lows on a relative basis using standard deviation to measure volatility and a moving average to measure time series.

To understand Bollinger Bands methodology is to know Bollinger's rules for use.

Bollinger Bands confirm W and M market patterns. They can be used for buy and sell decisions. Closing prices outside the bands don't necessarily mean market reversal; they may mean price continuation. Yet prices that touch the upper or lower band doesn't always translate to a buy or sell. Bandwidths can be adjusted. As moving averages increase or decrease so must standard deviations increase or decrease. Bollinger recommends two standard deviations for a 20-period moving average, 2.1 standard deviations for a 50-period moving average, and 1.9 standard deviations for a 10-period moving average. Moving average refers to simple moving averages and factored in the formula. Yet true sample size standard deviations are small so distributions are not normal. Indicators are normalized with percent b.

Parker Evans in the 2008 *Journal of Technical Analysis* performed a study employing percent b as adopted in the Bollinger Band calculation. He defines percent b as an oscillator that measures closing prices in relation to the upper and lower bands.

Many traders employ two sets of Bollinger Bands with various moving averages and standard deviations. Bollinger recommends confirmation by a sentiment or momentum indicator.

Simple Moving Averages

Precisely when a simple moving average was applied to a chart remains a mystery. It probably occurred after the first reported open interest in the 1920s but before the 1960s introduction of exponential moving averages. What is known as a simple moving average is an old indicator that survived the test of time for its effectiveness.

To calculate: add closing prices over X days and divide by X. A 20-day simple moving average is calculated by adding 20 closing prices and dividing the sum by 20. On the next day, the first day drops from the calculation and a new day is added to smooth the average.

Traders should focus on 10-, 20-, 50-, and 100-day averages and employ those as support and resistance levels as well as crossovers. Long crossovers occur when a 10-day crosses above a 20-day average and short crossovers occur when the 10-day crosses below a 20-day average. The same phenomena occur for 50- and 100-day averages. Many employ the 200-day average as well, but its accuracy deserves mention.

The most important simple moving average for a yearly view of the market has been the 200-day average. Factor trading days in the United States minus weekends and holidays, the 200-day average is actually 253 days, 249 for Canada, 249 for Australia, 253 for New Zealand, 245 for Japan, 258 for the euro, and 255 for the Swiss.

The 200-day average not only doesn't exist, but any yearly calculation based on it for trading purposes will be off by at least 45 days, possibly more, depending on the currency pair calculated.

The recommendation is to deploy the proper sized average to the currency pair in the respective market. For example, a long euro/U.S. dollar in Europe should employ the 258-day average, while a long U.S. dollar/ Swiss franc in the United States should employ the 253-day average. Further, employ the proper period for 100-day crossovers from above or below.

To employ a standard deviation moving-average indicator, subtract the moving average from each of the data points used in the moving-average calculation. This is a list of deviations from the average. Square each deviation and add them all together. Divide the sum by the number of periods selected and take the square root. This is a volatility indicator where high standard deviations will see prices fall and low standard deviations will see prices rise. The indicator will move opposite of prices.

Ichimoku Kinko Hyo

Ichimoku is an old Japanese indicator purportedly invented by a Japanese trader in the 1940s. Purportedly because the English and Japanese translation of the book can't be found, so it's assumed that Ichimoku methods exist today based on past Japanese tradition.

The widespread use of Ichimoku as a primary indicator in Japan and throughout Asia was highlighted by Nicole Elliott in her 2007 book *Ichimoku Charts*. It's imperative to understand the methodology of Ichimoku to measure not only Japanese yen pairs, but Ichimoku can be employed on any financial instrument. The success and further methodologies of Ichimoku can be found in a study in the Summer 2008 *Journal of Technical Analysis*.

Ichimoku Highlights

Ichimoku incorporates five moving average lines that work based on market highs and lows rather than closing prices. The Tenkan line is the shortest moving average and provides trade signals. The calculation is as follows: Subtract the lowest low over the past 9 days from the highest high in the same time period, then divide the sum by two. The Kijun line is a medium-term moving average calculated as follows: Add the highest high of the past 26 candles or days from the lowest low of the same time frame and divide that sum by two (Elliott).

Senkou Span A and Senkou Span B begin formation of the cloud, Kumo in Japanese, that provides an upper boundary of support and lower boundary of resistance. Senkou Span A calculation is:

$$\text{Tenkan} + \text{Kijun}/2 \text{ plotted 26 days ahead}$$

Senkou Span B calculation:

$$\text{Highest high in last 52 days} + \text{lowest low of the past 52 days}/ \\ 2 \text{ offset 26 days ahead}$$

Chikou Span is the momentum line calculated as today's closing price plotted 26 days back.

The basics of Ichimoku say buy when Tenkan crosses above Kijun and sell when Tenkan crosses below. Prices above the cloud signify a bullish situation while prices below the cloud is a bear situation. Tenkan and Kijun crossovers above and below the cloud must be managed due to its short-term duration and relation to cloud support and resistance. Ichimoku is a trend indicator that employs Fibonacci time series as a measure of price targets and wave pattern measurement. (Elliott).

As a personal favorite indicator, my sincere recommendation for the 9-, 26-, and 52-day periods is not to shorten the lengths of the periods, especially if a trade is managed throughout all markets. These are special time-tested numbers to measure time, price, and waves, that the overall features of Ichimoku use (Elliott). The inventor worked tirelessly for many years to perfect Ichimoku. Additionally, these numbers can measure currency-price congestion using the special day-count numbers. Used correctly, Ichimoku can stand alone as a primary indicator as the Japanese intended.

Baltic Dry Index

An important barometer to monitor commodity currencies and export-dependent nations such as Australian dollar, New Zealand dollar, and Japanese yen is the Baltic Exchange located in London. The Baltic Exchange advertises itself as the only independent source of maritime-market information. And rightly so since its existence traces back more than 250 years.

With a 550-member organization, the purpose of the group is arrange ocean transportation of bulk cargoes such as oil, coal, grain, iron ore, and sugar, to name a few categories, on behalf of ship owners and charterers (Baltic Exchange). The Baltic Exchange provides daily market information for the dry market for Capesize, Panamax, Supramax, and Handysize vessels (Baltic Exchange). Wet market products such as oil are also reported.

The main question for traders to monitor commodity currencies is who is shipping and where are shipments delivered or placed in storage. Most important is what is the price of shipping costs and is it rising or falling.

A downturn in the number of orders for freight deliveries and freight rates may mean a downturn in commodity prices, a downturn in expected profits for commodity currencies, and a downturn in spot prices. Likewise, a healthy commodity market is a rise in orders. Current 2010 dry-side orders in the first four months amounted to 18.8 million dry weight, while all 2009 saw 33.6 million dry orders. Compare that to Australian dollar/U.S. dollar and New Zealand dollar/U.S. dollar and notice a rise in spot prices. Dry

Supramax routes are reported during Asian sessions as of September 2010 while market information is reported Monday through Friday at 13:00 London time. Dry side orders are no longer reported due to the introduction and first trade on Baltex.

Baltex is an electronic marketplace introduced by the Baltic exchange to trade dry freight derivatives. The first trade began June 2011 and the exchange is regulated by the FSA in the UK.

The four Baltic indices include the Capesize, Panamax, Supramax, and Handysize with a separate category for Baltic International Tanker Routes. Currently 19 routes are mapped for oil deliveries, though a change is expected as the U.S. Gulf Coast oil route was closed for seven years. Oil routes will be rerouted from the United States to Brazil to China as new oil flows into China. U.S. oil rigs closed in the Gulf reopened in Brazil, and Brazilian oil flow is expected to flow to China (Baltic Exchange Site). The Baltic Dry Index (BDI) is the most prominent, as traders trade forward rate agreements against its price. The BDI is calculated by taking time-charted components of all indices. Currently 20 routes are covered within the BDI. Generally as the BDI rises, commodity currencies and major export nations' spot prices rise. The confirmation for any market is monitoring the respective nation's transportation indices and the indices of major export destinations.

IMF and Special Drawing Rights

Special Drawing Rights (SDR) traditionally never deserved special attention since their inception in 1969 but a number of recent developments may have implications for the future in terms of nation-to-nation trade, prices of commodities bought and sold in world markets, and central bank reserves.

From 1944 to 1973, the world operated on a fixed gold system—currencies were pegged to the price of an ounce of gold. Member nations of the IMF contributed a portion of their reserves to support the SDR system of trade on a voluntary quota system. Least-developed nations lacked gold and reserves so couldn't afford contributions in gold terms as a means to exchange their currencies. Plus gold was priced in U.S. dollars. So least-developed nations lacked the means to participate in global trade.

The main mandate of the IMF is ensure exchange rate stability. Their mandate worked for developed nations only so they devised the SDR as a "reserve asset to supplement reserves of all members" (IMF). The IMF definition of SDR is a "claim on freely usable currencies of members." The IMF has185 members, most who joined after 1981. Government-to-government relations are transacted by the SDR system.

From 1969 to 1973, SDR's value was pegged to gold at 0.888671 grams of gold as the U.S. dollar equivalent (IMF). After 1973, floating exchange rates were the new world order so SDRs were pegged to a basket of four currencies with various weights: U.S. dollar—44 percent, euro—34 percent, yen—11 percent, and British pound—11 percent (IMF).

The IMF sums the value of the four currencies in U.S. dollars measured to six decimal places directly after the London British Bankers Association (BBA) LIBOR release and reported on the IMF web site, with updates every 20 minutes. SDRs are then priced and exchanged by members on a voluntary basis or the stronger nations purchase from the weaker nations (IMF). Basket weights are reviewed every five years to determine changes. The factors considered are amounts of trade in goods and services. The November 2010 release of the new basket weights works as follows: US dollar 41.9, euro 37.4, British pound 11.3 and Japanese yen 9.4. For the first time since weights were first reported, the US dollar lost value.

Interest is credited or deducted every Friday based on SDR allocations. The euro is credited or debited based on Eurepo rates, United Kingdom based on Treasury Bills, Japanese based on Treasury Discount Bills, and the United States based on Treasury bills (IMF).

Two previous allocations were distributed to nations. The first was SDR $9 billion, distributed between 1970 and 1972. The second $12 Billion SDR was distributed between 1979 and 1981 (IMF).

The G-20 nations voted and approved a special allocation in 2009 of U.S. $250 billion, 74.3 percent of eligible participants' quota. This means each participating member receives their SDR quota equal to 74 percent of present totals (IMF Press Release). Emerging markets received U.S. $100 billion, with U.S. $18 billion to low-income nations. A special SDR $21.5 billion was allocated. The SDR $21.5 billion allocation brings the total SDR fund to U.S. $283 billion. The goal is to increase cumulative totals to US $1.1 trillion (IMF Press Release).

One fifth of new member nations that joined the IMF after 1981 never participated in the SDR program, yet the special allocation was available to them. Critics argued many allocated SDRs were sold and transferred back to the home currency and used to increase a nation's official reserves. China and Russia were beneficiaries, China by an increase and Russia by joining the SDR program for the first time, along with many African and South American nations.

SDRs can't be traded and only have ramifications for nation-to-nation business conducted through the IMF. The implications for future policy are what is important.

If nation reserves are increased due to SDR allocations, then SDR must be monitored as an indicator and insight into reserves. Spot prices will reflect any increases because economies and economic releases will improve.

Australia is a true commodity currency as defined by the IMF because more than 50 percent of exports are defined as commodities. Currently the Royal Bank of Australia (RBA) monitors the Australian commodity index, called the Index of Commodity Prices (ICP), by SDR rates. This is the first of its type and could have huge implications for future policy. A few questions to ponder include what if commodities were bought and sold strictly between governments? What if SDRs became the new reserve currency used as a sole method of trade? What are implications for private companies and importers and exporters who can't participate in the SDR system? As new SDR allocations are funded, old questions materialize in the research. Votes in the committee to determine any SDR policy is based on SDR holdings and the US currently by far represents the largest vote.

Australia's ICP is actually calculated in Australian dollar, U.S. dollar, and SDR terms, possibly because most Australian commodities are exported in non-Australia dollars and commodity exports comprise about 25 percent of Australia's Gross Domestic Product (GDP) (RBA). Possibly the reason to calculate the ICP in Australian dollar, U.S. dollar, and SDR terms is to determine which currency should be employed to export and measured against the profits of the imported nation's currency. All nations measure Home currency/SDR for evaluation terms. For the future, this development may deserve special attention as an economic indicator.

Pivot Points

The purpose for introduction of this old and reliable indicator is due to its widespread use by floor traders and other market professionals. The tradition continues to this day. Yet pivot points are important to measure other instruments such as stock indices against currency pairs.

The basic pivot-point calculation is provided, yet much experiment can be formulated for other uses. For example, Daniel Fernandez in the December 2010 *Currency Trader* magazine highlighted pivot points calculated to Fibonacci numbers.

Traditional pivot-point applications determined support and resistance levels, but as time progressed, trading methodologies were employed such as range and price breaks with addition of new sets of pivot points. It became a trading plan used as a single indicator.

The calculation is:

PP = (High + Low + Close)/3 1st Support = (2 × PP) – High

- 1st Resistance = (2 × PP) – Low
- 2nd Support = PP – (High – Low)
- 2nd Resistance = PP + (2 × High) – Low
- 3rd Support = 2PP – (High – Low)
- 3rd Resistance = 2PP + High – (2 × Low)

Currency Correlations and Trend Lines

An explanation of correlation coefficients is included to understand why and how currency pairs correlate or don't correlate.

Somewhere around the late 1800s or early 1900s, Karl Pearson was credited with Pearson's Product Moment Correlation Coefficient, the famous R. The formula is:

$$r = \frac{N\sum xy - \left(\sum x\right)\left(\sum y\right)}{\sqrt{n\left(\sum x^2\right) - \left(\sum x\right)^2}\ \sqrt{n\left(\sum y^2\right) - \left(\sum y\right)^2}}$$

This equation asks the question how strong and what direction is a linear relationship between X and Y? The purpose is only to determine if a positive or negative relationship exists. It's a measure on a number line with 0 as the middle bound between positive and negative values. A perfectly positive value means r = +1 and perfectly negative values means r = −1. This says both are perfect fits. As X increases or decreases, y increases or decreases in perfect unison. But currency pairs are never perfect fits.

To determine the fit, measure the proportion of the variance from one variable to the other, x and y by squaring the sums. This explains the percent variation determined by the variance and predicts future outcomes. Suppose the euro/U.S. dollar and British pound/U.S. dollar has a 0.70 positive relationship. Multiply by 100 and 70 percent is the correlation between the two pairs. The other 30 percent is unexplained and called randomness if no other considerations are factored in this regression model.

Many factor other pairs and plot the *x* and *y* results on a chart. A trend line called a regression line can be drawn using the equation

$$y = mx + b$$

where
      m = slope, and
      b = y intercept.

The slope is the change in *y* divided by change in *x*. The more positive the slope, the more the line will trend up. Likewise, the more negative the slope, the more the line will trend down. Much can be done with trend lines.

Edson Gould invented what was known as Speed Resistance Lines, today known as one-third—two-thirds lines and used to measure market corrections. Gould employed the lines to measure price points. For example, rising speed lines are measured by "taking the vertical distance between recent highs and lows and divide into thirds. Straight lines are drawn from the low through the one-third—two-thirds vertical distance. For a falling line, divide the vertical distance from high to low into thirds and draw straight lines from the high through the one-third—two-thirds point on the vertical distance" (Shade). Many still employ Edson Gould's long-ago invention by measuring other markets and currency pairs for one-third and two-thirds corrections.

The trend line drawn to measure highs to lows is not only popular today but used by a vast, vast majority to measure price points. Price points should always be measured in percents. It's an observation that various trend lines were the beginning of channel lines that boxes candlesticks and/or prices in a channel. All are viable technical tools and all work equally well.

The euro/U.S. dollar and British pound/U.S. dollar may be positively related, but that doesn't mean it will move in unison 100 percent of the time because it's not correlated to 100 percent, only 70 percent. Many times one pair will move without the other. That is a market gift and can be measured by the above formulas. If the euro trends without the British pound, it's only time before the British pound will trend. Why it didn't move is explained by randomness, the 30 percent unexplainable. Yet opposite correlations don't mean prices move pip for pip, because the correlations aren't perfectly fit to 100 percent.

The positive aspect about correlations is other markets can be measured in relation to currency pairs. Yet currency pairs can be measured against a bond's cash flows. These indicators are time tested by past generations of market professionals and all work as intended.

Whatever strategy is employed, the recommendation is use it, practice it, perfect it, and stay with the same methodology day after day. It's the market that may deviate, not the strategy. That can be expected from time to time, this is why they are called markets. Live with the idea of reasonable expectations where probabilities and risk are factored into every trade. The rewards of the markets will be seen.

Currency pairs can be volatile; they trend, range, cluster, and even stay congested for long periods of time. For the most part, currency pairs tend to range more than they trend and experience volatility. An essential ingredient to any trader's arsenal is to employ, to know, and to understand an indicator. One indicator may work to capture consistent profits but a risk factor—an error term must be employed. That is found in an opposite indicator rather than its complement. One risk measure is the second set of Bollinger Bands. If one set fails, the other set will alert to a problem, an unexpected market development. Unexpected market developments occur all the time so it's essential to always be ready.

Indicators such as the Baltic Exchange, the SDR, and COT reports have a worth for capturing consistent profits as much as a trading indicator because of its market alert to future price moves.

The purpose of this chapter was not only to highlight indicators that work to capture profits but to outline currency pairs and their movements. My hope is that this was a consistent theme throughout the book. This chapter focused on two consistent themes, trading indicators and market indicators. Each have a value of equal worth. One alerts to future market conditions and periods while the other alerts to price moves. One complements the other. Trading indicators together complement each other. Simple moving averages complement Ichimoku because simple moving averages focus on closing prices while Ichimoku focuses on market highs and lows. It's a continuous-market moving average.

Bollinger Bands work together with pivot points as a pivot-point support or resistance line may align to a band's support or resistance line. All indicators can be employed with a trend line whether it is a speed line, a regression line, or trend lines that comprise a channel. Different trend lines can be drawn simultaneously. A regression line complements a speed line.

Conclusion

My purpose for this book was to address the various issues involved that comprise a currency pair not only from a strict trading perspective but to bring an understanding from a whole host of perspectives. Part was historic to understand the full context for trade and approach the markets. To know where we were may help to know where we are.

The real purpose for my book is to understand the second side of a currency-pair equation so a pair is fully understood for its purpose, history, movements, and factors that make it move. Armed with this information, it is my hope that this book will be a continuous resource for not only those that know, understand, and trade the markets but for those who wish to learn, for some to be better at their craft. For those who wish to capture consistent profits with a full comprehension of market factors, much exists in this book for you.

Bibliography

ASEAN. March 24, 2010. "USD 120 Billion Chiang Mai Initiative Multilateralisation Swap Facility Comes Into Effect." ASEAN Secretariat Press Release. http://www.aseansec.org/24433.htm

Baba, Naohiko, and Yasunari Inamura. April 2002. "The Japanese Repo Market: Theory and Evidence." Financial Markets Department Working Paper 02-E-1.

Baba, Naohiko, Frank Packer, and Teppei Nagano. March 2008. "The Spillover of Money Market Turbulence to FX Swaps and Cross Currency Swap Markets." *Bank of International Settlements Quarterly Review.*

Baer, Julius, and George P. Woodruff. *Commodity Exchanges.* New York, London: Harper & Brothers, 1935.

Black, Fischer, and Myron Scholes. "The Price of Options and Corporate Liabilities." *Journal of Political Economy,* 1973.

Bank of International Settlements. 2009. "The Role of Valuation and Leverage in Procyclicality." Bank of International Settlements.

Bank of Japan. February 2009. "Guidelines on Eligible Collateral." Bank of Japan.

Becker, Chris, and Michael Davies. October 2002. "Developments in the Trade Weight Index." *Reserve Bank of Australia Bulletin.*

Bianchetti, Marco. "Two curves, one price." *Risk.* August 2010, Vol. 23, Issue 8, pp. 66–72, 7p.

Board of Governors of the Federal Reserve System. "Section 13. Powers of Federal Reserve Banks." Federal Reserve Act. http://www.federalreserve.gov/aboutthefed/section13.htm

Buldorini, Luca, Stelios Makrydakis, and Christian Thimann. "The Effective Exchange Rates of the Euro." ECB: Occasional papers by Stelios Makrydakis. Series No. 2, February 2002. http://www.ecb.europa.eu/pub/scientific/ops/author/html/author324.en.html

Chauvet, Marcelle, and Simon Potter. "Forecasting Recessions Using the Yield Curve." *Journal of Forecasting* 24, no. 2 (March 2005): 77–103.

Chionis, Dionisios, Perikils Gogas, and Ioannis Pragidis. "Predicting European Union Recessions in the Euro Era: The Yield Curve as a Forecasting Tool of Economic Activity." *International Advances in Economic Research* 16, no.1 (February 2010): 1–10, 6 Charts, 4 Graphs.

Cox, John, Stephen Ross, and Mark Rubenstein. "Option Pricing: A Simplified Approach." *Journal of Financial Economics*, 1979.

Elliott, Nicole. *Ichimoku Charts, An introduction to Ichimoku Kinko Clouds.* Hampshire, UK: Harriman House, 2007.

Evans, H. Parker. "An Empirical Study of Rotational Trading Using the % b Oscillator." *Journal of Technical Analysis*. Summer/Fall 2008.

"Export and Import Price Index Manual." Chapter 3: The Price and Volume of International Trade: Background, Purpose and Uses of Export and Import Price Indices. IMF Draft July 2003. http://www.imf.org/external/np/sta/tegeipi/ch3.pdf

Federal Deposit Insurance Corporation. "Depository Institutions Deregulation And Monetary Control Act of 1980." FDIC Law, Regulations, Related Acts. http://www.fdic.gov/regulations/laws/rules/8000-2200.html

Federal Reserve Bank of New York. The Foreign Exchange Committee, Annual Report. 2005.http://www.ny.frb.org/fxc/annualreports/fxcar05.pdf

Federal Reserve System. "Reserve Maintenance Manual." Federal Reserve System. December, 2010. http://www.frbservices.org/files/regulations/pdf/rmm.pdf

Fernandez, Daniel. "Daily Pivot Breakouts." Currency Trader Magazine, December 2010.

Fleming, Michael J., and Kenneth D. Garbade. "Repurchase Agreements with Negative Interest Rates." *Current Issues in Economics and Finance*, April 2004.

Fleming, Michael J., and Kenneth D. Garbade. "The Repurchase Agreement Refined: GCF Repo." *Current Issues in Economics and Finance*, June 2003.

Goldberg, Linda S. with Cedric Tille. "Vehicle Currency Use in International Trade", Journal of International Economics, December 2008

Groom, John. "The Development of the Kauri Bond Market." Reserve Bank of New Zealand, 2008. http://www.rbnz.govt.nz/research/workshops/capitalmarkets20june2008/3345557.pdf

Garman, Mark and Steven Kohlhagen. "Foreign Currency Option Values." *Journal of International Money and Finance*, 1983.

Haubrich, Joseph G. "Swaps and the Swaps Yield Curve." Federal Reserve Bank of Cleveland, December 2001. http://www.scribd.com/doc/19606659/Federal-Reserve-Bank-of-Clevland-Haubrich-Swaps-and-the-Swaps-Yield-Curve

Haubrich, Joseph G. "Does the Yield Curve Signal Recession?" Federal Reserve Bank of Cleveland, April 2006.

Haubrich, Joseph G., and Timothy Bianco. "Yield Curve and Predicted GDP Growth." Federal Reserve Bank of Cleveland, October 2010.

Hordahl, Peter, and Michael R. King. "Developments in Repo Markets during the Financial Turmoil." *Bank of International Settlements Quarterly Review*, December 2008.

Hurd, Matthew, Mark Salmon, and Christopher Schleicher. "Using Copulas to Construct Bivariate Foreign Exchange Distributions with Application to ERI." Center for Economic Policy Research, 2005.

Japanese Bankers Association. http://www.zenginkyo.or.jp/

Japanese Securities Dealers Association. "Review of Fails Practice for Bond Trading." Japanese Securities Dealers Association. 2009.

Jongmoo, Jay Choi, and Shmuel Hauser. "The Effects Of Domestic And Foreign Yield Curves On The Value of Currency American Call Options." *Journal of Banking & Finance* 14, no. 1 (March 1990): 41–53.

Jorian, Philippe. *Value at risk: The new benchmark for managing financial risk.* 3rd ed. New York: McGraw-Hill, 2007.

Kite, Hannah. "A Review of the Trade Weighted Exchange Rate Index." *Reserve Bank of New Zealand Bulletin*, June 2007.

Krause, Robert. "Volatility Contracts - A New Alternative." *The Journal of Alternative Investments.* Summer 2000.

Krause, Robert. "Volatility Trading: VolContracts™ Jump into the Mix." *Swiss Derivatives Review.* Autumn 2010.

Lynch, Birone, and Simon Whitaker. "The New Sterling." *ERI Quarterly Bulletin.* Winter 2004.

MacGorain, S. "Stabilising short-term interest rates." *Bank of England Quarterly Bulletin* (Winter, 2005): 462–470.

Market Technicians Association, MTA Knowledge Base. http://knowledgebase.mta .org/?fuseaction=kb.resource&kbDomainID=BDA870A8-CF1C-2465-1FE10C 6186345CA5&kbResourceID=13F1448F-AD6A-93F9-09E38B20030C01B4

Mehl, Arnaud. "The Yield Curve as a Predictor and Emerging Market Economies." European Central Bank, ECB Working Paper 691, 2006.

Morrow, Ron. "Repo, Reverse Repo and Securities Lending Markets in Canada." *Bank of Canada Review.* Winter 1994–1995.

New York Federal Reserve. "Tri Party Repo Infrastructure Reform and White Paper." New York Federal Reserve. May 17, 2010.

Olivei, Giovanni P. "Japan's Approach to Monetary Policy." *New England Economic Review*, 00284726, 2nd Quarter 2002.

Ong, Janone. "A New Effective Exchange Rate Index for the Canadian Dollar." *Bank of Canada Review.* Autumn 2006.

Reid, Christopher. "The Canadian Overnight Market, Recent Evolution and Structural Changes." *Bank of Canada Review.* Spring 2007.

Reserve Bank of New Zealand. "Operating Rules And Guidelines - Section 2 Domestic Market Operations." Reserve Bank of New Zealand Financial Markets, Department Domestic Markets Section, October 29, 2009, 18 pages, http:// www.rbnz.govt.nz/finmarkets/domesticmarkets/3519153.pdf

Royal Bank of Australia. "Open Market Operations." Royal Bank of Australia, http:// www.rba.gov.au/mkt-operations/open-mkt-oper.html

Securities Exchange Act of 1934. "Section 11A - National Market System for Securities." Securities Exchange Act of 1934. www.sec.gov/about/laws/sea34.pdf

Sengupta, Rajdeep, and Yu Man Tam. "The Libor-OIS Spread as a Summary Indicator." Federal Reserve Bank of St. Louis Economic Synopses, 2008, No. 25. http://research.stlouisfed.org/publications/es/08/ES0825.pdf

U.S. Securities and Exchange Commission, Regulation National Market System. "Rule 600 b 23." 17 CFR Parts 200, 204, 230, 240, 242, 249 and 270. 523 pages. http://www.sec.gov/rules/final/34-51808.pdf

Schade, George A. Jr. "Noted Market Technicians (Biographies) - Edson B. Gould" Technically Speaking authored by Michael Carr based on prior research presented at 2000 Annual MTA conference, Atlanta Georgia. mta.org.

———. "Forecasting Like the Technical Masters, Edson Gould's Three Steps and a Stumble Rule", *Stocks, Futures and Options Magazine*, September 2004, Vol 3, no 9, pgs 68-72

Shaleen, Kenneth. *Volume and open interest: Classic trading strategies for 24-hour market.* Revised edition. Chicago: Irwin Professional Publishing, 1997.

U.S. Department of the Treasury. "Treasury International Capital System (TIC)." U.S. Department of the Treasury, http://www.treasury.gov/resource-center/data-chart-center/tic/Pages/index.aspx

Volkman, David A., Olivier J. P. Maisondieu Laforge, and Donna Dudney. "The Effect of Federal Reserve Policy, Yield Curves, and Current Level of Interest Rates on Equity Returns." *Journal of Investing.* Winter 2009, Vol. 18, Issue 4, pp. 82–95.

Whitehouse, Mark. "Economists Ask if Bonds Have Lost Predictive Power." *Wall Street Journal*, December 29, 2005, eastern edition, C1–C3.

About the Author

Brian Twomey is an independent trader and a prolific writer on trading, having authored more than 60 articles in *Technical Analysis of Stocks and Commodities* and Investopedia. His article on Welles Wilder is one of the most heavily accessed pieces in *Technical Analysis of Stocks and Commodities* in recent years. Through his writings, he has established a strong following among traders and market analysts. He is an adjunct professor of Political Science at Gardner-Webb University. He has a BA in Political Science, a Masters in Public Administration and 24 graduate hours in Political Science from the University of Central Florida.

Index